KU-119-744

NEW CHALLENGES FOR EUROPEAN HUMAN RESOURCE MANAGEMENT

WITHDRAWN FROM STOCK

SHORT LOAN
One Week Only

New Challenges for European Human Resource Management

Edited by

Chris Brewster
Wolfgang Mayrhofer
and
Michael Morley

WITHDRAWN FROM STOCK

NATIONAL COLLEGE
OF IRELAND
LIBRARY

First published in Great Britain 2000 by
MACMILLAN PRESS LTD
Houndmills, Basingstoke, Hampshire RG21 6XS and London
Companies and representatives throughout the world

A catalogue record for this book is available from the British Library.

ISBN 0–333–74965–0

First published in the United States of America 2000 by
ST. MARTIN'S PRESS, LLC,
Scholarly and Reference Division,
175 Fifth Avenue, New York, N. Y. 10010

ISBN 0–312–22872–4 (cloth)

Library of Congress Cataloging-in-Publication Data

New challenges for European human resource management/edited by Chris Brewster, Wolfgang Mayrhofer, and Michael Morley.
p. cm.
Includes bibliographical references and index.
ISBN 0–312–22872–4
1. Personnel management–Europe–Case studies.
I. Brewster, Chris. II. Mayrhofer, Wolfgang.
III. Morley, Michael.

HF5549.2.E9 N48 2000
658.3′0094–dc21 99–088128

© Selection, editorial matter and Chapter 1 © Chris Brewster, Wolfgang Mayrhofer and Michael Morley 2000; individual Chapters © individual contributors 2000

All rights reserved. No reproduction, copy or transmission of this publication may be made without written permission.

No paragraph of this publication may be reproduced, copied or transmitted save with written permission or in accordance with the provisions of the Copyright, Designs and Patents Act 1988, or under the terms of any licence permitting limited copying issued by the Copyright Licensing Agency, 90 Tottenham Court Road, London WIP 0LP.

Any person who does any unauthorised act in relation to this publication may be liable to criminal prosecution and civil claims for damages.

The authors have asserted their rights to be identified as the authors of this work in accordance with the Copyright, Designs and Patents Act 1988.

This book is printed on paper suitable for recycling and made from fully managed and sustained forest sources.

10 9 8 7 6 5 4 3 2 1
09 08 07 06 05 04 03 02 01 00

Printed in Great Britain by
Antony Rowe Ltd
Chippenham, Wiltshire

Barcode No: 3900601008 4723
Dewey No: 658.3 (SC)
Date Input: 20/10/00
£59.15

Contents

OF IRELAND LIBRARY
WITHDRAWN FROM STOCK

List of Tables

List of Figures

List of Abbreviations

CEE	Central and Eastern Europe
Cranet-E	Cranfield Network on European Human Resource Management
DFA	Discriminant Function Analysis
EAPM	European Association of Personnel Management
HFO	High Flexibility Organisations
HR	Human Resources
HRD	Human Resources Development
HRM	Human Resource Management
IR	Industrial Relations
IRC	Industrial Relations Commission
LFO	Low Flexibility Organisations
MNE	Multinational Enterprises
SHRM	Strategic Human Resources Management

1 The Concept of Strategic European Human Resource Management

Wolfgang Mayrhofer, Chris Brewster and Michael Morley

INTRODUCTION

This book is about developments in the area of Human Resource Management (HRM) in public and private organisations in European countries. The basic data used for the chapters in this book were collected within the Cranfield Network on European Human Resource Management (Cranet-E). What was originally called the Price Waterhouse Cranfield Project and began in 1989 with five countries is now a research network consisting of 20 European and five non-European countries trying to analyse HRM issues in a national, cross-national and (quasi-)longitudinal way. The network, which is co-ordinated by the Centre for European Human Resource Management at Cranfield School of Management in the UK, consists of HRM experts from a leading business school or university department in each of the participating countries. Further details can be found at the web-page of Cranet-E (http://www.tu-dresden.de/wwbwlpew/cranfield/index.htm). These colleagues work together to collect comparable data from the senior Human Resources (HR) person in a representative cross section of organisations in each country in order to analyse and understand the similarities and differences they identify in that data. So far there have been four major rounds of the survey with more countries involved in each round: over 20 000 responses have been collected including over 6000 in the latest round. Full details of this research are given in Part VI on 'Research in Comparative Human Resource Management' and we have avoided repeating these details here or in any of the other chapters. Table 1.1 highlights the history and the development of Cranet-E.

Table 1.1 Member countries and years of surveys of Cranet-E

	Participation in year of survey					
Country	*1989*	*1990/91*	*1992*	*1993*	*1995/96*	*1997/98*
Germany (West)	•	•	•		•	
Germany (East)			•	•	•	
France	•	•	•		•	
Spain	•	•	•		•	
Sweden	•	•	•		•	
UK	•	•	•		•	
Danmark		•	•		•	
Italy		•			•	
Netherlands		•	•		•	
Norway		•	•		•	
Switzerland		•			•	
Finland			•		•	
Ireland			•		•	
Portugal			•		•	
Turkey			•		•	
Austria				•		
Czech Republic				•		
Greece				•		
Belgium					•	
Australia						•
Bulgaria						•
Hungary						•
Poland						•
Japan						*
New Zealand						•

* In preparation.

In addition, smaller groups within the network carry out other comparative research programmes, funded by Research Councils, the European Commission, the British Council and related bodies, major consultancy organisations and groups of employers. In the last few years these projects have examined a range of different topics, e.g. national differences in management styles; flexible working practices (three projects: one analysing the statistical data from 14 countries; one in-depth ideographic study in three countries; one study of short-term employment); the role of the line manager in HRM; communication and consultation in European organisations; training, development and learning in Europe; and the effects of the changing organisation of the European postal sector on employment.

DIFFERENT PARADIGMS IN HRM

Along with being done differently, things are also conceptualised differently in different countries. In the area under consideration in this book this includes both differences in the way HRM is conducted and the research traditions through which it is explored. These differences result in two different, 'ideal type', paradigms for research into HRM. These can be termed the *universalist* and the *contextual* paradigms. The term paradigm is used here in Kuhn's (1970) sense as an accepted model or theory, but with the clear implication that different researchers may be using competing models or theories. It is to some degree the difference between these paradigms which has led to the confusion noted by many (Conrad and Pieper, 1990; Guest, 1992; Singh, 1992; Storey, 1992; Boxall, 1993; Dyer and Kochan, 1994; Goss, 1994; Martell and Caroll, 1995) in the appropriate subject matter of HRM.

Our attempt to distinguish different paradigms is not unique: it mirrors those developed in Delery and Doti (1996) – and perhaps unfortunately shares a similar sounding, though differently defined, terminology – and in Wright and McMahan (1992). It is distinguished from them by contrasting a firm-internal with a firm-external perspective and by the linkage with methodology (see below). The aim here is not to categorise the different research perspectives used in studying HRM, but to identify the different paradigms which underlie these perspectives.

The *universalist paradigm*, which is dominant in the USA, but is widely used in many other countries, is essentially a nomothetic social science approach: using evidence to test generalisations of an abstract and law-like character. As in other related areas of the social sciences the universalist paradigm tends towards acceptance of convergence. In the organisational studies area, for instance, the Aston School argued strongly that context made little difference and only organisational characteristics mattered (Hickson *et al.*, 1974; Pugh and Hickson 1976; Hickson *et al.* 1979; Hickson and Macmillan, 1981). Although the Aston school and the contingency approach to organisation theory as a whole conceptually was open to various situational factors of the internal and external environment, in practice its research limited itself to a rather small segment of factors such as size, competitive structure, or environmental dynamics. Beyond that, this notion of the concept, implicitly, and consequently empirically, assumed that there is a quasi-deterministic link between situational characteristics and organisational structure, leading to the tacit conviction that there is a one-best-way of organising towards efficiency.

Closer to our own area of interest, Locke and Kochan (1995, pp. 380–1), who we will claim for the contextual paradigm later, ask whether national systems still exist or whether sector or company systems are taking over as industrial relations, for example, is increasingly decentralised.

This paradigm assumes that the purpose of the study of our area of the social sciences, HRM, and in particular 'strategic' HRM, SHRM (Tichy *et al.*, 1982, Fombrun, *et al.*, 1984; Ulrich 1987; Wright and Snell 1991; Wright and McMahan 1992), is to improve the way that HR are managed strategically within organisations, with the ultimate aim of improving organisational performance, as judged by its impact on the organisation's declared corporate strategy (Tichy *et al* 1982; Huselid, 1995), the customer (Ulrich, 1989) or shareholders (Huselid, 1995; Becker and Gerhart, 1996; Becker *et al.* 1997). Further, it is implicit that this objective will apply in all cases. Thus, the widely cited definition by Wright and McMahan states that SHRM is 'the pattern of planned human resource deployments and activities intended to enable a firm to achieve its goals' (1992, p. 298). The value of this paradigm lies in the simplicity of focus, the coalescing of research around this shared objective and the clear relationship with the demands of industry. The disadvantages lie in the ignoring of other potential focuses, the resultant narrowness of the research objectives, and the ignoring of other levels and other stakeholders in the outcomes of SHRM (Guest, 1990; Poole, 1990; Pieper, 1990; Bournois, 1991b; Legge, 1995; Brewster, 1995; Kochan, 1997).

Methodologically, the mechanism generally used to research this form of SHRM is deductive: to generate carefully designed questions which can lead to proof or disproof, the elements of which can be measured in such a way that the question itself can be subjected to the mechanism of testing and prediction. Built in to this paradigm is the assumption that research is not 'rigorous' unless it is drawn from existing literature and theory, focused around a tightly designed question and contains a structure of testing that can lead on to prediction. Literature in this paradigm often, therefore, follows a consistent structure and is often statistically based.[1] The research base is mostly centred on a small number of private sector 'leading edge' exemplars of 'good practice', often large multinationals and often from the manufacturing or even specifically the high-tech sector.

The strength of the approach is that good research based upon it tends to have a clear potential for theoretical development, it can lead to carefully drawn research questions, the research tends to be easily replicable and research methodologies sophisticated, and there is a coherence of criteria for judging the research. Of course, in any particular case, inappropriate techniques or dubious lines of causality can negate much of the value of this form of research (see Gerhart, 1997). Even where the data and analysis are sound, however, a disadvantage of this paradigm, perhaps of the US research tradition in particular, is that the pressure to publish and the restricted nature of what is acceptable has led to much careful statistical analysis of small-scale, often narrow, questions whose relevance to wider theoretical and practical debates is sometimes hard to see. This has been summed up, by an American commentator, in the notion of the 'drunkard's search' – looking for the missing key where visibility is good, rather than where the key was lost.

The *contextual paradigm*[2] by contrast is idiographic, searching for an overall understanding of what is contextually unique and why. In our topic area, it is focused on understanding what is different between and within HRM in various contexts and what the antecedents of those differences are. Among most researchers working in this paradigm, it is the explanations that matter – any link to firm performance is secondary. It is assumed that societies, governments or regions can have HRM practices and policies as well as firms. At the level of the organisation (not firm – public sector organisations are also included) the organisation's objectives (and therefore its strategy) are not necessarily assumed to be 'good' either for the organisation or for society. There are plenty of examples where this is clearly not the case. Nor, in this paradigm, is there any assumption that the interests of everyone in the organisation will be the same; or any expectation that an organisation will have a strategy that people within the organisation will 'buy in to'. It is argued here that not only will the employees and the unions have a different perspective to the management team (Kochan *et al.*, 1986; Barbash 1987; Keenoy, 1990; Storey, 1992b; Purcell and Ahlstrand, 1994; Turner and Morley, 1995), but also that even within the management team there may be different interests and views (Hyman, 1987; Kochan, *et al.*, 1986; Koch and McGrath, 1996). These, and the resultant impact on HRM, are issues for empirical study. As a contributor to explanation, this paradigm emphasises external factors as well as the actions of the management within an organisation. Thus it explores the importance of such factors as culture, ownership structures, labour markets, the role of the state and trade union organisation as aspects of the subject rather than external influences upon it. The scope of HRM goes beyond the organisation: to reflect the reality of the role of many HRM departments, particularly in Europe, for example, in lobbying about and adjusting to Government actions, in dealing with equal opportunities legislation or with trade unions and tripartite institutions, etc.

This paradigm is widespread in the UK and Ireland, Australia and New Zealand and in many of the northern European countries, but has some adherents in North America. Furthermore, if one were to judge by the journals and newsletters put out by the HR societies and consultancies, the interests of many HR practitioners in the United States are in many of the same legislative and labour market areas as those in Europe. This seems to apply particularly to the US public sector where, perhaps, the pressures of compliance are greatest. Interestingly, there are increasing calls from North Americans for a contextual paradigm or, to be precise, approaches which have considerable resonance with this paradigm, to be used in the USA (see, for example, Dyer, 1985; Schuler and Jackson, 1987; Dyer and Kochan, 1995; Kochan, 1997).

Methodologically, the research mechanisms used are inductive. Here, theory is drawn from an accumulation of data collected or gathered in a less directed (or constrained) manner than would be the case under the universalist paradigm. Research traditions are different: focused less upon testing and prediction and more upon the collection of evidence. There is an assumption that if things are important they should be studied, even if testable prediction is not possible or the resultant data are complex and unclear. The policies and practices of the 'leading edge' companies (something of a value-laden term in itself) which are the focus of much HRM research and literature in the universalist literature are of less interest to contextualists than identifying the way labour markets work and what the more typical organisations are doing. Much more work in, for example, Europe is, therefore, based on finding out and understanding what is happening. There is a stronger tradition of detailed idiographic studies and of large-scale survey work, both of which lend themselves to analyses of the different stakeholders and the environmental complexity of organisations. Similarly, research in Europe is more often focused on the services sector or the public sector of employment than is the case for HRM research work in the USA. Research there seems to evidence an interest in the manufacturing sector which is not only wholly disproportionate to its

NATIONAL COLLEGE OF IRELAND LIBRARY

share of employment but is also often discussed as if it is the whole of the economy – or at least the only sector of interest to specialists in HRM.

In Europe much of the research is located squarely in the contextual paradigm, concerned to develop a critique of the relationship between owners and/or managers and the employees and the society in which the organisations operate; and there is less likelihood of the researchers assuming that the purposes of the powerholders in the organisation are unchallengeable and that the role of research is to identify how their HRM contributes to those purposes.

It is quite obvious that the differentiation between the universalist and the contextual view of HRM is part of a larger discussion about the possibilities and the ways of gaining knowledge in general and scientific knowledge in particular. Occidental thinking for a long time has been characterised by a basic dichotomy which can be expressed in the following way: 'There is an uneasiness that has spread throughout intellectual and cultural life. It affects almost every discipline and every aspect of our lives. This uneasiness is expressed by the opposition between objectivism and relativism, but there are a variety of other contrasts that indicate the same underlying anxiety: rationality versus irrationality, objectivism versus subjectivity, realism versus antirealism. Contemporary thinking has moved between these and other related extremes' (Bernstein, 1983, p. 1). Possibilities and limits of gaining knowledge about reality are subject to different basic assumptions about the world and its accessability. Often in a simplistic notion these basic differences are linked to certain research methods and, therefore, called quantitative and qualitative approaches. However, this is much too simple, since the differences are not in the area of methods but are linked with basic epistemological and methodological positions: heuristic, interpretative ways of gaining knowledge on the one side and critical-rationalism and positivism on the other side.

The universalist and contextualist approaches are true paradigms in Kuhn's sense that they are in general unchallenged and are often held to be unchallengeable. Those researching in these paradigms are themselves often unaware of any alternatives. Like the fish's knowledge of water, these researchers not only see no alternatives but also do not consider the possibility that there could be any. Thus, as a small example, many of the papers published in the European journals make almost no reference to US texts – and vice versa. Some of those who become aware of the alternative paradigm respond, as the students of paradigms would expect, by denying the value of the alternative:

universalists arguing that, 'if it doesn't lead us to be able to say something that will help firms to become more effective, what use is it?' and, 'if you can't measure it', you can't research it'; contextualists arguing against, 'managerialist sub-consultancy' and, 'the narrow, overly statistical, chase for tenure'.

This is particularly unfortunate: just as the debate between the two paradigms can be depressingly sterile, or can lead to research which combines the worst of both, so the alternative can be stimulating and challenging. Insights from one paradigm can be powerful in the other; research in one paradigm can lead to lines of development in the other. In discussion of the closely related nomothetic and ideographic concepts of research Galtung (1990, p. 108) argues that 'although dramatically different, these should not be seen as antithetical, irreconcilable or mutually exclusive'. Thus, not only do we get different insights and findings from each paradigm, which overall strengthens our understanding of HRM and SHRM, but also the possibility that the challenge provided by these alternative paradigms can improve research in both is exciting. So the universalist tradition can include more important questions, take greater note of the environmental constraints and be more challenging in its approach to the multiple stakeholders within the organisation and beyond. And the contextual paradigm has much to learn from the tighter definition of research questions, more careful measurement and the more extensive use of statistics.

On the methodological front, the debate between these two leading paradigms in the field informs the rationale for research but says little about methodological tools. From either perspective the key question in research is what the research is trying to explain: different kinds of methodologies will be appropriate for different issues and there is much to be gained by drawing insights from different techniques (Jick, 1979).

This is not to argue for a melding of the two paradigms. Such a development is not only impossible, but also undesirable. There are different strengths in each paradigm and we can learn most by drawing on the best of both traditions[3].

OF NATURE LEVEL AND ACTORS

Contrasting these two different paradigms affecting the study of HRM and SHRM highlights three issues: the contested nature of the concept (what we are studying); the levels at which it can be applied (the range of our studies); and the actors concerned (who is involved).

The nature of HRM

Arguably, there is less room for debate in the universalist paradigm about the nature of what is being studied: there is greater coherence among the US universalist, for example, about what constitutes 'good' HRM: a coalescing of views around the concept of 'high performance work systems'. These have been characterised by the US Department of Labor (1993) as having certain clear characteristics: careful and extensive systems for recruitment, selection and training; formal systems for sharing information with the individuals who work in the organisation; clear job design; local level participation procedures; monitoring of attitudes; performance appraisals; properly functioning grievance procedures; and promotion and compensation schemes that provide for the recognition and financial rewarding of high performing members of the workforce. It would appear that, while there have been many other attempts to develop such lists, and they all differ to some degree, the Department of Labor list can be taken as an exemplar of the universalist paradigm: few researchers (or commentators or consultants) in the universalist tradition of HRM would find very much to argue with in this list.

The list is drawn from previous attempts to identify good practice in HRM. Mahoney and Deckop (1986) identify six elements that constitute HRM. In Europe, Beaumont 1992 finds five; and Storey (1992a) identifies 15 different practices. Many of the items in these lists are similar or are subsets of each other. Guest (1987) was one of the first to summarise his conception of what makes HRM distinctive (integrated into the general coordinating activity of line management; bottom line emphasis; management of corporate culture) and these lists still contain much in common with this outline. Later he expands this list to be more explicit ('innovative techniques of the sort typically associated with HRM' including such practices as flexible working, quality circles, training in participative skills and job enrichment: Guest, 1990, p. 385) – the soft version of HRM.

In many countries, however, where the contextual paradigm is more widespread, almost every item on these lists would be the source of debate among both practitioners and theorists. Thus, in much of southern Europe recruitment and selection schemes rely heavily on the network of family and friends (the *cunha* in Portugal for example). HRM experts in these countries would argue that this is a cheap and effective method of recruitment, and gives the organisation an extra means of motivating and controlling employees ('this behaviour will cause a lot of embarrassment to X and Y – perhaps members of your family – who persuaded us to employ you'). Formal systems for sharing information with individuals at their workplaces are significantly different from sharing information at the strategic level with trade union representatives skilled in debating the organisational strategy – a common requirement in Europe. Clear job design (which can presumably be linked with the performance appraisal and incentive schemes for the individual job holder) can be inimical to the need for flexibility, team work and responsiveness to the pace of change seen as important by most European organisations. And so on through the list.

One value of the contextualist paradigm can be seen in the 'test-bed' situation of the ex Communist states of Central and Eastern Europe (CEE). Our research into these countries (Brewster, 1992; Koubek and Brewster, 1995; Hanel *et al.* 1997; Chapter 13 in this book) indicates that while all of them have moved significantly away from the old models, the rate of change in the different countries has been very different. The greater explanatory power of the contextual paradigm in such cases at least is manifest; the poverty of attempts to explain developments there by contrasting them with the universalist conception of HRM is clear.

The universalist paradigm also assumes that HRM is concerned with the aims and actions of management within the organisation. In countries like the USA, which has as an avowed aim of most politicians the objective of 'freeing business from outside interference', or among commentators who share that approach, it is understandable that many researchers there develop a vision of HRM which takes as its scope the policies and practices of management.

There is indeed a school of authors in the universalist tradition who start from the premise that what distinguishes HRM from other approaches to employment is mainly that it is a set of policies and practices which are intended to be integrated with organisational strategies and objectives (Fombrun *et al.*, 1984; Guest, 1987; Schuler and Jackson 1987; Lengnick-Hall and Lengnick-Hall, 1988; Hendry and Pettigrew, 1990; Schuler, 1992; Wright and McMahan, 1992; Storey 1995). These authors see HRM as a particular set of practices which may or may not be appropriate depending upon the situation and the corporate strategy of each different organisation. This approach tends to follow one main strand of seminal US writing, the 'Michigan' school, initiated by Fombrun *et al.* (1984). For this school, business strategy, organisational structure and HRM are the three crucial, interactive, elements of strategic management. Other authors have referred to the need for HR strategy to be 'an integral part of business strategy, with labour utilisation approaches reflecting production and marketing priorities' (Ramsey, 1992, p. 233).

Boxall (1992) has used the instructive term 'matching' to encompass such an approach to HRM. Hendry and Pettigrew (1986) have summarised the approach clearly. They focus on HRM as strategic integration, defined by:

1. the use of planning;
2. a coherent approach to the design and management of personnel systems based on an employment policy and manpower strategy, and often underpinned by a 'philosophy';
3. matching HRM activities and policies to some explicit business strategy; and
4. seeing the people of the organisation as a 'strategic resource' for achieving
5. 'competitive advantage'

Hendry and Pettigrew, 1986, p. 4

Later they say explicitly, 'We see HRM as a perspective on employment systems, characterised by their closer alignment with business strategy' (Hendry and Pettigrew, 1990, p. 36).

In the hands of a different strand of the strategic HRM literature (Fombrun, *et al.*, 1984; Ackermann, 1986; Staffelbach 1986; Besseyre des Horts, 1987, 1988, Miller, 1989), this approach can lead to what might be characterised as 'contingent determinism'. The elements of the corporate strategy that dominate the HR strategy vary. Thus Purcell (1987) argues that certain organisational forms will find it virtually impossible to adopt strategic HRM, while Marginson *et al.* (1988) believe that foreign companies are more likely to adopt it. Other authors have linked HR strategies to different factors: Schuler has indicated that they should be based on the type of market, as defined by Porter (Schuler and Jackson, 1987), or on a particular position in a company's life-cycle (Schuler, 1989). The market approach has also been propounded by others (Baird *et al.*, 1983; Dertouzos *et al.*, 1989), while others have supported the life-cycle approach (Fombrun and Tichy, 1983; Kochan and Barocci, 1985). Cohen and Pfeffer (1986) argue that sector and type of organisation are the determining factors, with public sector and large, high visibility organisations more likely to adopt strategic HR practices.

What have been separated out here as distinct definitions can be, and often are, overlapping. Many of the texts assume that a focus on employee commitment or careful communication or employee development must, inevitably, be strategic. One of the problems in the literature is that individual texts either do not specify which of these broad definitional levels they are addressing, or assume mutual interlinking, or drift between them.

Theoretically it is quite possible that a closely integrated, strategic approach to HRM will involve nearly all the specific HRM objectives and practices and hence drive all aspects of the way labour is managed. Equally, however, it is possible that the close integration of HRM with corporate strategy could, in some sectors for example, lead to a heavy emphasis on cost-reduction, eliminating all 'people frills' such as training, communication with employees or employee benefits and making extensive use of outsourcing.

In Europe, however, many researchers find that the universalist paradigm, ironically, because it excludes a contextual element, inevitably excludes much of the work of HR specialists and many of the issues which are vital for the organisation. They are uncomfortable studying a subject in a way which excludes such areas as compliance, equal opportunities, trade-union relationships and dealing with local government, for example. Hence the development of a more critical, contextual paradigm based on increasing criticism of the universalist model of SHRM common in the USA. Looking at the UK, Guest sees 'signs' that what he calls 'the American model is losing its appeal as attention focuses to a greater extent on developments in Europe' (Guest, 1990, p.377); the same author is elsewhere sceptical of the feasibility of transferring the model to Britain. The inapplicability of the universalist approach in Europe has also been noted in Germany: 'an international comparison of HR practices clearly indicates that the basic functions of HR management are given different weights in different countries and that they are carried out differently' (Gaugler, 1988, p. 26). Another German surveying European personnel management, similarly concluded that 'a single universal HRM concept does not exist' (Pieper, 1990, p.11). Critiques of any simplistic attempts to 'generalise' the concept have also come from France (see, e.g. Bournois, 1991a, 1991b). European authors have argued that 'we are in culturally different contexts' and, that 'rather than copy solutions which result from other cultural traditions, we should consider the state of mind that presided in the search for responses adapted to the culture' (Albert, 1989, p. 75; translation in Brewster and Bournois, 1991).

The nature of SHRM assumed in the universalist paradigm provides for a more detailed examination and explanation of the policies and

established the notion of strategy as 'logical incrementalism'; with real strategies evolving 'as internal decisions and external events flow together to create a new, widely shared consensus for action among key members of the top management team. In well-run organisations, managers proactively guide these streams of action and events incrementally towards conscious strategies' (Quinn, 1980, p. 15). In the last few years the notion of incrementalism itself has been examined and seen as incorporating different interpretations (Mintzberg, 1990) and as having a number of different functions (Joyce, 1986).

'Strategy' as a concept has been used, whether recognised or not, in at least five separate ways (Mintzberg, 1987) – as: plan, ploy, pattern, position, and perspective. These definitions can be inter-related and in the real world strategic management 'inevitably involves some thinking ahead of time as well as some adaptation en route': effective strategies will encompass both (Mintzberg, 1994: 24). More recently still, it has been argued that control systems are the key means of managing and changing patterns in organisational activities (Simon, 1995).

Collins and Porras (1994) found that among their 18 high performing 'visionary' US companies there was no evidence of brilliant and complex strategic planning. Rather, their companies 'make some of their best moves by experimentation, trial and error, opportunism and – quite literally – accident. What looks *in retrospect* like brilliant foresight and preplanning was often the result of 'Let's just try a lot of stuff and keep what works' (Collins and Porras, 1994, p. 9). Behn (1988) had already found similar results in the public sector. None of this would have come as a surprise to Lindblom (1959) whose prescient article pointed out much the same thing many years ago, but which fell into disuse over the years of dominance of the 'command' model. Lengnick-Hall and Lengnick-Hall (1988) also challenged the assumption that strategic decisions were taken at a particular point in time such that the influence of HRM on that process could be measured.

In a more general way, the notion of strategic HRM can contain two core meanings. First, strategic HRM can focus on the link between organisational strategies and HRM as a central theme. Here the focus is on the place HRM has or does not have in the overall process of strategic decision making in the organisation. Secondly, strategic HRM can contain a strategic orientation of the HR function, i.e. the functional areas themselves. Here the discussion is focusing on the existence of various HR strategies and on the strategic orientation in the area of personnel planning or, in more detail, on the strategic orientation of various core functional areas of HR, e.g. recruitment and selection, training and development, appraisal, and compensation is discussed. Much of the discussion is, currently, centred around the first core meaning.

If the literature generally tends to assume that HRM is brought into the organisational strategy through some link to a formal 'predict and prepare' mode of strategy formulation, it makes two further assumptions: first, that this is solely a management issue; and secondly that, despite the debate about the role of line managers, HR issues are brought in to the strategic discussion by the HR specialists.

On the first issue, it has been pointed out that the rhetoric of the integration of the HR specialist function at the Board level has outpaced the reality (Legge, 1995). It has been argued, in contrast, that HRM participation can take many forms, from full membership of the Board to the design of implementation plans for the delivery of strategic goals (Caroll, 1987). Evidence from a substantial number of European countries has been used to assess the range of these forms (Brewster and Söderström, 1994; Brewster 1995; Brewster *et al.*, 1997a). The conclusion has been that previous discussions, mainly in the US but including significant examples from Europe too, miss important issues at the European level and at the European country level. Here, in a number of countries – most clearly, but not exclusively, Germany and the Netherlands – HRM issues are brought into the strategic level discussions by the presence of between one-third and one-half of the Board being representatives of the employees. In many organisations in these countries the HRM function is largely confined to an administrative role. In other cases, the presence of a legally required Works Council on which employee representatives have significant power, or pervasive unionism, mean that in practice the interests of the employees feature in all major operational decisions.

The debate about the growing role of line managers in strategic (and indeed in operational) HRM is widespread in Europe. Is HRM, as some would argue, now so well understood to be central to the well-being of an organisation and its ability to perform effectively that the subject has to permeate the responsibilities of every manager? Or is it the case that without a knowledgeable, experienced and influential human resource management department the organisation will be unable to give the subject the prominence that is needed? Perhaps more realistically, between these two extremes, what is the role of the HR function and how should its responsibilities be shared with line managers? In Europe the trend is clear: to give line managers more responsibility for the management of their staff and to reduce the extent to which human resources departments control or restrict line management autonomy in this area (Brewster and Hoogendoorn, 1992; Brewster and Söderström, 1994; Brewster, *et al.*, 1997a). This has created problems, with both personnel specialists and line managers unhappy about the way things are moving (Brewster and Hutchinson, 1994). The trend towards increased line management authority in this area, however, remains undeniable.

STRATEGIC HRM IN EUROPE

While in common with many other parts of the developed world, the major impact on labour management arrangements at the level of the individual organisation came indirectly from influences not specific to the employment relationship (Beaumont, 1995), European HRM differs from its US and Japanese counterparts in, among other ways, its relative emphasis on legislative frameworks (both supranational and national), trade unions and their role in the employment relationship, institutional arrangements relating to works councils, communication and consultation, managing diversity and its focus on competency and the development of human capital. While acknowledging that the definition, meaning and reliability of union membership figures vary across countries (Blanchflower and Freeman, 1990) and that trade union density varies considerably by country, and despite the fact that unions have always had a hard time in highly competitive product market conditions because of the difficulty they face in trying to take wages out of competition in such circumstances (Beaumont, 1995), in a majority of European economies membership remains significant.

In Europe employee communication and consultation remains centre-stage. However, while the prescriptive HRM literature advocates in employee communication the move from a more collective, negotiating focus to a more general approach to more direct communication with employees(Brewster and Bournois, 1991), there is European evidence to suggest that what we are witnessing is a general increase in all channels of communication (including collective) reflecting the desire to generate stronger identification and commitment among all employees.

A concentration on developing the skills of employees through HRM and training is evident in many organisations and sectors throughout Europe, and while differences may arise, they may be as much because of the differences in the overall thrust and provisions of the national educational system and the level of support given to employers by their governments, as opposed to underlying differences in organisational approaches.

Furthermore, while many of the pressures driving developments in Europe are a universal cry in the 1990s (national and organisational competitive advantage; increasing global competition and the resultant productivity pressures; the need for flexibility; technological sophistication and the emergence of the knowledge workforce), there have been a series of European specific developments which arguably will have a profound influence on the course and development of human resource management in Europe. Of particular significance here are the transforming economies of CEE, industrialisation/de-industrialisation and or re-industrialisation in different economies in Europe, falling birth-rates and increasing life expectancy, developments in European integration, the European Single Market and the launching of the Euro, and European work and labour legislation developments. But so too are countries within Europe rather distinctive from each other in terms of the architecture they rely on and the methodologies they employ in the management of their human resources. Thus it is common within Europe to talk about the existence of a Latin Model, or a Northern European/Nordic Model or an Anglo-Irish Model of HRM, or patterns of convergence and divergence in a continent characterised by diversity (for a more detailed contextual analysis see Brewster and Tyson, 1991; Brewster *et al.*, 1993; Brunstein, 1995; Sparrow and Hiltrop, 1994). It is precisely these differences within Europe and between Europe and other parts of the world which lend support to the argument for 'paradigm boundary-spanning' made earlier in order to unearth commonalties, differences and likely developments. Arguably only an approach of this nature is capable of investigating the 'paradoxical trends running through HRM in Europe' (Brewster and Bournois, 1991).

OUTLINE OF BOOK

This book is based on the empirical, conceptual and theoretical considerations that have been developed within Cranet-E about the current situation and the future development of HRM in Europe. Most of the contributions are written specifically for this book, though some draw on already published work. All of them, however, show the wide range of topics and frameworks that are used within the network, reflecting differing theoretical and national viewpoints.

The chapters of this book are grouped around five main topics: flexibility, training and development, industrial relations, regional aspects, i.e. central Europe and Pacific Rim, and problems of organising and undertaking comparative human resource management research.

First, in Part II, a number of contributions deal with various country-specific and comparative aspects of *flexibility* on the organisational as well as – to a lesser extent – on the individual level. Ricard Serlavós and Mireia Aparicio-Valverde in Chapter 2 use Atkinson's (1984) well-known framework about various forms of flexibility to develop a background against which they in a first step analyse the situation in Spanish organisations. They draw some conclusions about further developments and challenges in European HRM as well as point out promising lines of further research in this area. Andrea Friedrich, Rüdiger Kabst, Maria Rodehut and Wolfgang Weber (Chapter 3) concentrate on one specific aspect of organisational flexibility – job rotation – and proceed in three steps. First, they give an introduction to the field of labour flexibility, define the term job rotation, and distinguish it from other forms of flexibility. Secondly, they look at the relevance of job rotation in European companies. Thirdly, they analyse empirically whether job rotation in European enterprises is more likely to represent a solitary short-term instrument or whether on the other hand the implementation of job rotation is accompanied by a more long-term oriented integration of personnel strategies. In Chapter 4 Lesley Mayne, Olga Tregaskis and Chris Brewster deal with another aspect of flexibility and focus on the use of two particular forms of flexible or 'atypical' working patterns: part-time and short-term working. Based on the data of five large European countries they examine the proposition that there is little correlation between those employers who use a considerable amount of flexibility, defined in terms of part-time and short-term contracts, and those who take a more strategic approach to HRM. Dirk Buyens, Tine Vandenbossche and Ans de Vos (Chapter 5) point out that the application of flexible work structures and arrangements are vital for the competitiveness of organisations in today's markets. Given this assumption, they present an empirical analysis of the trends that can be observed in Belgium companies. In Chapter 6 Paul Gooderham and Odd Nordhaug analyse from the background of institutional theory and in a two country comparison the factors that influence the kind and level of organisational flexibility. In particular, they identify those factors which condition the use firms make of HR strategies aimed at enhancing their ability to respond flexibly to an increasingly changing environment. Specifically, they concentrate on the variations made by firms in their pursuit of greater levels of numerical flexibility. Nancy Papalexandris (Chapter 7) points out that flexibility is not only a tool for reducing labour costs and thus improving productivity and competitiveness; it might also be a means to fight unemployment and an important tool for reconciling work with family life. Thus, she examines the role of flexibility in addressing the important social issue of work and family reconciliation in Europe in general and in Greece in particular.

In Part III, some *training* and *development* issues are discussed in Chapters 8 and 9. In Chapter 8 Olga Tregaskis suggests that an organisation's HRD system is a key mechanism for enabling the achievement of business goals through people as one of the sources of competitive advantage. Given the importance of national contextual factors for the HRD system as well as the increasing presence of foreign multinationals or multinational enterprises (MNEs) in host countries, she compares the role of the host-national context to that of the parent in shaping MNE management practice. Specifically, she tests the relative impact of the host–national context, and the national origin of the parent company in shaping the HRD practices of foreign MNEs operating in Britain, drawing on data collected from European as well as US and Japanese multinationals. In Chapter 9 Henrik Holt Larsen concentrates on one specific element of personnel development systems i.e., high-flyer programmes. He suggests that the last decade with its emphasis on organisational culture, experiential learning, managerial competence, strategic HRM, the learning organisation, etc. has changed the demands and expectations of management development, as well as the methods and techniques by which these demands and expectations are met. He analyses the consequences of these developments on the role and effectiveness of high-flyer programmes in organisations. Furthermore, he presents survey data about high-flyer policy in a number of European countries and discusses the implications for practice and future research.

Part IV examines various aspects of the changing system of *industrial relations* in Europe. In Chapter 10 Michael Morley, Chris Brewster, Patrick Gunnigle and Wolfgang Mayrhofer deal with the developments of the industrial relations system from an overall European perspective. They draw on the ongoing debate about the increasing convergence or divergence of the national systems of industrial relations and the consequences this might have in particular for the trade unions. They investigate a number of key aspects of industrial relations at the level of the employing organisation (like levels of trade-union membership in organisations across Europe, the extent and nature of trade-union recognition, trade-union influence, and the locus of policy determination in industrial relations) as a means of evaluating developments in the nature and conduct of industrial relations. Wolfgang Mayrhofer, Chris Brewster, Michael Morley and Patrick Gunnigle (Chapter 11) argue that effective communication and consultation is at the heart of effective HRM. Furthermore, they point out that there has been a tendency to associate the concept of human resource management (HRM) with the individualisation of communication and a move away from, or even antagonism towards, the concept of industrial relations (IR) – communication and consultation which is collective and particularly that which is trade union based. Based on a comparative analysis of data from a number of European countries they examine the situation in Europe regarding the extent of communication and consultation that takes place in organisations in the various European countries and the extent to which that is individual or collective. They conclude by stating that the alternatives posited in the current models are inadequate to capture the reality of European organisations, that Europe (and perhaps other parts of the world) needs a conception of HRM which can encompass a positive collective relationship with employees and trade unions, that there are cases and evidence which suggests that there are already signs of the development of such a concept of HRM, and that, indeed, there may be positive advantages to such an approach.

Part V of the book covers some more general descriptions of HRM *in key regions of the world.* In Chapter 12 Wolfgang Weber, Rüdiger Kabst and Christopher Gramley relate to the convergence–divergence issue in terms of development of HRM across various countries in Europe. Based on existing frameworks they analyse HR policies in European organisations. Specifically, they analyse empirically whether organisation-specific variables have a major influence on the formulation of HR policies or whether country-specific circumstances bear more responsibility. Elizabeth Vatchkova (Chapter 13) comments on the developments in Bulgaria in the course of the transition to a market economy which is taking place under conditions of continuous eco nomic, political and social crisis. She examines some of the key chal lenges faced by Bulgarian organisations in the HRM area during the transition from a centralised planned economy to a market one. Thus, she offers an analysis of the changing nature of HRM which is accompanying the other major social and economic changes in

Bulgaria. Robin Kramar (Chapter 14) analyses the situation in Australia in the light of the major changes in methods of management and employment policies throughout industrialised countries during the 1980s and the 1990s. She argues that intense international competition and the internationalisation of labour markets have encouraged innovations in the way work is organised and the way people are deployed and managed. In particular, she examines the extent to which the management of labour has changed in Australia during the 1980s and 1990s and assesses whether these changes constitute a new approach to the management of labour and the degree to which the changes constitute an approach that is consistent with a 'human resource management' approach. Furthermore, she explores the factors which have encouraged these developments.

The final chapters in Part VI focus on *organisational and methodological questions of international comparative research* in the area of HRM. In Chapter 15 Wolfgang Mayrhofer suggests that the management of an international research network covers all areas that are well known in cross-border activities in the business field. Handling diversity, making use of economies of scale, dealing with cultural differences, working in multicultural teams, or balancing overall goals and local needs are some of the typical issues. However, international research networks cannot be equated with multinational companies, but differ in multiple ways. He argues that despite these differences an international research network can use the same forms of coordination and control as a (multinational) company. Furthermore, he claims that in order to contribute to the further existence of the network, to the efficient handling of the evolving tasks, and to a high quality output, managing the network requires the use of different forms of coordination and control at the same time. However, such a 'coordination mix' may lead to new problems like member ambiguity or conflict. These ideas are illustrated with examples from Cranet-E. Chris Brewster, Olga Tregaskis, Ariane Hegewisch and Lesley Mayne (Chapter 16) point towards the necessity and significance of international comparative research in general and, more specifically, in the area of HRM. However, research in this area is rare, largely because of the extra complexity created by international research. They explore some of the complexities of conducting comparative international research and in particular internationallly comparative surveys. The authors explore some of the issues that shape international research design and then examine some of the practical problems inherent in such research. Their considerations are illustrated with examples from Cranet-E.

Hanel, U., Hegewisch, A. and Mayrhofer, W. (eds) (1997) 'Personalarbeit im Wandel', *Entwicklungen in den neuen Bundesländern und in Europa*, München, Mering, Hampp.
Hendry, C. and Pettigrew, A. (1986) 'The practice of strategic human resource management', *Personnel Review* 15(5): 3–8.
Hendry, C. and Pettigrew, A. (1990) 'HRM: an agenda for the 1990s', *International Journal of Human Resource Management*, 1(1): 17–25.
Hickson, D. and Macmillan, C. J. (eds) (1981) *Organization and Nation: The Aston Programme IV*, Farnborough, Gower.
Hickson, D., Hinings, C. R., McMillan, C. J. and Schwitter, J. P. (1974) 'The culture-free context of organization structure: a tri-national comparison', *Sociology* 8: 59–80.
Hickson, D., McMillan, C. J., Azumi, K. and Horvath, D. (1979) 'Grounds for comparative organisation theory: quicksands or hard core?', in Lammers, C. J. and Hickson, D. J. (eds), pp. 24–41.
Huselid, M. (1995) 'The impact of human resource management practices on turnover, productivity and corporate financial performance', *Academy of Management Journal* 38: 635–72.
Hyman, R. (1987) 'Strategy or structure?: Capital, labour and control', *Work, Employment and Society* 1(1): 25–53.
Jick, T. (1979) 'Mixing qualitative and quantitative methods: triangulation in action' *Administrative Science Quarterly*, 24: 602–11.
Joyce, W. F. (1986) 'Towards a Theory of Incrementalism', *Advances in Strategic Management* 4: 43–58.
Keenoy, T. (1990) 'HRM: a case of the wolf In sheep's Clothing', *Personnel Review*, 19(2): 3–9.
Koch, M. J., McGrath, R. G. (1996) 'Improving labor productivity: human resource management policies do matter', *Strategic Management Journal* 17: 335–54.
Kochan, T., Katz, H. and McKersie, R. (1986) *The Transformation of American Industrial Relations*, New York, Basic Books.
Kochan, T. (1997) ' "Beyond myopia" ': human resources and the changing social contract', Research and Theory in Strategic Human Resource Management: An Agenda for the 21st Century Conference, Cornell University, 3–4 Oct.
Kochan, T. A. and Barocci, T. A. (1985) *Human Resource Management and Industrial Relations*, Boston, Little Brown.
Kogut, B. (ed.) (1993) *Country Competitiveness: Technology and the Organization of Work*, Oxford, Oxford University Press.
Koubek, J. and Brewster, C. (1995) 'Human resource management in turbulent times: the Czech case', *International Journal of Human Resource Management*, 6(2): 223–48.
Kuhn, T. (1970) *The Structure of Scientific Revolutions*, Chicago, University of Chicago Press.
Lamb, R. (ed.) (1983) Recent Advances in Strategic Planning, New York, McGraw-Hill.
Lammers, C. J. and Hickson D. J. (eds) *Organisations Alike and Unlike*, London, Kegan Paul.
Legge, K. (1995) 'HRM: rhetoric, reality and hidden agendas', in Storey, J. (ed.) pp. 33–59.

Lengnick-Hall, C. A. and Lengnick-Hall, M. L. (1988) 'Strategic human resources management: a review of the literature and a proposed typology', *Academy of Management Review*, 13(3): 454–70.

Lindblom, C. E. (1959) 'The science of "Muddling Through"', *Public Administration Review*, 19: 79–88.

Locke, R. and Kochan, T. (1995) 'Conclusion: the transformation of industrial relations?', in Locke, R., *et al.*, (eds), pp. 359–84.

Locke, R., Kochan, T., Piore, M. (eds) (1995) *Employment Relations in a Changing World Economy*, Cambridge, Mass., MIT Press.

Lundvall, B. A. (ed.) (1992) *National Systems of Innovation. Towards a Theory of Innovation and Interactive Learning*, London, Pinter.

Mahoney, T. and Deckop, J.R. (1986) 'Evolution of concept and practice in personnel administration/human resource management', *Journal of Management*, 12(2): 223–41.

Marginson, P., Edwards, P. K., Purcell, J. and Sissons, K. (1988) 'What do corporate officers really do?', *British Journal of Industrial Relations*, 26: 229–45.

Martell, K. and, Caroll, S. J. (1995) 'How strategic is HRM?', *Human Resource Management*, 34: 253–67.

Miller, P. (1989). 'Strategic HRM: what it is and what it isn't', *Personnel Management*, Feb.: 46–51.

Mintzberg, H. (1987) 'Crafting strategy', *Harvard Business Review*, (July–Aug.): 66–75.

Mintzberg, H. (1990) 'The manager's job: folklore and fact', *Harvard Business Review*, 68 (2): 163–76.

Mintzberg, H. (1994) *The Rise and Fall of Strategic Planning*, Hemel Hempstead, Prentice Hall International.

Nelson, R. R. (ed.) (1992) *National Systems of Innovation. A Comparative Analysis*. Oxford, Oxford University Press.

Oyen, E. (ed.), Comparative Methdology, London, Sage.

Pieper, R. (ed.) (1990) *Human Resource Management: An International Comparison*, Berlin, Walter de Gruyter.

Poole, M. (1990) 'Human resource management in an international perspective', *International Journal of Human Resource Management*, 1(1): 1–15.

Porter, M. E. (1990) *The Competitive Advantage of Nations*, London, Macmillan.

Pugh, D. S. and Hickson, D. J. (1976) *Aston Programme: Volume I*, London, Saxon House Press.

Purcell, J. (1987) 'Mapping management styles in industrial relations', *Journal of Management Studies* 24(5): 535–48.

Purcell, J. and Ahlstrand, B. (1994) *Human Resource Management in the Multi-Divisional Firm*, Oxford, Oxford University Press.

Quinn, J. (1980) *Strategies for Change: Logical Incrementalism*, Homewood, IL, ICC.

Ramsey, H. (1992) 'Commitment and involvement', in Towers, B. (ed.), pp. 208–37.

Rose (1991) 'Comparing forms of comparative analysis', *Political Studies* 39: 446–62.

Rowland, K. M. and Ferris, G. R. (eds) (1985) *Research in Personnel and Human Resources Management 3*, Greenwich, Coun., JAI Press.

Salaman, G. (ed.) (1991) *Human Resources Strategies*, Buckingham, the Open University.
Schuler, R. S. (1989) 'Human resources strategy: focusing on issues and actions', *Organisational Dynamics* 19(1): 4–20.
Schuler, R. S. (1992), Strategic human resource management: linking the people with the strategic needs of the business', *Organizational Dynamics*, summer: 18–32.
Schuler, R. S. and Jackson, S. E. (1987) 'Linking competitive strategies with human resource management practices', *Academy of Management Executive* 1: 207–19.
Simon, R. (1995) *Levers of Control*, Boston, Mass., Harvard Business School Press.
Singh, R. (1992) 'Human resource Management: a sceptical look', in: Towers, B. (ed.), *Handbook of Human Resource Management*, Oxford, Blackwell.
Sorge, A. (1991) 'Strategic fit and the societal effect: interpreting cross-national comparisons of technology, organisation and human resources', *Organization Studies* 12(2).
Sparrow, P. and Hiltrop, J. M. (1994), *European Human Resource Management in Transition*, Hemel Hempstead, Prentice Hall.
Staffelbach, B. (1986) *Strategisches Personalmanagement*, Bern-Stuttgart.
Standing, G.(1997) 'Globalisation, labour flexibility and insecurity: the era of market regulation' *European Journal of Industrial Relations*, 3(1): 7–37.
Storey, J. (1992a) *Developments in the Management of Human Resources*, Oxford, Blackwells. Oxford.
Storey, J. (1992b) 'HRM in Action: the truth is out at last', *Personnel Management*, Apr. 28–31.
Storey, J. (ed.) (1995) *Human Resource Management: A Critical Text*, London, Routledge.
Tichy, N., Fombrun, C. J. and Devanna, M. A. (1982) 'Strategic human resource management', *Sloan Management Review*, 23(2): 47–60.
Towers, B. (1992) *The Handbook of Human Resource Management*, Oxford, Blackwell.
Turner, T. and Morley, M. (1995) *Industrial Relations & the New Order: Case Studies in Conflict & Co-Operation*, Dublin, Oak Tree Press,.
Ulrich, D. (1987) 'Organizational capability as competitive advantage: Human resource professionals as strategic partners', *Human Resource Planning*, 10: 169–84.
Ulrich, D. (1989) 'Tie the corporate knot: gaining complete customer commitment', *Sloan Management Review*, summer 19–28.
US Department of Labor (1993) 'High performance work practices and firm performance', Washington, DC, US Government Printing Office.
Wright, P. M. and McMahan, G. C. (1992) 'Theoretical perspectives for strategic human resource management', *Journal of Management*, 18(2): 295–321.
Wright, P. M. and Snell, S. A. (1991) 'Toward an integrative view of strategic human resource management', *Human Resource Management Review*, 1: 203–25.

NATIONAL COLLEGE OF IRELAND LIBRARY

Part II
Aspects of Flexibility

pockets of poverty and marginalisation continue to exist in the developed countries with large degrees of labour flexibility.

Discussion about the need for flexible working practices often takes place within the framework of a discussion on job creation. It is true that job market deregulation and flexible labour practices do create jobs. But what kind of jobs? How do these jobs affect the macroeconomy? How do they affect social structures? Certain forms of flexibility mean that a considerable number of costs are shifted from companies to society in the form of taxes, unemployment benefits, health care and other kinds of spending, and risk is shifted to individuals and households in a move that could jeopardise social stability and cohesion. The prospects are not very bright and the outlook for the future is scarcely conducive to encouraging permanent learning and the attitudes of co-operation called for by a model of competition based on innovation and quality. Nevertheless, the alternatives proposed this far, among them a number of ways to redistribute employment, have not been very successful in terms of improving, or even maintaining, current employment levels.

Again according to Giarini and Liedtke (1996), the time has now come to look for new ways to combine theory and practice in an attempt to go beyond the manifestly inefficient standard approaches to, and perceptions of, the current state of affairs and use alternative tools for action that will enable us to shape a new vision of the future.

What kind of flexibility?

First of all, we must specify what we mean when we talk about flexibility. The concept of flexibility, understood as the *corporate objective of being able to quickly and effectively respond to the changing demands of the environment*, can be materialised under different forms. This variety of very diverse business practices generally comes under the umbrella heading of *flexible working practices*.

Atkinson provided the best known model of flexible working practices in 1984. His concept of a flexible company was based on observations and data from empirical research in British companies. Atkinson maintains that companies are striving for three types of flexibility:

1. *Functional flexibility*, whereby employees can perform different tasks and functions within their organisation. This means that the workforce must be trained in different fields and have a thorough

knowledge of the company and its processes. Functional flexibility tends to benefit both employees (by enriching their jobs) and employers (who acquire multi-skilled personnel with which to confront rapid change).
2. *Numerical flexibility,* whereby companies can easily and quickly reduce or expand their total number of employees in order to strike the perfect balance between the workforce employed and the workforce actually required. This kind of flexibility is usually achieved by using a variety of contract arrangements and varying the distribution of working time.
3. *Financial flexibility,* whereby companies attempt to link labour costs to performance both individual and corporate. This kind of flexibility is usually achieved through different variable remuneration systems, profit sharing, etc.

Given the needs for flexibility, Atkinson maintains that the typical hierarchical structure of many companies should be exchanged for a series of increasingly peripheral circles. Different hiring and HR policies can be applied to each of these circles (see Figure 2.1). According to this model, the core of the company consists of a group of employees who are offered long-term employment and career development plans. In exchange, these employees are expected to be versatile and able to perform a variety of functions related to the company's main activities. In other words, they will enable the company to attain functional flexibility. These key employees are usually managers, designers, technical experts, etc.

From here on out, there are several peripheral groups, each of which has increasingly loose links to the company. The first group might consist of specialised full-time employees who are not expected to develop their capacities to move horizontally or vertically within the company. The second peripheral group consists of permanent employees recruited from job promotion programmes (apprentices, business interns, etc.) to work on a part-time basis or in job-sharing arrangements. This second circle gives the company numerical flexibility as well as a certain extent of functional flexibility.

The outermost circle consists of people who work for the company but are not contracted employees. These include 'temps' and people who deliver services under the forms of subcontracting or outsourcing arrangements. This gives the company access to people who are specialists in activities that are not directly related to the company's core operations or who relieve the company of the need to worry about jobs

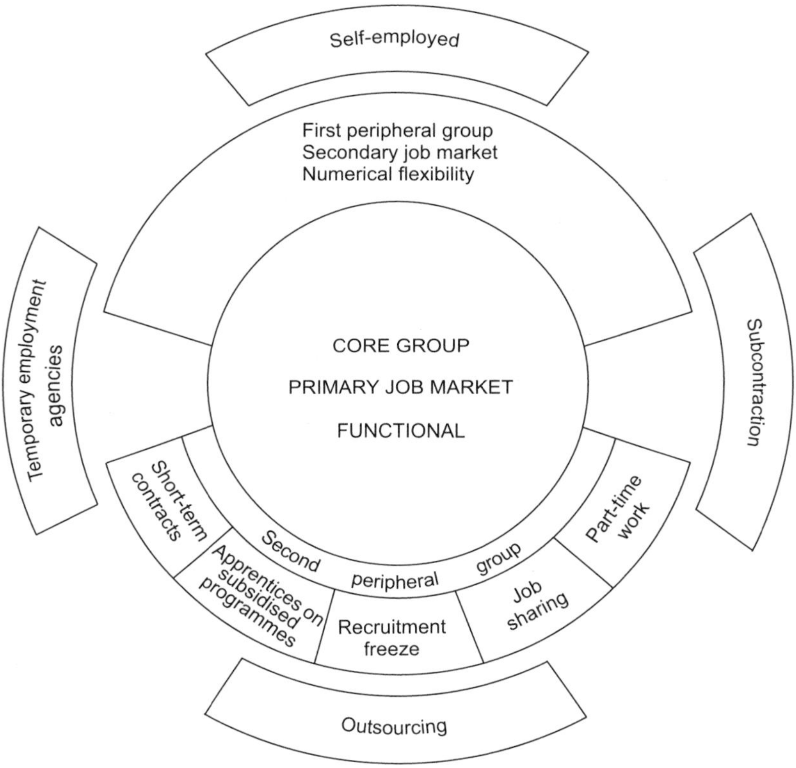

Figure 2.1 Atkinson's (1984) flexible firm model

that are necessary but not actually part of their core business (cleaning services, goods transport, maintenance, etc.)

Atkinson first used his model to explain and describe practices in the companies he observed. However, the model is frequently used as a prescribed formula for companies aiming to become flexible. As a result the model has been severely criticised by the academic community (see, for example, Pollert 1988, 1991, 1994). Moreover, and this is yet more worrying, it has been misinterpreted as a universal panacea, and corporate attempts to apply it indiscriminately have been unsuccessful. Obviously, cultural conditions differ from one country to the next and the particular economic structure and legal framework of each country is vital to determining the extent to which certain kinds of flexibility are necessary, desirable or even possible. The effect of socio-economic conditions on flexibility in European companies in general and Spanish companies in particular is discussed in the next section of this chapter. Other factors, such as economic sector and company size also help determine which specific practices should be applied.

Kinds of flexibility adopted by Spanish and other European companies in the 1990s

Data from Cranet-E in the past five years provide information on the kinds of flexible working practices being used in Spanish and other European companies (Cranfield Project Spanish Research Team, 1995) This information was collected from 283 Spanish companies employing more than 200 employees. The entire Cranet-E database from the 1995 survey round contains listings for more than 5000 organisations throughout Europe.

As an indicator of functional flexibility, the survey uses changes in the degree of specialisation of jobs in different professional categories that have taken place during the past three years. The findings reveal a general trend towards broader job content: but the trend is considerably less pronounced in Spain than in other European countries (see Table 2.1). It is particularly interesting to note that less than one-third of the Spanish companies surveyed has broadened the content of their managers' jobs. Moreover, and although 41% of the Spanish companies said that the content of their technical experts' jobs was now broader, 26% said that job content was yet more specific than before. This increase in the specificity of jobs can be explained by the fact that rapid technological developments in some industries require highly specialised skills and know-how.

Table 2.1 Percentage of companies who have broadened their employees' job content in the past 3 years (1995)

Job category	*Spain (%)*	*European average (%)*
Managers	30	44
Professional/technical	41	44
Clerical	36	44
Manual	30	34

Source: Cranet-E.

The difference between Spain and the rest of Europe is even more pronounced when it comes to the different forms of contracts used. Spanish companies on the whole have concentrated on the use of fixed-term contracts and subcontracting arrangements (see Figure 2.2). There are few cases in which companies combine and use other, more innovative forms. One praiseworthy exception is Danone (Martínez, 1996).

The extent to which temporary contracts are used by Spanish companies is clearly revealed not only by the number of companies who issue them but also by the proportion of employees hired on a temporary basis (see Figure 2.3).

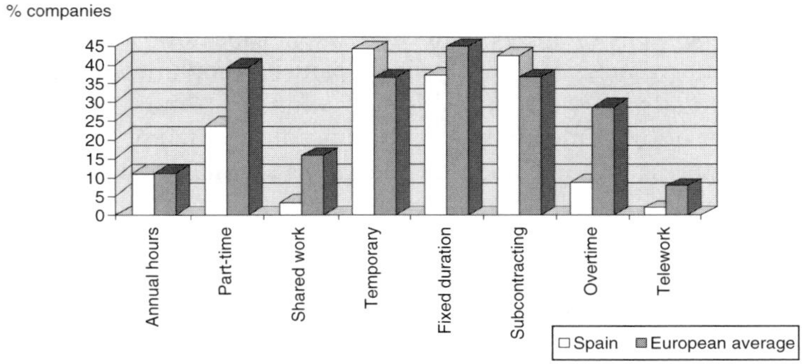

Figure 2.2 Percentage of Spanish and European firms that have increased their use of different kinds of job contracts during the past three years (1995)

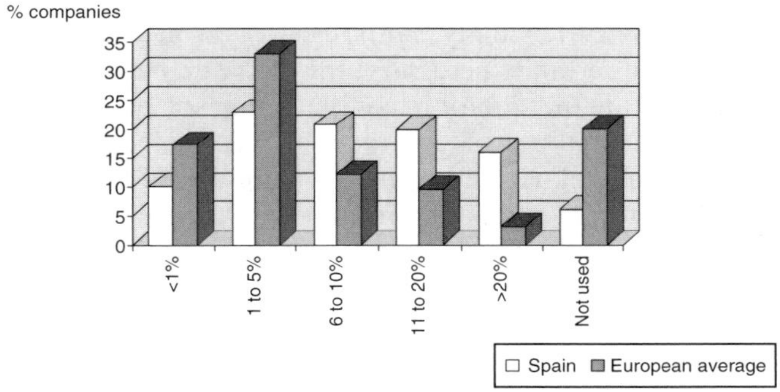

Figure 2.3 Proportion of workforce on temporary contracts in Spanish and European companies (1995)

One out of every three Spanish firms has no part-time employees. Nevertheless, once part-time positions are created or re-converted, they tend to endure. Still, in 1994 the number of part-time employees in Spain amounted to only 5.6 per cent of total employment in comparison with 14.1 per cent in the rest of Europe (Employment Observatory Trends, 1996). Moreover, only 3.5 per cent of Spanish part-time employees actually want to work on a part-time basis (*EPA*, 1995).

As in the rest of Europe, companies in Spain are proving very slow to adopt teleworking or distance working using electronic data transmission techniques. Apart from IBM, only 1 per cent of the companies in Spain have employees working from their homes and they account for only 1–2 per cent of their total staff. Moreover, in 2 per cent of these companies, teleworkers are used only sporadically and do not amount to even 1 per cent of the regular staff. New legislation on temporary employment agencies is now causing Spanish companies to gradually reduce their use of overtime. Although allowances must be made for the number of overtime hours worked but not reported or remunerated (though figures are not available, indications are that they are high), 36 per cent of the Spanish companies surveyed for the Cranfield project stated that their employees were working fewer overtime hours than three years ago and 20 per cent said that their employees no longer worked overtime at all.

Structure and culture: conditioning factors

Discussion on flexible working practices too often focuses almost exclusively on legislation governing the job market and particularly on employee in-and outflows, as though flexibility was only limited to Atkinson's *numerical* flexibility. Although recent negotiations among social agents were certainly necessary, they have actually done nothing more than aggravate the situation, concentrating solely on reducing the number of different types of contracts and defining the causes and conditions of dismissal. However, there is a number of other conditioning factors that prevent companies from becoming truly flexible and we will examine them in the following paragraphs.

The first type of conditioning factors is *structural* in nature and involves issues that affect the smooth functioning of the job market. Primary among them are the barriers to relocation caused by a poorly functioning housing market (in which the cost of relocation is so high as to make it virtually inadvisable) and an educational system that makes changing children from one school to another a high-risk undertaking. With conditions like these it is not surprising that people are reluctant to relocate or, if they are unemployed, look for jobs that would involve a change of residence.

The educational system is also an important obstacle to functional flexibility. Schooling in general, and occupational training in particular, continues to have little to do with what companies really need in their employees. Moreover, and despite notable efforts to remedy the situation (the Catalan regional government's Servei Català d'Occupació is a good example) job markets are still not sufficiently transparent, and therefore matching supply and demand is an awkward process.

At a European level, although obstacles to free movement of Europe's labour force were theoretically eliminated in 1995, the workforce is no more mobile than it was before. This can be partly explained by high rates of unemployment in all the largest European Union countries, but there are other structural factors that are important here as well. Among them are language barriers, problems in getting academic degrees and professional accreditations recognised, and differences in social security systems from one country to the next.

A second type of conditioning factors is *cultural* in nature and related to psychological, personal and family obstacles to the changes required by the new conditions on the job market. Despite pronounced migratory movements in recent history, local roots continue to go very deep in Spain. However, it is these very roots and the strength of family ties that have enabled the country to withstand the tremendous social costs of unemployment without the situation giving rise to major tension or conflict.

Other cultural conditioning factors have to do with deeply ingrained patterns of behaviour, among them the generalised practice of concentrating summer holidays in August; the belligerent stance of a faction of the Catholic Church which is strongly opposed to certain proposals involving relocation; the introduction of fourth and fifth shifts which require employees to work on Sundays and holidays, and the notable reluctance of many families to accept vocational educational (occupational) training as a reasonable and worthy form of education for their children.

Limits to flexibility

The positive features of flexibility have been amply described by a variety of authors and some social agents. In addition to enabling organisations to quickly and effectively adjust to changing demands in their environment without suffering major upheaval, there are concrete advantages such as lower wage and extra-salarial costs, the possibility of quickly finding substitute employees, and increased opportunities for employers to acquire employees with specific skills (Lenz, 1996).

They also point out more general advantages. Some authors consider part-time employment as a good way of reconciling work and family demands (DeRoure, 1995; Papalexandris, 1996) in a setting like Europe, where although 40 per cent of the women are part of the labour market, the family is still considered to have the lion's share of responsibility in caring for children and other dependents and transmitting social and cultural values.

Furthermore, and particularly in countries like Spain where unemployment is high, there is a good deal of discussion about temporary employment agencies and other arrangements which promote short-term contracting as ways to keep down unemployment figures. When faced with the choice between precarious employment or unemployment, the former tends to be considered the lesser evil. Nevertheless, it should be noted here that no European country has as yet been able to demonstrate a direct link between an increase in temporary hiring arrangements and a decrease in unemployment (Cranet-E, 1996).

Flexibility, then, should not in itself be a goal. Instead it should be a strategy for responding to certain needs. Even though flexible companies do have certain advantages, indiscriminate use of flexible working practices can cause a series of problems. Four of them are discussed below:

1. Flexible working practices, performance and industrial safety

In an ideal situation, employees would be able to take their skills and know-how from one company to another without any problems. In reality, and depending on the specific nature of each job, entering a company involves a period of adaptation to both the corporate culture and the specific job to be performed. This necessary learning curve means that performance at the outset tends to be poorer and novices are more likely to make mistakes and have accidents.

In the case of temporary employment, adaptation and learning is a recurrent process, multiplying the risks mentioned above. Although accidents are only one of many indicators of industrial safety, they are by far the easiest way to measure the differences between the industrial safety of temporary and permanent employees. The most complete and complex studies of these differences were carried out in France (François, 1991) and demonstrate that the risk of industrial accidents is consistently higher among temporary employees. In contrast, the 1979–87 campaign to reduce industrial accidents in France led to a considerable decrease in industrial accidents among permanent employees. The campaign consisted largely of assessing the inherent risks of each job, making employees aware of these risks and providing them with suitable training. Such measures are difficult and/or costly to apply when these jobs are to be performed by temporary employees.

Figures for Catalonia in particular and Spain in general point to a similar situation. According to figures from the Labour Relations Authority (DGRL, 1995) there are 92.6 accidents for every 1000 temporary employees in Catalonia and 52.8 per 1000 employees with permanent contracts. At nation-wide level, the figures are similar, as is shown in Table 2.2, which lists the percentages of accidents suffered by permanent and temporary employees in every sector of the Spanish economy and demonstrates that the likelihood of accident is far higher among temporary employees (Aparicio and Masip 1996).

2. *Organisational health and sustainable flexibility*

Flexibility also requires setting certain limits at the organisational level. Flexible contracting is HRM's equivalent of just-in-time or lean production (Cranet-E, 1996). With these systems, only the resources actually in use are physically present in the company, thus saving warehousing costs and the need to manage idle resources. Despite the

Table 2.2 Accidents in Spain: breakdown by type of contract and sector of economy.

	% Accidents permanent employees	*% Accidents temporary employees*	*% of Temporary employees in sector*	*Ratio accidents temporary/ permanent employment*
Industry	60.9	39.1	21.7	1.80
Construction	20.4	79.6	52.8	1.51
Services	49.3	50.7	33.2	1.53
Total	47.2	52.8	31.4	1.68

Sources: Aparicio-Valverde and Masip 1996, based on information from the Direcció General d'Informàtica i Estadística (1995) and the Instituto Nacional de Seguridad e Higiene en el Trabajo (1994).

proven virtues of these systems, they are only successful if a whole series of internal and external conditions are met, among them available and efficient suppliers, reliable means of transport, etc.

Similarly, if a company has only the minimum number of employees and they are able to keep the company going if they operate at 100 per cent of their capacity, the company is liable to find itself short of employees at any given time. This shortage could be strictly numerical or it could be a shortage of employees with certain necessary skills. Thus, one wonders if the company should not have a certain number of 'idle' people or hours which could serve as a reserve when necessary. Companies need to strike the right balance between the minimum number of employees necessary and the number of reserves which would enable the company to react rapidly to changes in its environment (Mayrhofer, 1996).

Moreover, the more components of flexibility there are in an organisation (the more peripheral circles) the harder it is to draw the limits between the company's internal and external environments. This permeation capacity of the organisation, in principle, is not a problem, but rather it can be said that organisations, as open systems, should take advantage of this exchange with their environment. Nevertheless, it is also true that an important part of business management is based on the influence of, and changes in, organisational culture. But this usually affects only the core members of the organisation, which means that if they account for only a small portion of the people working in the company, efforts to influence culture could become increasingly watered-down as they spread to the periphery and end up having little or no impact. It is therefore necessary to review what is meant by culture, whose culture is important and how this culture can be influenced in organisations whose boundaries are not clearly drawn. Similarly, we should re-assess the meaning and importance of concepts such as commitment, involvement or leadership and their relationship to organisational efficiency.

3. The dual labour market and a decrease in aggregate demand

The growing number of people with short-term contracts and no idea of what their job and economic situation will be like in the near future makes the emergence of a dual labour market seem likely (on the one hand, people who have permanent jobs and, on the other, those who do not). Generally speaking, temporary employees are paid less (Marsden, 1989; Rodgers and Rodgers, 1989) and have fewer chances for training and development (Brewster *et al.*, 1994). This combination of factors and study. Academics and social agents alike must rise to this challenge.

The academic contribution

Academics began to turn their attention to the subject of flexible working practices when these were first formalised by Atkinson. Although some authors did mention flexibility prior to 1984, their work usually focused on its economic and legal aspects and explored the evolution of different kinds of contract arrangements. It was not until the 1980s and 1990s that there began to be a body of management and human behaviour literature that dealt with what had up until that time been the employment market's 'missing persons' (Feldman and Doerpinghaus, 1992).

Outstanding among these studies are those which explore the effects of particular kinds of flexible working practices (part-time employment, variable remuneration systems, etc.) on human and organisational behaviour. But rarely has there been any direct relation discovered between a particular practice and corporate performance. In addition, a number of case studies have been written, most of which describe examples of 'best practice' in the use of different kinds of flexibility. But it must be pointed out that few case studies explore the unsuccessful companies that also apply flexible working practices.

There is, then, a whole list of specific issues which need to be systematically and thoroughly studied in both their qualitative and quantitative aspects and from multi-disciplinary viewpoints. Among them are:

- The actual costs and benefits of using particular flexible working practices and combinations thereof.
- Integrating flexible working practices in corporate strategies.
- The effects of legislation and regulations on the use and extent of flexible working practices.
- Differences in employee salaries, benefits and working conditions for different kinds of flexible working arrangements.
- How to get short-term employees committed and involved, as well as keeping corporate data confidential.
- The use and efficiency of functional flexibility and its relation to other kinds of flexibility.
- The role of trade unions: their importance and the kind of actions they can take in a situation in which their normal representatives

(permanent employees) account for an increasingly smaller share of the workforce.
- The significance and practicality of flexible working practices in small and medium-sized companies.

Lastly, because it seems likely that jobs as they have been known for generations will soon cease to exist, research should address the subject of what work actually means in terms of the individual's life experience. Such studies should be almost philosophical in nature and involve observing and studying other societies, cultures and religions whose concepts differ from those of our Western world.

The contribution of the social agents

This contribution is decisive because the flexible working practices that make any economy and its constituent companies truly competitive are those that are the result of consensus among the parties involved. If this consensus is to be achieved and, above all, maintained, employers and employees alike will have to revise their traditional stances and be willing to jointly take the risks that are an inherent part of all major processes of social change.
Some of the possible lines of work could be:

- Exploring the possibility of reaching employer–employee agreements on flexible working practices in sectors where conditions are appropriate. This would involve first selecting these sectors and defining the terms of possible agreements.
- Bringing the true 'victims' of flexible working practices into the discussion and seriously listening to their opinions and experiences. This means involving people who are really affected by the situations and conditions resulting from corporate-imposed flexible working practices. The Petras Report (Petras, 1996) is a good example of this kind of study.
- Undertaking actions to promote the changes in culture (working / living) and the structural changes needed to facilitate geographic and functional mobility. However, we must not lose sight of the priority goals of economic, social and personal growth and development. In short, flexibility is no more than a means towards an end.
- Introducing the issue of secondary education into the discussion. The system of secondary education in Spain has recently been reformed and although the intention is praiseworthy, differences in

Pollert, A. (1988) 'The "flexible firm": fixation or fact?', *Work, Employment and Society*, 2(3): 281–316.
Pollert, A. (1991) *Farewell to Flexibility?*, Oxford, Basil Blackwell.
Pollert, A. (1994) *Adiós a la Flexibilidad?*, Madrid, Ministerio de Trabajo y Seguridad Social.
Rifkin, J. (1996) *El fin del trabajo. nuevas tecnologías contra puestos de trabajo: el nacimiento de una nueva era*. Barcelona, Paidós.
Rodgers, G. and Rodgers, J. (ed.) (1989) *Precarious Jobs and Labour Market Regulation: the Growth of Atypical Employment in Western Europe*, Geneva, International Institute for Labour Studies.

3 Job Rotation: An Empirical Analysis on the Utilisation and Strategic Integration in European Companies

Andrea Friedrich, Rüdiger Kabst, Maria Rodehuth and Wolfgang Weber

INTRODUCTION

In this chapter the topic of job rotation will be dealt with in three steps. It is first necessary to give an introduction to the field of labour flexibility, define the term job rotation, and distinguish it from other forms of flexibility. Secondly, the relevance of job rotation in European companies will be looked at. The third step will be a statistical analysis of whether job rotation in European enterprises tends more to represent a solitary short-term instrument or whether on the other hand the implementation of job rotation is accompanied by a more long-term oriented integration of personnel strategies.

LABOUR FLEXIBILITY

Firms have developed different methods of adapting to economic and business changes in which the modification of employment practices plays a central role (Pinfield and Atkinson, 1988, p. 18). In the past, organisations tried to govern the increasing complexity of tasks with division and specialisation of labour, but it seems that we have reached the limit of possibilities in this direction (Bleicher, 1991, p. 3). One reason is that with professional specialisation the departments of organisations have tended to develop their own subcultures, which can cause conflicts and problems over integration and build barriers between functions, inhibit teamwork and distract attention from customer needs (Leveson, 1996, p. 36). A second reason is that strong, temporary team structures gain in importance, starting with the trend that a falling share of jobs can be completely formalised and thus electronically automated, while on the other hand the share of jobs with a high degree of complexity is constantly growing (Ruf, 1991, pp. 30ff.). This development has clear repercussions for the company's hierarchical structure, the company's internal formalism, the specific communication structure, and also the spatial and temporal dimensions of HRM. For the employer, labour flexibility is the ability to quickly reshape the existing supply in terms of configuration, deployment, and cost (Olmsted and Smith, 1989, p. 51). So in recent times, more and more organisations have increasingly sought to adopt work structures which are characterised by their flexibility and adaptability (Wood, 1989). In many instances this has involved redesigning jobs around a functionally flexible worker (Katz, 1985; Cordery *et al.*, 1993: 705).

In the discussion of labour flexibility the model of the 'flexible firm' developed at the Institute of Manpower Studies (Atkinson, 1984; Atkinson and Gregory, 1986; Atkinson and Meager, 1986; IMS, 1986) has enjoyed widespread acceptance, despite its conceptual simplicity and lack of theoretical underpinnings (Pollert, 1988; Pinch *et al.*, 1991: 208).

One approach to employment flexibility sets four broad categories: numerical flexibility, functional flexibility, distancing, and pay flexibility (Pinfield and Atkinson, 1988: 18ff.; Olmsted and Smith, 1989: 51). Firms use these types of employment flexibility in different dimensions depending on their specific competitive circumstances, the business strategy they develop to meet this competitive situation, and the constraints and opportunities they face as they attempt to adjust their employment policies (Pinfield and Atkinson, 1988: 19).

These different types of flexibility have the effect of restructuring the labour market in firms into 'core' and 'peripheral' workers. Simplified, the core group consists of multiskilled, permanent employees, who are also flexible in working time, in terms of adjusting more closely to production demands. The peripheral group provides numerical flexibility in the form of, for example, less job security, part-time work, working on temporary contracts, or being involved in subcontracting (Atkinson 1984, pp. 29, NEDO, 1986; Bagguley, 1990, pp. 737ff.).

JOB ROTATION AS AN INSTRUMENT TO ENHANCING FUNCTIONAL FLEXIBILITY

Functional flexibility can be defined as the process of increasing the skill repertoire of workers in such a way that in the outcome the employees acquire the capacity to work across traditionally distinct occupational boundaries (IMS, 1986; Cordery, 1989, p. 13; Olmsted and Smith, 1989, pp. 51ff.; Mueller, 1992; Cordery *et al.*, 1993, pp. 705ff.).

Functional flexibility can have various advantages for the employer as well as for the employee. The principal argument often mentioned in the literature states that functional flexibility enables organisations to respond more flexibly to future changes (Cordery, 1989, p. 20). Against the background of turbulent and competitive international markets it is more and more important that the workforce be able to change along with product or production method changes by redeploying between activities and tasks (Atkinson, 1984, p. 28). At the same time the employer can obtain a good recruiting tool. The increasing pool of skills generates greater labour flexibility and thus reduces labour costs and improves organisational efficiency and productivity. Additionally, as people at the lower organisational levels become horizontally and especially vertically more skilled, this may, for example, lead to a reduction in supervisory personnel – and may lead to a reduction in indirect labour costs. On the employees' side there is the presumption that flexibility gives rise to an increase in the humanisation of work, greater security of employment, and more interesting and varied work. Due to the costs, organisations have to decide for what types of jobs it will be efficient to increase the labour skills and in which way other personnel management practices should support such investment in human capital, for example in the development of internal labour markets.

Functional flexibility is often associated with different models of work systems such as job enlargement, job enrichment, and job rotation (Cordery *et al.*, 1991; Cordery *et al.*, 1993, pp. 705ff.), which represent a reaction to the Tayloristic work system associated with scientific management (Ulich, 1992, p. 374; Cappelli and Rogovsky, 1994, p. 206).

Job enlargement consists of expanding the field of activity horizontally, i.e. quantitatively, by extending the content of work and joining several successive work steps. The individual tasks that are to be fulfilled are not or only slightly changed with regard to their degree in Western Germany 16.0 per cent report using this instrument whereas only 9.9 per cent of the East German companies mention implementing job rotation in a systematic way.

With the help of multiple regression analysis it is possible to see which countries deviate significantly from the European trend. The results confirm the differences: firms in Belgium, Finland, Ireland, the Netherlands, Norway, Spain, Switzerland, and Turkey show a significantly higher probability of implementing job rotation systematically than the totality of the European companies surveyed. France and Eastern Germany show a significantly lower probability of using job rotation systematically and Denmark, Western Germany, Italy, Sweden, and the United Kingdom do not show any significant deviation from the European mean.

Osterman (1994, p. 176) finds when analysing 694 American firms that in principle 43.4 per cent of them use job rotation. Even intuitively this result is astonishing in view of the existing variance in European practice. However, this share sinks to 26.6 per cent of the companies surveyed, when at least 50 per cent of the core-employees are involved in job rotation. It could be supposed that the share of American corporations surveyed with more than 50 per cent of the core employees involved in job rotation corresponds more to the findings of Cranet-E, which asked about the systematic implementation of job rotation.

Table 3.1 Systematic implementation of job rotation according to countries

Systematic implementation of job rotation	%
Belgium	27.5
Denmark	19.7
Finland	32.3
France	9.7
Germany (East)	9.9
Germany (West)	16.0
Ireland	22.5
Italy	13.9
Norway	22.7
Spain	23.7
Sweden	20.2
Switzerland	28.9
Netherlands	22.7
Turkey	28.6
UK	17.6

Most often job rotation is employed in the manufacturing industry (22.5 per cent of the companies surveyed), followed by the service industry (21.2 per cent) and agriculture (20.1 per cent). In the public sector only 15.1 per cent of the organisations surveyed reported implementing job rotation. The dominance of the manufacturing industry is not surprising, while the relatively low use of job rotation in the public sector is of particular note.

Table 3.2 Systematic implementation of job rotation in European companies according to economic sectors

	Agriculture (%)	*Manufacturing (%)*	*Services (%)*	*Public sector (%)*
Systematic use of job rotation	20.1	22.5	21.2	15.1

This dominance of the manufacturing sector in the use of job rotation is supported by other studies, while the role played by the service sector tends to be assessed at a lower level. Osterman (1994, p. 177) investigated the degree of dissemination of various innovative work practices (teams, job rotation, Total Quality Management, Quality Circles, none) in American firms and found that 43.4 per cent of the companies surveyed used job rotation, whereas the figure for the manufacturing sector was 55.6 per cent. Pinch *et al.* (1991, pp. 209ff.) make a similar point: 'Compared with manufacturing, the service sector appears to be progressing more slowly with changing its employment strategies and there does not seem to be the same pressure for change as in the manufacturing sector.'

Company size as measured by the number of employees reveals a significantly positive influence on job rotation. The larger the company, the higher the probability of a systematic use of job rotation.

Table 3.3 Systematic use of job rotation according to the number of employees

	1–199 (%)	*200–499 (%)*	*500–999 (%)*	*1000–1999 (%)*	*2000–4999 (%)*	*> 5000 (%)*
Systematic use of job rotation	15.5	19.5	22.8	21.2	25.0%	28.5

personnel planning or the measures taken for the qualification of the personnel.

References

Ackermann, K. -F. and Wührer, G. (1984) *Personalstrategien in deutschen Groaunternehmen – Ergebnisse einer empirischen Untersuchung*, Stuttgart.

Atkinson, J. (1984) 'Manpower strategies for flexible organizations', *Personnel Management*, (8): 28–31.

Atkinson, J. and Gregory, D. (1986) 'A flexible future: Britain's dual labour force', *Marxism Today*, 30: 12–17.

Atkinson, J. and Meager, N. (1986) 'Is flexibility just a flash in the pan?', *Personnel Management*, 9: 26–9.

Bagguley, P. (1990) 'Gender and labour flexibility in hotel and catering', *Service Industries Journal*, 10(4): 737–47.

Bleicher, K. (1991) *Organisation: Strategien–Strukturen–Kulturen*, 2nd edn, Wiesbaden.

Brewster, C. and Hegewisch, A. (1994) *Policy and Practice in European Human Resource Management: The Price Waterhouse Cranfield Survey*, London, New York, pp. 1–21.

Brewster, C., Hegewisch, A. and Mayne, L. (1994) 'Flexible working practices: the controversy and the evidence', in Brewster, C. and Hegewisch, A. (eds), pp. 168–93.

Bruch, H. and Kuhnert, B. (1994) 'Projekte als Kernelement einer ganzheitlichen Flexibilisierungsstrategie', *Arbeit – Zeitschrift für Arbeitsforschung*, 3: 220–37.

Bühl, A. and Zöfel, P. (1994) *SPSS für Windows Version 6: Praxisorientierte Einführung in die moderne Datenanalyse*. Bonn.

Campion, M. and McClelland, C. L. (1993) 'Follow-up and extension of the interdisciplinary costs and benefits of enlarged jobs', *Journal of Applied Psychology*, 78(3): 339–51.

Cappelli, P. and Rogovsky, N. (1994) 'New work systems and skill requirements', *International Labour Review*, 2: 205–20.

Chearskin, L. and Campion, M. A. (1996) 'Study clarifies job-rotation benefits', *Personnel Journal*, 75(11): 31–8.

Cordery, J. (1989) 'Multi-skilling: a discussion of proposed benefits of new approaches to labour flexibility within enterprises', *Personnel Review*, 18(3): 13–22.

Cordery, J., Mueller, W. and Smith, L. (1991) 'Attitudinal and behavioral effects of autonomous group working: a longitudinal field study', *Academy of Management Journal*, 34: 464–76.

Cordery, J., Sevastos, P., Mueller, W. and Parker, S. (1993) 'Correlates of employee attitudes toward functional flexibility', *Human Relations*, 46(6): 705–23.

Devanna, M. A., Fombrun, C. and Tichy, N. (1984) 'A framework for strategic human resource management', in Fombrun, C. *et al.*, (eds), pp. 33–51.

Doeringer, P. B. and Piore, M. J. (1971) *Internal Labor Markets and Manpower Analysis*, Lexington, Mass.

Drumm, H. J. (1989) *Personalwirtschaftslehre*, Berlin, Walter de Gruyter.
Eckstein, P. P. (1997) *Angewandte Statistik mit SPSS: Praktische Einführung für Wirtschaftswissenschaftler*, Wiesbaden.
Festing, M. (1996) *Strategisches internationales Personalmanagement: Eine transaktionskostentheoretisch fundierte Analyse*, München, Mehring.
Fombrun, C., Tichy, N. and Devanna, M. A. (eds) (1984) *Strategic Human Resource Management*, New York, John Wiley.
Freimuth, J. (1992) 'Die personalpolitische Absicherung von Projektmanagement', *Zeitschrift Führung und Organisation*, 61(4): 220–25.
Frese, E. (ed.) (1992) Handwörterbuch der Organisation, 3rd edn, Stuttgart.
Gaugler, E. and Weber, W. (eds) (1992) Handwörterbuch des Personal Wesens, 3rd edn, Stuttgart.
Hartly, J. and Stephenson, J. N. (eds) (1992) *Employment Relations: The Psychology of Influence and Control at Work*, Oxford.
Hendry, C. and Pettigrew, A. (1990) 'HRM: An Agenda for the 1990s', *International Journal of Human Resource Management*, 1(1): 17–25.
Joerger, G. (1987) 'Job Rotation – oft propagiert, selten praktiziert', *VOP – Verwaltungsführung, Organisation, Personal*, 6: 262–7.
Katz, H. (1985) *Changing gears*, Cambridge, Cambridge University Press.
Klimecki, R. and Remer, A. (eds) (1997) *Personal als Strategic*, Neuviwed.
Kreikebaum, H. (1992) 'Humanisierung', in Frese, E. (ed.), pp. 816–26.
Kullak, F. (1995) *Personalstrategien in Klein-und Mittelbetrieben: Eine transaktionskostentheoretisch fundierte empirische Analyse*, München, Mering.
IMS (Institute of Manpower Studies) (1986) *Changing Working Patterns*, London, National Economic Development Office.
Lengnick-Hall, C. A. and Lengnick-Hall, M. L. (1988) 'Strategic human resource management: a review of the literature and a proposed typology', *Academy of Management Review*, 3: 454–70.
Leveson, R. (1996) 'Can professionals be multi-skilled?', *People Management*, 2(29): 36–8.
Mag, W. (1992) 'Bildungsplanung, Betriebliche', in Gaugler, E. and Weber, W. (eds), pp. 687–98.
Mentzel, W. (1992) 'Trainingsmethoden', in Gaugler, E. and Weber, W. (eds), pp. 2209–20.
Miller, P. (1991) 'Strategic human resource management: an assessment of progress', *Human Resource Management Journal*, 1: 23–39.
Mintzberg, H. (1987) 'The strategy concept I: five Ps for strategy', *California Management Review* 30(1): 11–24.
Mueller, W. S. (1992) 'Flexible working and new technology', in Hartley, J. and Stephensou, J. N., (eds) (1992).
NEDO (1986) *Changing Working Patterns*, Report prepared by the IMS for the NEDO in association with the Department of Employment.
Olmsted, B. and Smith, S. (1989) 'Flex for success!', *Personnel* (6): 50–5.
Osterman, P. (1994) 'How common is workplace transformation and who adopts it?', *Industrial and Labor Relations Review*, 47(2): 173–88.
Pinch, S., Mason, C. and Witt, S. (1991) 'Flexible employment strategies in British industry: evidence from the UK "Sunbelt" ', *Regional Studies*, 25(3): 207–18.

Pinfield, L. T. and Atkinson, J. S. (1988) 'The flexible firm', *Canadian Business Review*, 15(4): 17–19.
Piore, M. (1978) 'Lernprozesse, Mobilitätsketten und Arbeitsmarktsegmente', in Sengenberger, W. (ed.), pp. 67–98.
Pollert, A. (1988) 'Dismantling flexibility', *Capital and Class*, 34: 42–75.
Purcell, J. (1989) 'The impact of corporate strategy on human resource management', in Storey, J. (ed.).
Rodehuth, M. (1997) *Weiterbildung und Personalstrategien: eine ökonomisch fundierte Analyse der Bestimmungsfaktoren und Wirkungszusammenhänge*, Dissertation, Universität Paderborn, München, Mering.
Ruf, F. (1991) 'Baby Boomer stellen Forderungen', *TopBusiness* Report VI(VI): 28–32.
Schuler, R. S. (1992) 'Strategic human resource management: linking the people with the strategic needs of the business, *Organisational Dynamics*, Summer: 18–32.
Schuler, R. S. and Jackson, S. (1987) 'Linking competitive strategies with human resource management practices', *Academy of Management Executive*, 1(3): 207–55.
Schuler, R. S., Dowling, P. J. and De Cieri, H. (1993) 'An integrative framework of strategic international human resource management', *Journal of Management*, 19(2): 419–59.
Sengenberger, W. (1987) *Struktur und Funktionsweise von Arbeitsmärkten: Die Bundesrepublik Deutschland im internationalen Vergleich*, Frankfurt am Main, New York.
Sengenberger, W. (ed.) (1978) *Der abgespaltene Arbeitsmarkt: Probleme* der *Arbertsmarktsegmentation*, Frankfurt aun main, New York.
Storey, J. (ed.) (1989) *New Perspectives on Human Resource Management*, London.
Treu, T. (1992) 'Labour flexibility in Europe', *International Labour Review* 131(4–5): 496–512.
Ulich, E. (1992) 'Arbeitsstrukturierungsmodelle', in Gaugler, E. and Weber, W. (eds.), pp. 374–87.
Weber, W. (1989) 'Betriebliche Personalarbeit als strategischer Erfolgsfaktor der Unternehmung', in Weber, W. and Weinmann, J. (eds.), pp. 3–15.
Weber, W. and Kabst, R. (1997) 'Personalwirtschaftliche Strategien im europäischen Vergleich: Eine Analyse organisations-und landesspezifischer Prädiktoren', in Klimecki, R. G. and Remer, A. (eds.).
Weber, W. and Klein, H. (1992) 'Strategische Personalplanung', in Gaugler, E. and Weber, W.(eds), pp. 2142–54.
Weber, W. and Weinmun, J. (eds) (1989) *Strategisches Personal management*, Stuttgart.
Williamson, O. E. (1985) *The Economic Institutions of Capitalism*, New York.
Wood, S. (1989) 'The transformation of work?' in Wood, S. (ed.) *The Transformation of Work*, London, Hutchinsen.
Wright, P. M. and McMahan, G. C. (1992) 'Theoretical perspectives for strategic human resource managment', *Journal of Management*, 18(2): 295–320.

4 A Comparative Analysis of the Link Between Flexibility and HRM Strategy

Lesley Mayne, Olga Tregaskis and Chris Brewster

INTRODUCTION

Flexible working patterns have been the focus of considerable comment and much controversy for some years. The spread of what the European Union refers to as 'atypical' working patterns is now widely recognised and is a key issue for personnel specialists across Europe. It is a subject which has also been attracting the attention of senior line managers, trade unions, national governments and the European Commission, as well as academics. Much of this discussion has focused on the issue of managerial policies: whether the growth in flexible working mainly reflects structural changes and is a by-product of changes in the labour market or is the result of purposeful managerial choice, an aspect of strategic approaches towards HRM.

Much of the writing on flexibility has been criticised for being 'characterised by a style of global prophesying, sweeping generalisation from very limited evidence, economical or technical determinism and an assumption of a radical break from the past' (Pollert, 1988b). By basing this chapter on carefully collected, representative data covering all sectors of the economy, we seek to overcome these cited shortcomings and to explore further one of the central questions the literature raises; whether the increase in flexibility is the result of a deliberate strategy by organisations or, rather, just a reaction to circumstances.

This chapter focuses on the use of two particular forms of flexible or 'atypical' working patterns: part-time and short-term working. In doing so no assumption is made regarding the definitional validity of part-time work as a flexible form of working. Rather, the focus on part-time and short-term contracts is based on the fact that together they make-up a significant part of the flexible working patterns across Europe. Part-time working is one of the fastest growing forms of flexible working while short-term contracts, although less significant in growth terms, are still among the most widely adopted forms of contractual flexibility used by employers.

We make no attempt here to outline the advantages and disadvantages of flexible working patterns for employers or employees; nor to explore the different meanings that the associated terms have in the different European countries (see, for a discussion of these matters, Brewster *et al.*, 1994);

What this chapter aims to do is examine the proposition that there is little correlation between those employers who use a considerable amount of flexibility, defined in terms of part-time and short-term contracts, and those who take a more strategic approach to HRM. To do this, we outline briefly the extent and growth of flexibility and summarise the debate about its link to HR strategy; then after outlining the nature of our data, which establishes a clear link between the use of part-time and temporary employment contracts and a strategic approach to HRM, we develop the core of our argument. This is that strategy is a more incremental and less formal process than is recognised in much of the writing on HRM; when this more realistic view of strategy is adopted, our finding that high use of flexibility is correlated with a more strategic approach to HRM can be reconciled with previous studies.

THE EXTENT AND GROWTH OF FLEXIBILITY

Among management in particular the drive towards more flexible working has reached almost the state of an orthodoxy. Over the last decade or so many assumptions about working time have been broken down. While the 'standard' 9 am–5 pm, 5 days a week permanent contract has never been universal, what has happened in the last decade or so is that non-standard patterns have spread extensively – causing a re-evaluation of the nature of employment

Associated with this development is the breaking down of the assumed links within organisations between tasks and jobs. Until recently most managers saw a direct relationship between the two: reduced work meant fewer jobs; more work, more jobs. This relationship is now seen as much less direct. More work may or may not mean more jobs – there is a considerable range of ways other than direct employment in which the work might be covered. At the furthest extreme the work can be subcontracted, so that the organisation achieves the extra work without any increase in numbers employed. Other options (government trainees, job-sharing, home working and so on) may involve different numbers of people, for different periods of time or employed in different formats. These options are now more widespread, more complex and more difficult to evaluate and manage (Hutchinson and Brewster, 1994). What is contentious is the precise meaning of this growth and its impact within and beyond employing organisations.

There is considerable ambiguity regarding the definition of flexibility. It has been argued, for example, that part-time work should be excluded on the grounds that, for the employee, particularly in organisations with many part-timers, there may be little flexibility involved in part-time work (Walsh, 1990); though most commentators include it on the grounds that it does increase flexibility from the employer's perspective. Even if this is resolved, Hunter *et al.* (1993) commenting on the UK, note that part-time work covers everything from a few hours a week to the conventional cut-off of 30 hours a week; that the distinction between temporary and permanent work is not so clear-cut as it may at first seem, with some permanent workers losing their jobs at very short notice; and that self-employment is a notoriously grey area. Internationally the issue becomes even more complicated. For example, European comparisons of part-time working are made difficult by the lack of uniform statistical definitions (see Konle-Seidl *et al.*, 1990; Bruegel and Hegewisch, 1994). Research in the field in Europe tends to concentrate more on the employment effect of flexible working, that is, the notion that deregulation of employment protection and the introduction of more flexible working encourages organisations to create additional employment (see, for example, Boyer, 1990; Büchtemann, 1994). Elsewhere in the world, in Japan and the USA for example, the debate is notably distinct and more limited (see, as an introduction, Koshiro, 1992).

Despite the different legal, cultural and labour traditions around Europe there is a clear trend among employers in all sectors towards increasing their use of flexibility (Bielenski *et al.*, 1992). This trend varies by country, sector and size and has been slowed down by the impact of the recession. It is nevertheless a clear and largely consistent development (Brewster *et al.*, 1994). A few details on the two most common forms of 'atypical' working, part-time and temporary employment will both indicate the position and provide the basis for our later analysis.

Part-time employment is playing an increasingly important role in Europe. One in seven people in the European Community is working part-time, and part-time employment has been the major area of employment growth during the last decade. Even taking account of the varying definitions, the levels of part-time work vary greatly between different European countries (Commission of the EC, 1992). There are also variations in the treatment of part-time workers in legal and social security systems (Brewster *et al.*, 1993).

The share of part-time as a proportion of total employment differs greatly between countries. Broadly, there is a North–South divide. Part-time employment is highest now in the Nordic countries, with the exception of Finland (Brewster *et al.*, 1993). Within the EC, part-time work is highest in the Netherlands where, after very rapid growth during the last decade, by the end of the 1980s over 30 per cent of the labour force, and six out of ten women, worked part-time. Denmark, Norway, Sweden and the UK also have an overall part-time share of over 20 per cent, with more than four out of ten women working part-time. At the other end of the spectrum are the southern and more agricultural countries such as Greece, Portugal, Spain and to some extent Italy, and Ireland, where part-time employment is well below 10 per cent of all employment (Commission of the EC, 1992).

Apart from Denmark, Portugal and Greece all countries within the European Community saw a growth in the relative share of part-time employment in their work-forces during the 1980s. The size of this increase was generally less than 2.5 per cent, except in the Netherlands with an increase of 10 per cent. In Greece the share of part-time employment dropped by 2 per cent, while in Denmark and Portugal there was a more marginal decline (Commission of the EC, 1992). At the organisational level, recent research shows that while the growth in part-time employment has slowed down during the recession, there is still growth nearly everywhere (Brewster *et al.*, 1994).

Non-permanent (temporary or fixed term) contracts play a lesser role in the overall labour market in Europe than part-time employment and their growth during the 1980s is less dramatic; however, as with part-time employment, levels and growth rates of non-permanent employment vary substantially across Europe, but remain an important feature of flexible employment patterns for many organisations. In general it is the poorer countries of the European Community which have the highest levels of employees on such contracts. Non-permanent employment is highest in southern countries such as Greece, Portugal and Spain where the percentage of the workforce involved is over 15 per cent and lowest in Luxembourg, Belgium and Italy at around 5 per cent (Commission of the EC, 1992).

At organisational level, research shows that the use of non-permanent employment is widespread: used by 8 or 9 out of every 10 employers in all countries except Denmark and Turkey. The 'wealth divide' however is clearer when we look at the share of those organisations in each country which are high temporary/casual or fixed-term users (those where at least 10 per cent of the workforce are on such contracts); in Spain, Portugal, Turkey and the Netherlands more than one-fifth of organisations are 'high users' (Brewster *et al.*, 1994). Growth rates for non-permanent employment varied substantially during the 1980s, increasing rapidly in some countries while remaining at a low level or declining in others (OECD, 1991). The largest increases occurred in France, where the proportion of non-permanent employment for both men and women more than doubled between 1983 and 1989 (to 9.4 per cent of the female and 7.8 per cent of the male workforce); Ireland, Greece and the Netherlands also show positive increases (Commission of the EC, 1992).

FLEXIBILITY AND STRATEGY: THE DEBATE

The academic discussion of human resource flexibility at the level of the firm has been led by British commentators, starting with the work of Atkinson (1984a, 1984b, 1985; Atkinson and Meager, 1986a, 1986b) and attacks on the concept led by Pollert (1987, 1988a, 1991). The model of the 'flexible firm' put forward by Atkinson focused on the type of contracts offered by employers and proposed a differentiation between a core workforce of (generally) full-time permanent employees, for whom functional flexibility was seen to be appropriate; and a peripheral workforce of part-time, temporary and subcontract workers for whom numerical flexibility was relevant. A further development adds in the concept of 'distancing', which includes even more peripheral, non-employment relationships such as franchising, self employment, home working, networking and subcontracting. However, a distinction between core and peripheral workers on the basis of functional and contractual flexibility is problematic; many part-timers, for example, are engaged in jobs which in all other senses are core for the organisation. Therefore, the examination of those on such contracts does not necessarily imply the exclusion of core workers.

The attacks on the model have argued that it is not a new theory; that there is little evidence that the growth in flexibility is more than a reflection of a sectoral shift to the service sector; that the core/peripheral distinction is not useful; and that it confuses analysis with prescription. Many of the attacks on the concept reflect a distaste for the effects on the individuals involved, but analytically a central plank of the attack on the flexible firm concept has been the argument that there is no evidence that employers in the real world have such manpower strategies: various authors have argued that managerial motives of reducing costs are the fundamental cause of certain types of flexibility (Piore and Sabel, 1985) or are evidence that the approach to flexibility is not strategic (Pollert, 1987, 1991). Rubery (1988) has pointed out that a coherent managerial strategy in this area is merely a spin-off from some wider strategy. Other authors have attempted to identify whether there is a relationship between different forms of flexibility, such that employers might have been seen to be developing a 'full set' of peripheral workers, or setting use of one type against another (Blanchflower and Corry, 1987; Hakim, 1990; Casey, 1991).

One group of authors have used a variety of forms of survey to explore these issues. They include Marginson *et al.* (1988); Wood and Smith (1989); Hakim (1990); IRS (1990); Hunter and MacInnes (1992); McGregor and Sproull (1992). Most of the commentators here have failed to find evidence of written, or worked through, strategies aimed at the creation of a core/peripheral workforce per se. They have concluded that there is, therefore, no strategy, and that the introduction and expansion of flexible working has been merely *ad hoc* and reactive. Commenting on the 'key research finding' of one of these studies, that 'little evidence existed to show increased labour "flexibility" was the result of a coherent management strategy', one British trade union leader wrote 'This conclusion sits uneasily with the experience of many unionists' (Monks, 1994).

Those who have undertaken research at the case-study level have been inclined to be cautious about denying the absence of any link between flexibility and strategy. Geary (1992) found evidence to suggest few 'British firms actively pursue a core/peripheral strategy of the type outlined by Atkinson' (p. 266). Nevertheless, there was a recognition in his examination of recruitment of temporary workers in three electronic firms, that the choice to use more flexible forms of working was related to a range of factors including a 'more strategic' (p. 267) approach to the utilisation of employees. An examination of functional flexibility leads O' Reilly (1992) to the conclusion that the flexibility debate needs to differentiate more clearly between deliberate and 'inadvertent' strategies. These and other case studies have revealed evidence of strategies of a more incremental or emergent nature (Collinson *et al.*, 1990) and in some cases of a very considered kind (O'Connell Davidson, 1993).

It is clear that many of the discussions of strategy in the flexibility (and wider IR and HRM?) literature assume that strategy formulation is a rational, deliberate process instituted and controlled by senior management; this is what the strategy specialists termed the 'commander model' (Bourgeois and Brodwin, 1984). This classical view of strategy was intellectually destroyed by Lindblom's seminal article on 'muddling through' over 35 years ago (Lindblom, 1959). Current debates are more about the relationship between deliberate and enacted strategy and the ways in which incremental decisions coalesce within an organisational culture to define direction (see e.g. Johnson and Scholes, 1988). The counterposing of 'strategic' to 'reactive to circumstances' in some of the flexibility literature leads one to question the reality of a view of strategy that implies that it should not be responsive to developments in the real world. One classic text even argued that good managers tend deliberately to avoid being clear about their strategies partly so that they do not get 'straightjacketted' (Wrapp, 1967).

This distinction between classical and incremental models of strategy development are discussed further in relation to the implications of these research findings.

THE RESEARCH DATA

We set out to contribute to this debate by utilising both qualitative and quantitative data. In each case, in order to limit our enquiry, we have restricted our secondary analysis and discussion to the most common forms of flexible working, namely; part-time, temporary/casual and fixed-term contractual work.

Quantitatively, we conducted secondary analysis of existing data we have collected as part of a wider research project examining HRM strategies and practices in Europe (Brewster and Hegewisch, 1994). The survey provides broadly representative data across all sectors of the economy of organisations with more than 200 employees. This illuminates the issue of flexibility on a broad, international basis and allows us to draw clear comparisons of the degree of flexibility typical in the different countries.

The data limits our analysis in two important ways. First, the data is limited to organisations with more than 200 employees. It is likely that smaller organisations have quite different approaches to flexibility. Secondly, because of the nature of our survey, which is fact-based rather than an attempt to explore opinions, we have had to use a limited number of general, surrogate measures to identify HR strategies. In this respect our method has equivalence to that used for similar purposes by Hunter *et al.* (1993); though they were looking for strategy at the workplace level, rather than the organisational level from which our data is taken, and were only examining the UK. Identification of strategy via a survey means the measures can test classical notions of strategy as opposed to the incremental perspectives.

In order to address the question of whether there is a systematic difference in the characteristics of organisations utilising flexibility we identified organisations making high or low use of part-time and temporary contracts. In order to do this the sample was split into high and low users of flexibility on the basis of a question asking organisations to indicate the proportion of employees on part-time or short-term contracts. Responses to this question were normally distributed. Organisations at the two extreme ends of the distribution were selected for analysis. This resulted in a definition of high flexibility organisations (HFOs) as organisations where at least 20% of the workforce was employed either on a part-time, temporary or fixed-term contract; and low flexibility organisations (LFOs) as those where at most 2 per cent of the workforce was employed on one of the above forms of contract. These 'cut-off' levels were selected on a statistical rather than theoretic basis in order to provide a more polarised and precise sample for the examination of differences.

The areas examined in relation to flexibility were: organisational demographics, training and communication policy, line management involvement, and organisational strategy. Full details of the issues covered within each of these areas and the results of statistical analyses are outlined in Appendices I and II. In most cases the survey asked for 'yes/no' answers; or for details of numbers or percentages. An exception was the series of questions on the role of line management (questions asked if the topics were the responsibility of line managers, line managers supported by personnel specialists, specialists supported by line managers or personnel specialists alone). Full details of the survey,

the sampling and the frequency counts of the results are available in Brewster and Hegewisch (1994).
On this basis we established four propositions:

1. that HFOs are concentrated among certain groups of employers;
2. that HFOs are likely to be those organisations that are involved in a variety of linked HR practices, such as a substantial investment in training.
3. that HFOs are more likely to have a substantial involvement of line management in HR policy-making; and
4. that HFOs take a more strategic approach to HRM.

The analysis was restricted to five countries, namely the UK, France, Germany, Sweden and Norway, to ensure that the sample size of high and low users was large enough for quantitative analysis. This sample constituted 494 HFOs and 730 LFOs. The statistical procedure adopted was discriminant function analysis (DFA). This is a technique that makes it possible to test for significant differences between groups on the basis of specific criteria. This procedure therefore made it possible to explore differences between high and low flexible users in each country, as outlined in the four propositions.

Inevitably, however, with such a research approach the explanatory value available through company-level studies is lost. For that purpose other research methods are more powerful and we have, therefore, supplemented this material with qualitative data gathered through interviews conducted on behalf of the European Association of Personnel Management (EAPM). Interviews were conducted with senior personnel specialists, and in some cases also senior line managers, in their native language, in organisations in Austria, Belgium, Denmark, Finland, France, Germany, Italy, the Netherlands, Norway, Portugal, Spain, Sweden, Switzerland and the United Kingdom. Between one and three organisations were interviewed in each country, giving a total of 32 cases (Hutchinson and Brewster, 1994). This approach also allowed for the exploration of less rigid and narrowly defined concepts of strategy than those examined via the questionnaire.

FLEXIBILITY AND STRATEGY: THE EVIDENCE

When the data from all five countries was combined the results showed significant differences in the practices of high and low flexible users

than jobs. In many cases it was difficult to tease out the exact relationship between flexibility and other managerial objectives because the change was seen as contributing to two or three different objectives (Hutchinson and Brewster, 1994, pp. 20–1).

If flexibility is more closely linked to strategy than has been thought hitherto, perhaps this is because previous commentators have taken a rather unrealistic view of what 'strategy' involves. The concept of strategy is far from simple or straightforward and needs to be treated with caution (Crow, 1989; Morgan, 1989). In practice there is no exact point of determination of strategy and no direct link to implementation. A perspective which assumes that there is and that takes no account of the effects of actors, processes and contextual conditions, will lead inevitably to a finding of absence of strategy (Child, 1985).

Mintzberg (1978, p. 935) argued that 'formulation' of strategy does not take place – it is much less explicit, conscious or planned than that implies. He suggests using the term 'formation' instead. The development of strategy is in fact a complex, interactive, incremental and restricted process (Johnson, 1987), so that it is difficult to define a point at which the corporate strategy can be 'finalised' sufficiently to allow the 'HRM strategy' to be created. (For a brief, clear view of this issue see Hendry and Pettigrew, 1990, p. 34.) Some concepts of HRM, particularly those drawn from or following the 'traditional' United States literature complicate this picture by restricting the elements of what constitutes HRM to imply that, for example, legislation and employee representatives play no role in strategic considerations (Guest, 1990; Brewster, 1995). Again, Mintzberg (1987) argues for a view of strategy which allows for influence from below.

On this understanding of strategy our data becomes even more intriguing. It indicates that, if we are prepared to accept that strategy is not the simplistic, linear process that has been sought for in the past, managements often are taking a strategic view of the introduction or extension of flexible working into their organisations. Our statistical survey indicates this, even though our tests for strategy (head of department on the Board of Directors or the equivalent; written corporate and HR strategies) are drawn from the more limited perspective of the formalised 'strategy formulation' approach. In this respect, one advantage of the international comparison of data may be the opportunity to compare evidence across more and less formalised cultures. Our qualitative evidence is more direct and less equivocal. All 32 of the case-study companies argued that they had entered into flexible working as part of a strategy to meet corporate objectives (though, of course, the nature and scope of the strategies varied) (Hutchinson and Brewster, 1994).

CONCLUSION

This analysis has implications for several of the groups of commentators on flexible working practices. For the British trade unions, for example, it raises some questions about their opposition to flexible working and not just because it is clear that employees are, for whatever reason, accepting flexible working practices. John Monks, TUC general secretary, has argued that the drive for a deregulated flexible labour market must be rejected in favour of high-quality, secure employment; and argued that they can look to the rest of Europe for examples of how that works (Monks, 1994). The evidence here is that such a call is flying in the face of current managerial strategies across Europe. The unions will have a difficult case to make.

For policy-makers at organisational and governmental level, there may be less concern in the finding that the moves towards flexible working are correlated with strategic approaches to HRM. The finding is based on the experience of employing organisations. Many governments across Europe have, in the last few years, taken action to free employers from some of the legislative constraints in order to encourage employers to adopt policies of flexibility.

For similar reasons, though with perhaps opposite effect, the debates within the European Union about protection for flexible workers (what the Commission often calls 'vulnerable workers') assume a new perspective in the light of evidence that the growth of flexibility is indeed linked to managerial strategies. On the one hand, the EU is most effective when it builds upon a foundation of broad consensus, as in the case of European legislation on equal opportunities for women. It finds it harder to act against widespread trends where the consensus among employers is against EU policy. Thus while EU action to protect vulnerable workers has been valuable in raising the debate, it has also, arguably, been late and watered down to the point where it will have little impact in practice. It may be, paradoxically, that such action becomes even more necessary.

Our analysis also has implications for researchers. Our data is taken from a broad, 'thin-slice' survey. It is valuable to discover that it supports the evidence of many of the case studies that found that flexibility was introduced as part of a deliberate strategy. However, large-scale survey research, while it is irreplaceable in setting other work into context and in identifying the unspectacular average, has important limitations in addressing the kind of issues raised by a more 'modern' view of managerial strategy (see the debate started by McCarthy, 1994 and responses from Fernie and Woodland, 1995 and Millward and Hawes, 1995). There is a need for more detailed work on the rationale, and the rationality, of the drive for flexibility. There is also a need for a new examination of the meaning of HRM strategies within organisations. Finally, there are serious questions raised beyond the scope of this article about the position of the flexible workers themselves and the long-term economic impact of a continued growth in these kinds of employment relationships.

APPENDIX I

Secondary analysis of survey data

Secondary analysis of the Price Waterhouse Cranfield Survey data was carried out using DFA. This identified the organisational factors which characterised low and high users of flexibility as significantly different in the UK, France, Germany, Norway and Sweden.

High flexible organisations, or HFOs, were defined as those organisations employing more than 20 per cent of employees on part-time, temporary or fixed term contracts. In contrast low flexible organisations, or LFOs, were defined as those organisations employing less than 2 per cent of employees on part-time, temporary or fixed term contracts.

In Appendix II, Tables 4AII.1–4AII.5 detail the results of the DFA analyses conducted on the data for each of the five countries independently. In Appendix II, Table 4AII.6 shows the results for the data of the five countries combined, i.e. the European results.

Determinants of flexible practices

Examination of the standardised coefficients and Wilk's lambda figures (Appendix II, Tables 4AII.1–4AII.5) shows which organisational characteristics are the most important predictors of flexibility. In all countries industry sector was consistently found to be one of the primary indicators of flexibility. Expansion of the workforce, targeting of women in recruitment and the presence of an HR/personnel representative on the board of directors also figured strongly as predictors of flexibility across Europe. However, the diversity in the individual country profiles indicates that the operation of flexible practices is country specific and thus implications for the organisation must be considered within the national context.

Table 4AI.1 Discriminant function analysis (DFA) – summary table

Statistics	*Europe*	*UK*	*France*	*Denmark*	*Sweden*	*Norway*
Eigen value	0.5964	0.8968	0.4083	0.4331	1.414	1.319
Canonical correlation	0.6112	0.6876	0.5385	0.5497	0.7654	0.7542
Wilk's lambda	0.6264	0.5272	0.7100	0.6978	0.4142	0.4312
Chi-square	567.37	334.17	70.02	77.72	103.12	101.78
D.f.	18	16	11	10	14	16
Significance	0.0001	0.0001	0.0001	0.0001	0.0001	0.0001

Table 4AI.2 Classification results

Country	*% Correct low users*	*% Correct high users*	*N*
UK	91	74	532
France	86	58	212
Germany	95	55	223
Sweden	80	90	126
Norway	88	87	131
Europe	87	68	1224

Table 4AI.1 provides a summary of the DFA statistics for each country and Europe as a whole, indicating the success of each of the discriminant models. The percentage of variance accounted for by each of the DFA solutions ranges from 59 per cent in Sweden to 29 per cent in Germany (Norusis, 1988).

The results also show the high level of predictive accuracy of each model (Table 4AI.2). In the UK 91 per cent of low users were predicted correctly and 74 per cent of high users. The figure for Europe shows correct prediction for low users was 87 per cent and 68 per cent for high users.

Table 4AI.3 summarises the relationships between flexibility and HRM practices across Europe. The left-hand column of the table details the organisational characteristics examined. The letter 'H' indicates that high flexible organisations (HFOs) were more likely to be active in relation to the organisational characteristics examined. The letter 'L' indicates that low flexible organisations (LFOs) were more active. The horizontal heading indicates the country categories: D = Germany, F = France, N = Norway, S = Sweden, UK = United Kingdom, with EUR indicating the combined figures for the five countries examined.

Table 4AI.3 Characteristics of high and low users of flexible working practices

Organisational characteristics	*Eur*	*D*	*F*	*N*	*S*	*UK*
Organisational demographics						
High trade union membership	H		L	H		L
Service sector	H	H	H	L	H	H
Public sector	H	H	H	H	H	H
Increased number of employees	H	H	H	H		H
Increase in product/service	H			H	H	H
Organisational policy						
Monitoring and targeting						
Monitor women's recruitment			H	L	H	H
Monitor ethnic recruitment					H	H
Target older workers		H	H	L		
Target disabled				L	H	
Target ethnic minorities				H		
Target women	H		H	H		H
Training						
No. of days spent on training		H	L			
Analyse training needs			L		L	
Evaluate training	L				H	L
Communication						
Communicate through immediate supervisor	L					
Use of trade unions/works councils	H			H		H
Use of workforce meetings	L	L	H		L	
Use of quality circles						
Use of suggestion schemes		L		L		
Use of attitude surveys	H					H
No formal communication		H			L	
Line management						
Line managed pay & benefits		H			L	
Line managed recruitment	L					L
Line managed training	L		L			L
Line managed IR						
Line managed health/safety				L		
Line managed labour demand		L				L
Organisational strategy						
Head of HR on main board	H			H	H	
Written corporate strategy	H					
Written HR strategy	H					H
HR dept. involved from the outset in corporate strategy	H			L		

Table 4AI.3 (Cont.)

Organisational characteristics	*Eur*	*D*	*F*	*N*	*S*	*UK*
Strategy translated into work programmes					L	
Manpower planning	L			L	L	L

Notes: L=used significantly more by LFOs; H=used significantly more by HFOs.

APPENDIX II – COUNTRY DFA RESULTS

Table 4AII.1 DFA results for UK data

Variable	*Standard coefficients*	*Wilks lambda*	*Significance*
Public sector*	1.0154	0.6458	0.0001
Service sector*	0.5276	0.5688	0.0001
Target women	0.1362	0.5621	0.0001
Written corporate strategy	–0.2036	0.5552	0.0001
Increased no. of employees	0.1113	0.5518	0.0001
Evaluate training	–0.1559	0.5490	0.0001
Written HR strategy	0.1164	0.5457	0.0001
Communicate through trade unions/ works councils	0.1346	0.5429	0.0001
Line managed training	–0.1302	0.5404	0.0001
Line managed labour demand	0.1143	0.5378	0.0001
Monitor ethnic recruitment	0.1774	0.5352	0.0001
Manpower planning	–0.1036	0.5328	0.0001
Communicate via surveys	0.0871	0.5312	0.0001
Increase in products/services	0.0814	0.5297	0.0001
High trade union membership	–0.0818	0.5284	0.0001
Monitor women's recruitment	–0.0966	0.5272	0.0001

Notes: N=532.
*Production is equal to the constant to which all others are compared.

Table 4AII.2 DFA results for Norwegian data

Variable	*Standard coefficients*	*Wilks lambda*	*Significance*
Public sector*	1.1681	0.6590	0.0001
Service sector*	0.4569	0.6055	0.0001

Table 4AII.2 (Cont.)

Line-managed health/safety	−0.2225	0.5702	0.0001
Head of HR on main board	0.2230	0.5457	0.0001
Target disabled	−0.2485	0.5295	0.0001
Target women	0.3284	0.5128	0.0001
Target ethnic minorities	0.2959	0.4969	0.0001
High trade union membership	−0.3064	0.4838	0.0001
Increased no. of employees	0.3097	0.4756	0.0001
Target older workers	−0.1480	0.4666	0.0001
Use of suggestion schemes	−0.2254	0.4589	0.0001
Increase in product/service	−0.2115	0.4527	0.0001
Use of trade unions/works councils	0.1687	0.4474	0.0001
Monitor women's recruitment	−0.1566	0.4426	0.0001
HR dept involved from the outset in corporate strategy	0.2127	0.4368	0.0001
Manpower planning	−0.1639	0.4312	0.0001

Notes: N=131.
*Production is equal to the constant to which all others are compared.

Table 4AII.3 DFA results for Swedish data

Variable	*Standard coefficients*	*Wilks lambda*	*Significance*
Public sector*	1.1421	0.8276	0.0001
Service sector*	1.1183	0.5849	0.0001
Manpower planning	−0.4105	0.5585	0.0001
Regular workforce meetings	0.3131	0.5281	0.0001
Increase in product/service	0.3599	0.5043	0.0001
Target disabled	0.2154	0.4860	0.0001
Line managed pay & benefits	−0.2485	0.4715	0.0001
Head of HR on main board	0.2154	0.4616	0.0001
Evaluate training	0.2824	0.4453	0.0001
No formal communication	−0.2355	0.4368	0.0001
Strategy translated into work programmes	−0.1580	0.4294	0.0001
Monitor women's recruitment	−0.2084	0.4224	0.0001
Analyse training needs	−0.1932	0.4163	0.0001
Monitor ethnic recruitment	0.1706	0.4109	0.0001

Notes: N=126.
*Production is equal to the constant to which all others are compared.

Table 4AII.4 DFA results for German data

Variable	*Standard coefficients*	*Wilks lambda*	*Significance*
Service sector*	0.7010	0.8896	0.0001
Public sector*	0.7538	0.7797	0.0001
Increased no. of employees	0.3103	0.7490	0.0001
No. days spent on training	0.2109	0.7399	0.0001
Regular workforce meetings	0.2875	0.7322	0.0001
Use of suggestion schemes	−0.2154	0.7238	0.0001
No formal communication	0.2403	0.7126	0.0001
Target older workers	0.1612	0.7068	0.0001
Line managed labour demand	−0.2016	0.7024	0.0001
Line managed pay & benefits	0.1632	0.6978	0.0001

Notes: N=223.
*Production is equal to the constant to which all others are compared.

Table 4AII.5 DFA results for French data

Variable	*Standard coefficients*	*Wilks lambda*	*Significance*
Increased no. of employees	0.4024	0.9154	0.0001
Public sector*	6759	0.8472	0.0001
Target older workers	0.2234	0.8177	0.0001
Service sector	0.3335	0.7952	0.0001
Written corporate strategy	0.2604	0.7775	0.0001
Analyse training needs	−0.3304	0.7616	0.0001
Target women	0.3218	0.7446	0.0001
Line managed training	−0.3009	0.7303	0.0001
Regular workforce meetings	0.2631	0.7207	0.0001
No.s days spent on training	−0.1771	0.7138	0.0001
High tradeunion Membership	−0.1404	0.7101	0.0001

Notes: N=212.
*Production is equal to the constant to which all others are compared.

Table 4AII.6 DFA results for the five country European data

Variable	*Standard coefficients*	*Wilks lambda*	*Significance*
Public sector*	0.9766	0.7610	0.0001
Service sector*	0.5878	0.6810	0.0001
Increased no. of employees	0.0663	0.6629	0.0001

Table 4AII.6 (Cont.)

Head of HR on main board	0.1559	0.6556	0.0001
Target women	0.1361	0.6496	0.0001
Manpower planning	0.1657	0.6441	0.0001
Use of trade unions/works councils	−0.1565	0.6396	0.0001
Regular workforce meetings	0.1013	0.6375	0.0001
Communication via superior	−0.0938	0.6358	0.0001
Increase in product/service	−0.1084	0.6346	0.0001
Line managed training	0.1095	0.6336	0.0001
Line managed recruitment	−0.0718	0.6323	0.0001
Evaluate training	−0.0881	0.6311	0.0001
Written HR strategy	0777	0.6297	0.0001
High trade union Membership	−0.0879	0.6285	0.0001
Written corporate strategy	0.0663	0.6277	0.0001
Communicate via attitude surveys	0.0564	0.6270	0.0001
HR involved in corporate strategy			0.0001
from the outset	0.0539	0.6264	

Notes: N=1224.
*Production is equal to the constant to which all others are compared.

References

Atkinson, J. (1984a) 'manpower strategies for flexible organisations', *Personnel Management*, Aug.; 32–5.

Atkinson, J. (1984b) 'Flexibility, uncertainty and manpower management', Brighton, *IMS Report No. 89.*

Atkinson, J. (1985) 'Flexibility: planning for the uncertain future', *Manpower Policy and Practice*, 1, Summer: 26–9.

Atkinson, J. & Meager, N. (1986a) 'Is flexibility just a flash in the pan?', *Personnel Management*, Vol. 18, No. 9, Sept. 26–9.

Atkinson, J. and Meager, N. (1986b) *New Forms of Work Organisation*, Brighton, *IMS Report No. 121.*

Bielenski, H., Alaluf, M., Atkinson, J., Bellini, R., Castillo, J.J., Donati, P., Graverson, G., Huygen, F. and Wickham J. (1992) 'New forms of work and activity: a survey of experiences at establishment level in eight European countries', *European Foundation for the Improvement of Working and Living Conditions*, Working papers, Dublin.

Blanchflower, D. and Corry, B. (1987) 'Part-time Employment in Great Britain: an analysis using establishment data', *Department of Employment Research Paper 57.*

Bourgeois, L. J. and Brodwin, D. R. (1984) 'Strategic implementation: five approaches to an elusive phenomenon', *Strategic Management Journal*, 5, 3: 241–64.

Boyer, R. (1990) 'The impact of the single market on labour and employment', *Labour and Society*, 15,7: 109–42.

Brewster, C. (1995) 'Towards a "European" model of human resource management', *Journal of International Business Studies*, 26(2): 1–21.
Brewster, C. and Hegewisch, A. (eds) (1994) *Policy and Practice in European Human Resource Management: The Price Waterhouse Survey'*, London, Routledge.
Brewster, C., Hegewisch, A. and Mayne, L. (1994) 'Flexible working practices: the controversy and the evidence', in Brewster C. and Hegewisch A. (eds).
Brewster, C., Hegewisch, A., Lockhart, T. and Mayne, L. (1993) 'Flexible working patterns in Europe', *Issues in People Management*, Wimbledon, IPD.
Brown, P. and Crompton, R. (eds) (1994) *A New Europe?: Economic Restructuring and Social Exclusion,* London, UCL Press.
Bruegel, I. and Hegewisch, A. (1994) 'Flexiblisation and part-time work in Europe', in Brown. P. and Crompton, R. (eds), pp. 33–57.
Büchtemann, C. (1994) 'Does (de-) regulation matter?: employment protection and temporary work in the Federal Republic of Germany', in Standing, G. and Tokman, V. (eds.).
Casey, B. (1991) 'Survey evidence on trends in "non-standard" employment', in Pollert A (ed.), pp. 179–99.
Child J (1985) 'Managerial strategies, new technology and the labour process' in D. Knights et al. (eds), pp. 107–41.
Collinson, D., Knights, D. and Collinson, M. (1990) *Managing to Discriminate*, London, Routledge.
Crow G. (1989) 'The use of the concept of "strategy" in recent sociological literature', *Sociology*, 2, 3 (1): 1–24.
Commission of the EC (1992) 'The position of women on the labour market: trends and developments in the 12 member states', *Women of Europe supplements*, No 36, Brussels, EC.
Fernie, S. and Woodland, S. (1995) 'HRM and workplace performance evidence using WIRS3 – a reply to McCarthy', *Industrial Relations Journal*, 26, 1: 65–8.
Geary, J.F. (1992) 'Employment flexibility and human resource management: the case of three American electronics plants', *Work, Employment and Society*, 6,2: 251–70.
Guest D (1990) 'HRM and the American Dream', *Journal of Management Studies*, 27,4: 377–97.
Hakim, C., (1990) 'Core and periphery workers in employers' workforce strategies: evidence from the 1987 ELUS survey', *Work, Employment and Society*, 4,2: 157–88.
Hendry, C. and Pettigrew, A. (1990) 'HRM: an agenda for the 1990s', *International Journal of Human Resource Management*, 1,1: 17–25.
Hunter, L., McGregor, A., McInnes, J. and Sproull, A. (1993) ' "The Flexible Firm": Strategy and Segmentation', *British Journal of Industrial Relations*, 31, 3: 383–408.
Hunter, L. and McInnes, J. (1992) 'Employers and labour flexibility: the evidence from case studies', *Employment Gazette*, June: 307–15.
Hutchinson, S. and Brewster, C. (1994) *Flexibility at Work in Europe: Strategies and Practice*, Report prepared for the European Association of Personal Management, London, IPD.

IRS (1990) 'Temporary working 2: how employers use temporary workers', *IRS Employment Trends*, 469: 5–14.
Johnson, G. (1987) *Strategic Change and the Management Process*, Oxford, Blackwell.
Johnson, G. and Scholes, K. (1988) *Exploring Corporate Strategy*, Hemel Hempstead, Prentice Hall.
Knights, D., Willmott, H. and Collinson, D. (eds) (1985) *Job Redesign: Critical Perspectives on the Labour Process*, Aldershot, Gower.
Konle-Seidl, R., Ullmann, H. and Walwei, U. (1990) 'The European social space – atypical forms of employment and working hours in the EC', *International Social Securities Review*, 43,2: 151–87.
Koshiro, K. (ed.) (1992) *Employment Security and Labour Market Flexibility: An International Perspective*, Wayne State, Detroit.
Lindblom, C. E. (1959) 'The science of "Muddling Through" ', *Public Administration Review*. 19: 79–88
Machin, S. and Stewart, M. (1992) 'Unions and the financial performance of British private sector establishments', *Journal of Applied Econometrics*, 5, 327–50.
Marginson, P., Edwards, P.K., Purcell, J. and Sissons, K. (1988) 'What do corporate officers really do?', *British Journal of Industrial Relations*, 26: 229–45.
McCarthy, W. (1994) 'Of hats and cattle; or the limits of macro-survey research in industrial relations', *Industrial Relations Journal*, 25, 4: 315–22.
Metcalf D. (1993) 'Industrial relations and economic performance', *British Journal of Industrial Relations*, 31, 2: 255–84.
McGregor, A. and Sproull, A. (1992) 'Employers and the flexible workforce', *Employment Gazette*, May: 225–34.
Millward, N. and Hawes, W. R. (1995) 'Hats, cattle and IR research: a comment on McCarthy', *Industrial Relations Journal*, 26,1: 69–73.
Mintzberg, H. (1978) 'Patterns in strategy formation', *Management Science*, 24(9): 934–48.
Mintzberg H (1987) 'Crafting Strategy', *Harvard Business Review* (July–Aug.): 66–75.
Monks, J. (1994) 'The trade union response to HRM: fraud or opportunity?', *Personnel Management*, Sept.: 42–7.
Morgan, D. (1989) 'Strategies and sociologists: a comment on Crow', *Sociology*, 23 (1): 25–9.
Norusis, M. J. (1988) *SPSS X Advanced Statistics Guide*, 2nd edn, SPSS Inc.
O'Connell Davidson, J. (1993)*Privatisation and Employment Relations: The Case of the Water Industry*, London, Mansell.
O'Reilly, J. (1992) 'Where do you draw the line?: functional flexibility, training and skill in Britain and France', *Work, Employment and Society*, 6,3: 369–96.
OECD (1991) *Employment Outlook*, Paris.
Piore, M. J. and Sabel, C.F. (1985) *The Second Industrial Divide: Possibilities for Prosperity*, New York, Basic Books.
Pollert, A. (1987) 'The flexible firm: a model in search of reality (or a policy in search of a practice)?', *Warwick Papers in Industrial Relations*, no. 19, Warwick University.
Pollert, A. (1988a) 'Dismantling flexibility', *Capital and Class*, 34: 42–75.

Pollert, A. (1988b) 'The "flexible firm": fixation or fact?', *Work, Employment and Society*, 2,3: 281–316.

Pollert, A. (ed.) (1991) *Farewell to Flexibility?*, Oxford, Blackwell.

Rubery, J. (ed.) (1988) *Women and Recession*, London, Routledge and Kegan Paul.

Standing, G. and Tokman, V. (eds) (1994) *Towards Social Adjustment*, Geneva, ILO.

Walsh, T. (1990) 'Flexible labour utilisation in the private service sector', *Work, Employment and Society*, 4(4): 517–30.

Wood, D. and Smith, P., (1989) *Employers' Labour Use Strategies First Report on the 1987 Survey*, Department of Employment Research Paper 63, London, HMSO.

Wrapp, E. H. (1967) 'Good managers don't make policy decisions', *Harvard Business Review*, Sept.–Oct.: 91–9.

more and more supple (Reveley, 1995; Anonymous, 1996; Wallace, 1997). Sliding working times, a flexible working week or overtime are some examples of the working day becoming more flexible. According to the alliance of Belgian companies the number of wage-earners performing irregular hours is increasing every year (VBO Bulletin, 1997). When we look at the Belgian figures, we see that 46 per cent of the participating organisations makes use of flexible working hours/time. Almost half of the participating organisations (46 per cent) increased their use of this kind of flexible working arrangement over the last three years. In 52 per cent of the organisations the use of this method stayed the same over the last 3 years. Only 2 per cent of the participating organisations decreased their use of flexible working hours/time over the last three years.

Home-based working and teleworking

Home and teleworking, sometimes also called 'flexiplace', have been promoted as the working method of the future (England, 1996; Raghuram, 1996; Guthrie 1997; Nilles 1997). Among the factors driving the growth of telecommuting are economic trends towards downsizing, increasing market competition, faster and better technology, and a greater emphasis on hiring and retaining qualified workers (Anonymous, 1995). Information and communication technology provides organisations with a whole range of new possibilities for performing work and structuring the organisation (Lindstrom, *et al.*, 1997). Technology can be used by companies so that the work doesn't have to be carried out at the office or in the immediate environment of the office. Employees don't have to waste their time and energy in traffic jams, which fosters their efficiency. Research conducted in the US has shown that advanced technology and its use has a small role in telework (England 1996). According to England (1996), telework has more to do with HR planning and task design than with technology. And that is because telework is a management strategy enabling performance of work at another place than the traditional workplace. But, perhaps, the main advantage for employees is the greater flexibility it affords to coordinate work schedules with personal and family responsibilities.

Yet our results indicate that teleworking is seldom used in practice. Only a small part of the participating companies (10 per cent) use teleworking. Moreover, companies remain careful with the utilisation of teleworking. In 68 per cent of the companies teleworking involves less than 1 per cent of the workforce (see Table 5.3). On the other hand teleworking seems to show a positive evolution over the past three

Table 5.3 Proportion of workforce who are on specific contracts

%	*Shift work*	*Annual hours*	*Part-time work*	*Temporary/ casual*	*Fixed-term contracts*	*Home-based work*	*Tele-working*
<1	9	46	22	37	32	69	69
1–5	15	24	42	40	47	14.5	15
6–10	6	5	16	14	14	8.5	8
11–20	13	5	10	7	6	4	4
>20	57	20	9	2	3	4	4

years. In half of the companies using teleworking it increased, while only 3 per cent of the companies decreased their use of teleworking.

The use of home-based working, which means working at home without necessarily being on-line connected with the company, is limited within the participating organisations (only 12 per cent). Furthermore, 69 per cent of the organisations using home-based working do so for less than 1 per cent of their workforce : it remains rather limited at the level of the organisation. When we look at the change in the utilisation of this working arrangement over the last 3 years an increase can be observed in almost half of the participating organisations (47 per cent), while the utilisation of it remained stable in 47 per cent of the participating organisations. Only 4 per cent of the organisations using home-based working report a decrease of this method over the last 3 years.

Amongst the reasons that telecommuting programmes, launched by companies, did not succeed are poor technology planning, unrealistic expectations, culture shock and lack of trust. Important for the success of home and teleworking is that there is a climate and culture based on trust, instead of control. But tele-and home-working as flexible working practices do also have disadvantages. For instance, this method requires discipline. Employees could work too little or too much. The division between work and family could tend to disappear because the employees' working instruments (laptop computers, cellular phones, beepers, etc.) are always in front of them at home. It is also suggested in the literature that telework alters the context within which teleworkers acquire knowledge (Raghuram, 1996). Because of sophisticated information technologies, teleworkers have greater access to on-line information and documentation. According to the author, this access creates the potential for higher explicit knowledge in comparison with the traditional work environment. However telework increases the physical distance from work and decreases the ability to socialise. And Raghuram (1996) argues that increased physical distance would create a challenge in the teleworkers' abilities to acquire tacit knowledge. Socialisation, mentoring, training and documentation practices, therefore, become important for maintaining knowledge in the organisation. According to Guthrie (1997) teleworking offers a challenge to the issues of trust, time versus quality, and the definition of what work entails. In spite of the many advantages home and teleworking offer, one has to realise that communication between employees is a crucial factor and irreplaceable.

Annual hours contract

Among the most important innovations in flexible working time arrangements is the annual hours contract (Holder, 1995; McMeekin, 1995; Thatcher, 1995). Annual hours contracts aim to provide a more cost-effective way than overtime of dealing with cyclical variations in demand. So the competitive pressure for closer control of labour costs is one of the important stimulating factors. The annual hours arrangement involves determining the actual demand pattern of the (manufacturing) process during the course of the year and then allocating labour accordingly. Maximum labour costs accrue when there is insufficient work to keep the workforce occupied, while minimum labour costs will be achieved during periods of peak demand because employees are motivated to use their time effectively. According to Holder (1995) the trick is to attain the latter situation on a regular basis. In the past, annual hours systems were associated with shiftworkers and manufacturing companies, but now we also find them in the service sector (McMeekin, 1995). Of all the participating organisations 18 per cent say they use annual hours. In addition to that, 30 per cent of the respondents reports an increase of this method over the last 3 years, while 61 per cent of the respondents report that the use of the annual hours contract stayed the same. Only 9 per cent of the organisations decreased their use of annual hours. With reference to the organisations involved, the utilisation of the method is rather limited: in 71 per cent of the organisations it involves less than 5 per cent of the workforce.

Outsourcing

As more companies focus on their core business, outsourcing of activities which are not core activities, is on the rise (Correia, 1994; Sweeny, 1995; Benson and Ieronimo, 1996; Elliott and Torkko, 1996; Deavers,

1997; Vaughn, 1997). According to Elliott and Torkko (1996) companies today are using outsourcing in order to achieve strategic advantages, such as a management focus on core businesses, long-term flexibility, regular access to leading practices, new skills and culture, and an internal customer/supplier orientation. Elliott and Torkko (1996) call this practice 'strategic outsourcing'. According to Deavers (1997) several factors tend to increase outsourcing simultaneously, such as rapid technological change, increased risk and the search for flexibility, greater emphasis on core corporate competencies and globalisation. Deavers (1997) argues that, in this broader context, outsourcing is the result of a complex change in the cost boundaries facing firms as they choose between inside and outside production. So outsourcing can be considered as an arrangement promoting flexibility. By doing so the company gets more space to concentrate on its core activities and develop a flexibility-based policy on the core activities: 70 per cent of the participating organisations report that they outsource certain activivities. The results show an increase over the last 3 years: 65 per cent of the participating organisations increased their use, while only 3 per cent decreased their use, of outsourcing or subcontracting.

An important implication of outsourcing for HRM is that, as outsourcing becomes more widespread within organisations, HR professionals need to sharpen their negotation skills when selecting and working with outside vendors that provide a number of services. The HR department has to act as a broker of talent and expertise, has to develop screening and selection criteria, has to coordinate training, and has to oversee budgeting and billing practices (Correia, 1994).

Specification of jobs

A very important aspect of flexibility is concerned with how jobs themselves are organised. In addition to the use of flexible working arrangements, there is a change in the specification of jobs over the last 3 years. There is a strong drive to open jobs up and make them intrinsically more flexible. The majority of the respondents indicate that there have been changes in job content. The question on the specification of jobs was asked with reference to four categories (see Table 5.4).

Of all the participating organisations 68 per cent report a major change in the specification of management jobs: the same number of companies sees a change in the specification of professional/technical jobs. 61 per cent of the respondents report a change in the specification of clerical jobs, while 66 per cent report a change in the specification of manual jobs.

6 Flexibility in Norwegian and British Firms: Competitive Pressure and Institutional Embeddedness

Paul N. Gooderham and Odd Nordhaug

INTRODUCTION

The purpose of this chapter is to broaden our understanding of those factors which condition the use firms make of HR strategies aimed at enhancing their ability to respond flexibly to an increasingly changing environment. In particular, we will focus on the variations made by firms in their pursuit of greater levels of numerical flexibility. The main thrust of our argument is that such pursuits will not simply be a rational, firm-based response to market conditions, but will not least be a product of the institutional context within which firms are embedded. In order to test this proposition, developments in Norwegian and British firms will be compared.

First, we sketch the main arguments which suggest that firms are, to an increasing degree, having to confront heterogeneous, dynamic and therefore uncertain environments. This development is the base from which the so-called 'soft' variants of HRM have evolved. It is, however, maintained that these variants are inadequate in that they fail to address the needs many firms have for a substantial degree of numerical flexibility. However, simply arguing that numerical flexibility must be incorporated in delineations of HR strategies would be too simplisitic. There is an additional need to incorporate perspectives from the new institutionalism in organisation theory, which emphasise that the autonomy a firm enjoys to enact strategies for achieving numerical flexibility is largely determined by the national context. In other words, the choices available to Norwegian and British firms will be significantly coloured by their respective institutional contexts, not least in regard to laws governing employment and the power of trade unions. In order to test this argument, we will compare Norwegian and

British firms in relation to three methods for generating numerical flexibility: temporary employment, part-time employment and the use of sub-contractors. The choice of these two countries as test cases for our argument is occasioned by their very different institutional trajectories since the early 1980s. Whereas the institutional parameters British firms operate within have been significantly liberalised, those of Norwegian firms have remained unchanged and relatively highly regulated.

TOWARDS NEW ORGANISATIONAL FORMS

Within recent organisation theory it has become commonplace to argue that firms are making radical changes to their organizations (Stone and Eddy, 1996). It is argued that the traditional organisational form characterised by specialisation, vertical control and centralised decision making is inadequate in relation to the external demands being made on firms. These demands may be summarized in terms of two dimensions (see Figure 6.1). Environmental stability refers to the pace of technological change that has to be dealt with. The greater the pace, the more critical the innovative ability and HR development capability of the firm become. The other dimension, environmental complexity, refers to the degree to which product standardisation may be achieved. Mass production and corresponding economies of scale are problematic if the firm has to meet the needs of increasingly heterogeneous customers who demand personalised products or services.

The two dimensions of Figure 6.1 produce four generic situations to which firms may be assigned.

		Environmental Stability/Change	
		Stable	*Dynamic*
Environmental Complexity	Homogeneous	II Machine, centralised, standardised	I Simple, centralised
	Heterogeneous	III Professional, decentralised	IV Organic, decentralised

Figure 6.1 Organisational environments and types

Traditionally, manufacturing firms have moved from quadrant I to quadrant II as they have succeeded in developing the routines required for successful mass-production. Service industries such as banking have on the other hand been located in quadrant III because they serve a variety of different groups. Environmental stability has meant though that it has been possible to develop a formalised division of labour which is reflected in the formation of professions. Increasingly though, it is argued, firms are being pushed into quadrant IV by a mix of forces that include the globalisation and fragmentation of markets and rapid technological change (Pfeffer, 1994). This quadrant is characterised by dynamic and heterogeneous external conditions (Burns, 1963). This fosters a need for a strong customer focus and a management approach that ensures that quality control is conducted, not on the basis of routines and vertical control, but on the basis of flexible, decentralised systems. Such systems are dependent on the establishment of a new psychological contract between firm and employee in which employees at all levels are empowered. In addition, a decentralisation of authority means that the need for hierarchy diminishes, which results in delayering whereby the number of middle managers is reduced. The result is a flatter organisation comprised of multidisciplinary teams assembled on a project by project basis.

HRM

One version of what a move to a quadrant IV existence implies for firms is represented by HRM. HRM as a concept was launched around 1980, it being contended that there was now a need for a fundamental alternative to traditional personnel management (Hendry and Pettigrew, 1986; Nordhaug, 1993; Olberg, 1995). Whereas traditional personnel management had as its aim to ensure stability and predictability by for example the maintainance and development of standardised sets of firm-employees agreements and accords, HRM heralded a need to link the deployment and development of human resources with strategy. Furthermore, HRM represented a new perspective on the value of a firm's human resources for the realisation of its strategy in that quadrant IV firms are dependent on substantial employee commitment and innovativeness coupled with an ability to work in interdisciplinary teams.

However, the HRM perspective has increasingly become to be regarded as too limited a paradigm to account for what has actually taken place in work life. The goal of increased flexibility, which is the starting point for HRM, is a response to an environment which has become increasingly less certain and therefore more demanding. Given that this is the case, it must be expected that firms are not only seeking to generate commitment and creativity but are also focusing on disengaging those parts of its staffing which are extraneous to its core operations. This would account for the rise of such phenomena as 'downsizing' (Freeman and Cameron, 1993) and 'outsourcing' (Lacity *et al.*, 1995), both of which represent attempts to reduce transaction costs (Williamson, 1985) and neither of which is a feature of HRM.

NUMERICAL FLEXIBILITY

In essence HRM stands accused of having failed to address firms' needs for forms of flexibility other than that of functional flexibility. Atkinson (1985) indicates that the functional flexibility espoused by HRM characterised by empowerment and creativity may be achieved without involving the whole work force. Indeed, it is positively advantageous for firms facing uncertain market conditions, and therefore fluctating staffing needs, not to do so. Manpower needs over and above those required to maintain the firm's core activities can either be acquired using subcontractors or labour hired through a temporary or part-time basis, thus granting firms numerical flexibility.

Generally speaking, according to Atkinson, 'externals', that is personnel acquired on a temporary, part-time or subcontractual basis, are subject to a substantially different developmental and managerial regime than that of core employees. Their work is more closely controlled than empowered core employees and payment is either hourly or fixed at a piece-rate. Moreover, training paid for by the firm is limited. Hence, external employees achieve only a peripheral status in relation to the firm.

Atkinson's model has been subjected to a number of criticisms, not least that it mixes description, prediction and prescription (Hendry and Pettigrew, 1986; Pollert 1988). Nevertheless, although undoubtedly there are elements of 'best practice' thinking in his model, it is relatively unproblematic to leave its prescriptive features to one side and focus on the issue of whether it captures current trends in employment practice. In our case, as we have indicated, we are particularly concerned with the development of numerical flexibility.

Table 6.2 Reported changes in the influence of unions within the firms during the last 3 years (percentages of firms)

	Norway		*UK*	
	1991	*1995*	*1991*	*1995*
Increased	41.8	22.0	3.8	2.8
Unchanged	51.6	69.8	42.6	58.7
Decreased	6.6	8.2	53.1	38.2
'Net change'	35.2	13.8	−49.3	−35.2
N =	168	182	984	786

argument that Norway and Britain represent two fundamentally different institutional contexts, are the substantially different perceptions held by top personnel managers in the two countries of trends in union influence.

As Table 6.2 indicates, whereas only 8.2 per cent of Norwegian firms report a decline in union influence over the period 1993–95, the figure is 38.2 per cent for British firms. Indeed, 22.0 per cent of the Norwegian firms in the sample report an increase for the period, as opposed to a mere 2.8 per cent of the British firms.

IMPLICATIONS FOR NUMERICAL FLEXIBILITY

Given these two substantially different institutional regimes, the question that will now be addressed is: What are the consequences of these divergent institutional regimes for the growth and development of numerical flexibility strategies? As indicated, the increased use of temporary employees, part-time employees and sub-contractors are critical indicators of a trend toward numerical flexibility. Furthermore, we have distinguished between two different sources of what DiMaggio and Powell (1983) label as coercive institutional pressures. The first of these is trade union power. Although we have demonstrated that Norwegian unions are generally perceived as being more powerful at the firm level than their British counterparts, there will be some exceptions in that some British firms will be faced with powerful unions while some Norwegian firms will be confronting unions whose power is relatively weak. Put differently, the critical test of the new institutional thesis is whether managerial perception of union power per se has an influence on changes in numerical flexibility.

Hypothesis 1: Firms in which management perceives trade unions as being powerful will be less prone to implement strategies for numerical flexibility.

The second coercive institutional pressure we have distinguished is the national legislative regime. Although firm perceptions of their respective regimes will vary, their influence will inevitably be significantly less open to negotiation than the influence of trade unions. Consequently, in their general pervasiveness, national legislative regimes may simply be conceived of as national regimes. In the Norwegian context, we have noted the existence of legislation restricting the use of temporary employees and sub-contractors, but none on the use of part-time employees. In the British context, none of these are restricted by legislation. Thus we hypothesise that:

Hypothesis 2: Norwegian firms will be less likely to implement strategies for numerical flexibility than British firms with the execption of part-time employment.

As noted earlier, Atkinson has suggested that the implementation of numerical flexibility will vary from sector to sector. Although Atkinson fails to acknowledge it, this assumption is very much in accordance with the new institutionalism in that it recognises that the 'normative institutional pressures' (DiMaggio and Powell, 1983) are unevenly spread. Not least will employee expectations differ according to the degree of professional training they have received. As professional training is particularly weak in the personal services sector which includes hotels, restaurants, bars, retail outlets and cleaning in Norway and Great Britain (Gooderham and Hines, 1996), we expect the following:

Hypothesis 3: Firms within the personal services sector will be more likely to implement strategies for numerical flexibility than firms operating in other sectors.

Opposed to new institutionalism is the view implicit in Atkinson's model that the drive towards numerical flexibility is a product of rational processes within the firm itself. That is, the implementation of numerical flexibility is a response to fluctuating market fortunes. In particular it may be argued that firms which have experienced increased competitive pressures over an extended period of time will be particularly motivated to increase their numerical flexibility.Our hypothesis is thus:

Hypothesis 4: Firms which have confronted an increased degree of competition during the past 3 years are more likely to have introduced strategies for numerical flexibility than firms which have not experienced any such increase.

EMPIRICAL ANALYSIS

The data which will be employed to test our hypotheses is derived from Cranet-E (Brewster *et al.*, 1994b). The response rate for Norway and Great Britain has been typical for such surveys, that is between 25 and 30 per cent. Brewster *et al.* (1994) have concluded that the response rate does not appear to have impaired representativity.

The operationalisations are shown in Table 6.3.

NATIONAL COLLEGE OF IRELAND LIBRARY

Table 6.3 Operationalisation of variables

Operationalisation	*Measurement*
Numerical flexibility: Changes in the use of temporary, part-time and subcontracting in the past three years	1 = increased 2 = unchanged 3 = decreased or not used
Trade union power	1 = The firm does not recognise unions as counterparts in bargaining, or if it does, it reports a decline in the influence of unions in the past 3 years. 2 = The firm accepts trade unions for the purpose of negotiations and reports no decline in the influence of unions the past 3 years. 3 = The firm accepts trade unions for the purpose of negotiations and reports an increase in the influence of the union the past 3 years.
National context	1 = Great Britain 0 = Norway
Sector (Dummy)	Manufacturing Construction Transportation Financial services Personal services (refence category)
Degree of competition	1 = increased 0 = decreased

In Table 6.4, we present a linear regression analysis which displays the effects of the independent variables on changes in the use of the three numerical flexibility strategies.

First, it was found that hypothesis 1, which states that firms who perceive trade unions as being powerful will be less prone to implementing strategies for numerical flexibility, is supported by the findings.

Hypothesis 2 contends that Norwegian firms will be less likely to implement strategies for numerical flexibility than British firms with the execption of part-time employment. As Table 6.4 shows, while there are relatively powerful effects for both the use of temporary employees and the use of sub-contractors, there is no such effect for the use of part-time employees. The hypothesis is therefore supported.

In hypothesis 3 it was proposed that firms within the personal services sector will be more likely to implement strategies for numerical flexibility than firms operating in other sectors. In regard to financial services, the hypothesis is not supported since there are no significant differences between financial services and personal services. The picture for the other sectors is far more complex than the anticipated realities encompassed in the original hypothesis. In both manufacturing and construction, significantly more use is made of sub-contractors but significantly less of part-timers than is the case for personal services. There is no significant difference in the use of temporary employees. In regard to transport, significantly more use is made of temporary

Table 6.4 Effects of trade union power, national context, sector and degree of competition on changes in the use of (I) temporary employees (I), part-time employees (II) and subcontracting (III) (standardised regression coefficients)

	I	*II*	*III*
Trade union power	.076**	.094**	.128**
National context	.287**	.058	.154**
Sector			
Manufacturing	−.049	.274**	−.109**
Construction	−.014	.093**	−.139**
Transport	−.077**	−.018	−.095**
Financial services	−.010	−.021	−.045
Degree of competition	.053*	.086*	.074*
R2	.116	.113	.077

** p<.05; * p<.10.
N=964.

employees and sub-contractors, but there is no difference in the use of part-time employees. In sum, the hypothesis is clearly too simplistic and therefore cannot be substantiated.

In hypothesis 4 it was argued that firms which have confronted an increased degree of competition over the past 3 years are more likely to have introduced strategies for numerical flexibility than firms that have not experienced any such increase. This hypothesis is supported by the findings in Table 6.4.

CONCLUDING COMMENTS

Our analysis reveals that Atkinson's thesis that numerical flexibility is a response to market conditions cannot be rejected. However, our analysis also reveals that new institutional explanations must be included in any comprehensive understanding of the processes that generate numerical flexibility. Moreover, our analysis suggests that the latter represent more powerful explanations of firms' pursuit of numerical flexibility than the former. For example, in those areas where Norwegian employment law is particularly restrictive, that is in the use of temporary employees and sub-contractors, national context represents a considerably more potent effect than firm perceptions of changes in the level of competition. In addition, trade union power has a consistently more powerful effect on all three indicators of numerical flexibility than changes in the level of competition.

In practice, this means that even when we control for the effect of changes in the level of competition, the drive towards numerical flexibility is substantially stronger among British firms than among Norwegian firms. The latter not only have to adapt to more rigid employment laws with respect to the use of temporary employees and sub-contractors but they also to have to contend with an institutional environment comprising relatively powerful unions. It must be borne in mind though that the effect of trade union power is not restricted to Norwegian firms. Our findings indicate that those British firms which face powerful unions are also less inclined to introduce numerical flexibility.

Our analysis has also controlled for the effect of sector. As we have conceded, our hypothesis at this point was shown to be too simplistic. Clearly there is a need for further theoretical and empirical work in order that we might more fully comprehend cross-sectoral differences.

References

Atkinson, J. (1985) 'The changing corporation', in Clutterbuck, D. (ed.), pp. 13–34.

Brewster, C. (1994) 'European HRM: reflection of, or challenge to, the American concept?', in Kirkbridge, P. S. (ed.), pp. 56–89.

Brewster, C. and Hegewiseh, A. (eds), (1994) *Policy and Practice in European Human Resource Management*, London, Routledge.

Brewster, C., Hegewisch, A. and L. Mayne (1994a) 'Flexible working practices the controversy and the evidence', in Brewster, C. and Hegewisch, A. (eds), pp. 168–93.

Brewster, C., Hegewisch, A., Mayne, L. and Tregaskis, O. (1994b) 'Methodology of the Price Waterhouse Cranfield Project', in Brewster, C. and Hegewisch, A. (eds) pp. 230–45.

Bridges, W. P. and Villemez, W. J. (1991) 'Employment relations and the labour market: integrating institutional and market perspectives', *American Sociological Review*, 56: 748–64.

Burns, T. (1963) 'Industry in a new age', *New Society*: 17–20.

Clutterbuck, D. (ed.) (1985) *New Patterns of Work*, Aldershout, Gower.

Davis-Blake, A. and Uzzi, B. (1993) 'Determinants of employment externalization: a study of temporary workers and independent contractors', *Administrative Science Quarterly*, 38: 195–233.

DiMaggio, P. J. and Powell, W. W. (1983) 'The iron cage revisited.: institutional isomorphism and collective rationality in organizational fields', *American Sociological Review*, 48: 147–60.

DiMaggio, P. J. and Powell, W. W. (1988) 'Introduction', in DiMaggio, P. J. and Powell, W. W. (eds), pp. 1–38.

Dobbin, F., Sutton, J. R., Meyer, J. W. and Scott, W. R. (1993) 'Equal opportunity law and the construction of internal labour Markets', *American Journal of Sociology* 99: 396–427.

Edelman, L. E. (1990) 'Legal environments and organizational governance: the expansion of due process in the American workplace', *American Journal of Sociology*, 75: 1401–40.

Freeman, S. J. and Cameron, S. J. (1993) 'Organizational downsizing: a convergence and reorientation framework', *Organization Science*, 4: 10–29.

Gallie, D. (1994) 'Pattern of skills change: upskilling, deskilling, or polarization?', in Penn, R., Rose, M. and Rubery, J. (eds), pp.

Gooderham, P. N. and Hines, K. (1995) 'Trends in employer funded training as an indicator of changes in employment: the case of Norway in the 1980s', *Adult Education Quarterly*, 45 (4): 213–26.

Hakim, C. (1990) 'Core and periphery in employers' workforce strategies: evidence from the 1987 ELUS Survey', *Work, Employment & Society*, 4 (2): 157–88.

Hatch, M. J. (1997) *Organization Theory: Modern, Symbolic and Postmodern Perspectives*, Oxford, Oxford University Press.

Hendry, C. and Pettigrew, A. (1986) 'The practice of strategic human resource management', *Personnel Review*, 15 (5): 3–8.

Kirkbridge, P.S. (ed.) (1994) *Human Resource Management in Europe*, London, Routledge.

Lacity, M. C., Willcocks, L. P. and Feeny, D. F. (1995) 'IT outsourcing: maximise flexibility and control', *Harvard Business Review*, May–June: 84–93.

Marchington, M., Wilkinson, A., Ackers, P. and Goodman, J. (1994) 'Understanding the meaning of participation: views from the workplace', *Human Relations*, 47 (8): 3–31.

Nordhaug, O. (1993) *Strategisk personalledelse (Strategic Human Resource Management)*, Oslo, Tano.

Olberg, D. (1995) *Endringer i arbeidslivets organisering (Changes in the Organization of Worklife)*, Oslo, Fafo.

Penn, R., Rose, M. and Ruberg, J. (eds) (1994) *Skilland Occupational Change*, Oxford, Oxford University, Press.

Pfeffer, J. (1994) *Competitive Advanatge Through People: Unleashing the Power of the Work Force*, Boston, Harvard Business School Press.

Pollert, A. (1988) 'The "flexible firm": Fixation or fact?', *Work, Employment & Society*, 2 (3): 281–316.

Rubery, J. and Wilkinson, F. (1994) *Introduction: Employer Strategy and the Labour Market*, Oxford, Oxford University Press.

Rumelt, R. P., Schendel, D. E. and Teece, D. J. (eds) (1994) 'Fundamental issues in strategy', *Fundamental Issues in Strategy: A Research Agenda*, Cambridge, Mass., Harvard Business School Press.

Scott, W. R. and Meyer, J. W. (eds) (1994) 'The rise of training programs in firms and agencies: an institutional perspective', *Institutional Environments and Organizations*, London, Sage.

Sparrow, P. and Hiltrop, J. M. (1994) *European Human Resource Management in Transition*, New York, Prentice Hall.

Stone, D. L. and Eddy, E. R. (1996) 'A model of individual and organizational factors affecting quality-related outcomes', *Journal of Quality Management*, 1 (1): 21–48.

Williamson, O. E. (1985) *The Economic Institutions of Capitalism*, New york, The Free Press.

7 Flexible Working Patterns: Towards Reconciliation of Family and Work

Nancy Papalexandris

INTRODUCTION

In the past decade, especially in Northern countries of the European Union, some major changes have occurred regarding labour matters. The conventional and legal framework regulating employment has become more flexible as new patterns of employment have gained popularity. Part-time work, one of the oldest and most common forms of flexibility, has shifted from involving unqualified women to qualified men and women, while a number of other flexible working patterns involving contract, place and pay flexibility have emerged.

Flexibility is seen as a tool for reducing labour costs and thus improving productivity and competitiveness. Research has shown that flexible working is correlated with strategic approaches to HRM (Brewster *et al.*, 1994) and as, suggested by the model of the flexible firm described by Atkinson (1984), companies are externalising peripheral functions by subcontracting and restructuring working hours.

This growing shift towards flexibility may, however, have, apart from its impact on competitiveness, some positive social effects. It is more and more seen as a means to fight unemployment and as an important tool for reconciling work with family life (DeRoure, 1995). This chapter will examine the role of flexibility in addressing the important social issue of work and family reconciliation in Europe in general and in Greece in particular.

TRENDS AFFECTING THE LABOUR SITUATION IN EUROPE

In traditional pre-industrial societies, work and family were united as a whole with the family being the main production unit. It is worth mentioning that the word economy comes from the Greek words meaning home and care. So economy meant originally taking care of home matters.

Later, in industrial societies the division between work and private life became sharp. However, the percentage of married women working outside their home was still low while the extended family came in to support the working mother in meeting her family obligations.

Today the family may differ in size from a one parent wage-earner to a dual career professional couple, while the extended family is becoming a rare phenomenon. Regardless of differences in family structure there is a common wish on the part of the working population at all levels: for reducing the separation between family and work and achieving a better balance between working life, family obligations, leisure and socialising. This has led to a serious debate and policy formulation in the EU concerning the reconciliation of family and work and to a number of activities which are adopted both by countries and organisations.

In order to understand the general context in which this balance of family and work can be achieved we need to refer briefly to the main changes in the external environment of organisations affecting the work and family situation in Europe.

Changes affecting work

In the economic setting, Europe is facing intense international competition as the globalisation of production and markets is a clear reality. Newly industrialised countries are producing good quality products at a low cost (one dollar per hour or even less) and production which was until now local and national is under threat. Industry has thus to work under a constant pressure to reduce costs while diversifying its range of products and services to meet the demand of customers and consumers. Industrial skills are increasingly based on information systems and development of the service sector is more and more dependent on the new communication technologies. The change towards a computer-based society demands a great capacity to adapt and increases the risk for exclusion from the workforce for a part of the working population (DeRoure, 1995).

In an effort to meet economic and technological changes the organisational setting is changing drastically. Organisations have adopted new principles all aimed at the suppression of non-profit-making operations. Employees have to develop versatility and a variety of competencies as part of the tasks traditionally carried out by administrative services are transferred to operational posts. Thus we see a shortening of the hierarchical chains, greater employee autonomy through work teams, greater demand for optimisation of professional skills including capacity for curiosity, initiative and continuous learning.

This is the overall situation for those who have the chance to get a job and keep it. But we know that as fewer and fewer employees are producing more and more goods and services, unemployment, now amounting to approximately 20 million in the EU is likely to increase. For the member states of the EU improvement in employment figures is a top priority. One of the ways proposed to achieve that has been to decrease working hours and increase part-time employment. Employment on a permanent contract or lifetime employment in the same company are on the decrease. So we now refer to the employability of workers and their capacity to keep a job in the future and no longer, 'their' job.

Changes affecting family

Today 40 per cent of women of the EU are in the labour market, while at the same time there is a high appreciation of family as an institution and of family values. However, the families' living circumstances and the requirements imposed by work make child rearing more and more expensive and difficult. As a result, those who have children work harder overall and have less money, while those who are childless have more freedom and more money. The situation appears to be equally difficult in the US where despite corporate and public policies the work-family dilemma is still very strong (Smolowe, 1996).

Thus we can see a conflict emerging between work and family. This conflict may lead either to a clear dominance of work over the family life and a 'fully mobile society of single persons' or to a reshaping of the present everyday lives of families through changes in existing family policies (DeRoure, 1996). If we all agree that the second alternative is the most desirable for the major part of the population, an adjustment in the organisation of work is needed in order to facilitate the upbringing of children, bring paid work into line with family responsibilities and create employment opportunities, especially for women, who still bear the major part of family obligations. This cannot occur without the equitable sharing of duties between husband and wife since the need to overcome the gender-related distribution of roles seems today a most appropriate and fair solution coinciding with aspirations towards a better control over time and life which are becoming stronger and stronger both among men and women (Moussourou, 1996).

The need of people to have better control over working time and the hours they wish to devote to work varies according to their age, sex, mobility, qualifications, pay, professional aspirations and family status. For example, availability of professional time is lower for women when they have young children and for people in general when they feel the need for training or retraining or when they approach the end of their careers. On the contrary people feel the need to put more hours in their work just after studies, before starting a family and during stages of their career when they assume greater responsibilities and see opportunities in their career development. All this points toward the need for increased flexibility at work.

FLEXIBILITY AT WORK AND EUROPEAN UNION POLICY

Companies and organisations have received the message and several work methods are being offered allowing people to choose from a number of flexible working patterns and career options designed to achieve a balance between working, personal and family life while also fighting unemployment and creating job opportunities. These include:

1. flexibility in working time arrangements (flexi-time, annualisation of working time, four-day week, individual/collective management of working hours);
2. flexibility in the number of hours worked (part-time work, job-sharing, 32–or even shorter hour-week, compressed week, etc);
3. flexibility in the way that periods of work can be broken up (career breaks, parental leave, sabbatical leave, etc);
4. flexibility with regard to place of work (teleworking, combination of working some days in the office and some days home).

To these are added support measures designed for families with young children such as:

- childcare services;
- workplace catering and laundry service;
- support when returning to work after maternity;
- paternal leave.

At the European Union policy level certain serious initiatives have taken place to promote work and family reconciliation. The first, created in 1986, is called 'Childcare and other measures aimed at reconciling working and family responsibilities for women and men'. The second, created in 1993, is called 'Coordination group on positive action and aims at positive action for women'. The third, created in June 1994, is called 'Families and work network'.

The Network was set with the following objectives (Stewart, 1994):

1. to promote organisation methods designed to achieve balance between personal and family life.
2. to support measures for families and mobile professionals; and
3. to award the European social innovation prize to companies which have started practices enhancing a better balance between working and family.

In June 1995 in Stockholm one large company from Germany, one SME from Denmark and one State owned organisation from France won the prize for their category. The Network also organises national seminars in each member state and circulates a publication under the name 'New ways' to promote its objectives. Its contribution so far has been positive and it has stimulated a number of further initiatives in different EU countries on the work and family balance issue.

EXAMPLES FROM EU ORGANISATIONS

As described by Frederick DeRoure, coordinator of the Family and Work Network (DeRoure, 1996), in EU countries workers choose a part of their working hours in certain professional sectors. Public services offer flexible working hours with core working hours. Many organisations in the tertiary sector (insurance companies, banks, social security) have applied flexi-time, giving their employees certain options concerning the beginning and the end of the working hours. These hours are crucial for the organisation of family life (shopping, children, meals). The service sector in general offers employees a certain 'chosen' flexibility whereas the industrial sector remains more rigid, especially for people employed in production. Shift work is often the rule, required by a discontinuous or continuous production systems. The distribution sector, health (hospitals), transport (air, sea, trains, roads) and the Post Office are sectors at 'high-risk' with anti-social working hours incompatible with family life. Some among these organisations have encouraged the opening of commercial Childcare facilities open 24 hours a day or have defined collective time management systems. Here it is worth mentioning a few examples showing ways in which European member states apply flexibility in an effort to bring better balance between work and family while also fighting unemployment.

In *France* some companies apply the 4-day working week but on the basis of more or less 10 hours work a day. However, opinion polls show that workers and employees think that 3 days of freedom a week largely make up for the 4 intensive working days. These changes are not contested by workers. At company level, the example of one service company's worth mentioning. Parents who take parental leave to bring up their child receive compensatory benefit, are guaranteed a job to come back to and are replaced during this period by a job-seeker of the same sex (preservation of the proportion of women in work).

In *Germany*, the Volkswagen case is interesting because almost 100,000 workers in this car manufacturing sector, work and will continue to work for 4 years on the basis of 28.8 hours a week. The case of Volkswagen remains an example of collective agreement of the redistribution of working hours and its reduction to avoid numerous redundancies. Also, in Germany the new term *mobilzeit* (moving time) is replacing the term part-time which carries a negative connotation (European Community, 1996). Mobilzeit includes various options such as job sharing, longer summer holidays, compressed week and involves also qualified professionals of both sexes. Companies are encouraged to create mobile posts and are offered consultants' advice which is partly funded by the state.

In *Denmark* a rotational system became systematic in 1994, with a law allowing paid leave on the basis of unemployment benefit to any worker who has been present for over 5 years in an organisation (right to leave for various reasons). A new worker enters the organisation during the period of leave which can range from a few hours over any week to a few weeks or a year. Job-sharing formulae have been invented this way. After a year of application, the law has been a success and will continue, with a sliding scale system for the amount of benefit entitlement.

In the *United Kingdom* a non-profit organisation 'Parents at Work' is campaigning against people staying too long hours in the office. The 'go home on time' seminar held in June 1996 aimed at showing that working too many hours does not necessarily mean increased productivity while it is makes a normal family and personal life difficult.

In *Belgium* and in *Sweden* various campaigns aim at promoting the equal sharing of family responsibilities by the two sexes.

THE GREEK SITUATION

The need for reconciling work and family appears quite intense in Greece as it may help in three of the major problems the country is facing. These are (Papalexandris, 1996):

1. demographic problems showing a lowering birth rate and the ageing of the population.
2. unemployment problems with official figures reaching 10 per cent although figures among young people are well above that percentage; and
3. economic problems due to slow rate growth and the urgent need to raise competitiveness.

According to a recent report by the Association of Greek Industries, to which most companies belong, the lack of flexibility in the labour market and the existing rigid legal framework limit competitiveness and increase unemployment since they do not attract future investments.

Interestingly enough, flexibility and deregulation in labour markets which usually appear following stages of regulation and consolidation are common in many small and medium-sized Greek firms which are owned and run by family members. *Work at home* in the form of 'facon' is a very common source of employment for women with workers sewing clothes or producing handicrafts, jewellery and toys. These workers are paid on a piece basis. *Outsourcing* and *subcontracting* is a common way of working in engineering, mining and constructing firms where there is no regular demand and companies prefer to subcontract according to their needs. *Contract flexibility* is used extensively by the State which hires temporary and seasonal employees for certain jobs, (fire department, post office) by tourist enterprises which use seasonal employees, by the merchant marine, where seamen have to stop after 7 months of travel and by agriculture where both farming and industrial processing units require a seasonal type of employment. *Job sharing* can be found in nursing, house cleaning or distribution posts. *Flexibility in tasks* is also very common and is considered one of the major advantages of small companies, allowing them to survive and face the competition of larger firms.

Until recently a considerable percentage of people working under this type of flexible patterns, especially in small–medium-sized firms, did not enjoy the corresponding benefits of regular workers and were in an unfavourable situation compared to larger firms where labour issues are officially controlled by legislation. Only recently part-time employment gained official legal status.

Part-time work

Part-time employment was established officially in Greece in 1990 with Law 1892 although under the form of the fixed term contract has been practised since 1925. As official statistics show, only 4.5 per cent of the labour force works on a part time basis in Greece against the 14 per cent of the European Union. However Greece has the highest percentage in temporary employment (17.6 per cent) against 9.6 per cent of the European Union. According to a recent survey, part-time workers number to approximately 162,000 persons and of these 38 per cent could not find a full-time job, 30 per cent did not want a full-time job, 6 per cent were students and the rest declared various reasons for this type of job. Thus there is a general belief that in times of economic difficulty full-time jobs are replaced by part-time employment.

Part-time work is higher in the service sector and lower in industries where a convenient solution is offered by 'facon', with 225,000 persons employed, and by subcontracting. Labour unions are reserved and sceptical about the part-time model as revealed by recent research carried out by the Institute of Work of the General Conference of Greek Workers on 'New Ways of Working in Greece'. In a public debate on the issue appearing in the Greek Press, Employers associations said 'yes, in necessity only' and workers said 'no, if reduction of salaries is included' (Greek workers are the lowest-paid in Europe).

THE CRANFIELD SURVEY IN GREECE

In view of this general situation it is interesting to look closely at the Cranet-E data from Greece. Data from 112 companies mainly in the private sector employing more than 200 employees were gathered through the questionnaire developed by Cranet-E between autumn 1995 and spring 1996.

Table 7.1 shows the percentage of organisations in the Greek sample with a change in the use of flexible practices.

Table 7.1 Percentage of organisations with a change in the use of flexible practices in Greece

Practice	*Increased*	*Same*	*Decreased*	*Not Used*
Weekend work	11	46	13	26
Shift work	14	61	6	14
Overtime work	15	46	34	3
Annual hours contract	3	26	0	58
Part-time work	14	22	5	52
Job sharing	7	5	0	78
Flexible working hours	21	24	0	47
Temporary/casual work	18	43	8	28
Fixed-term contracts	16	46	4	30
Home-based work	1	5	0	87
Teleworking	1	2	0	89
Subcontracting/outsourcing	13	13	2	64

Source: Cranet-E survey Results (1995/96/97), Centre for European HRM, Cranfield School of Management, UK.

As can be seen, contrary to what was mentioned before concerning small–medium-sized firms, the larger companies which were represented in the sample make very little use of annual hours contracts, job sharing, home-based work and teleworking. The most important increase can be seen in flexi-time which means arriving or leaving earlier or later from work provided that the daily amount of working hours remains stable. This, as a measure, favours working mothers who can thus take children to school and is largely practised in banks or service companies.

Shift work is also extensively used since many companies in the sample belong to the manufacturing sector which works on a shift basis. Part-time work shows some increase which comes mainly from respondents in retail service companies following legal authorisation in 1990.

Finally, the decrease in overtime work is due to legal reasons. In order to encourage the creation of new jobs, the Labour Department asks companies to apply for a special permit in order to use overtime work above the limit of 48 hours per week. Thus companies are encouraged to hire new staff and discouraged from the over-use of the existing one.

Table 7.2 shows the percentage of organisations using flexible practices for more than 5 per cent of their workforce across European countries.

Greece shows a low percentage of part-time contracts (12 per cent) with Turkey, Bulgaria, Spain, Hungary having even less and some

Table 7.2 Percentage of organisations using flexible practices for more than 5 per cent of their workforce

Country Practice	*OZ*	*B*	*BL*	*CH*	*D (W)*	*D (E)*	*DK*	*E*	*F*	*FN*	*GR*	*H*	*I*	*IRL*	*N*	*NL*	*S*	*T*	*UK*
Part-time contracts	35	30	6	73	50	22	47	7	32	15	*12*	10	17	23	72	69	55	5	43
Temporary / casual contracts	45	18	16	15	6	3	18	55	26	18	*21*	12	4	43	17	27	29	5	28
Fixed-term contracts	17	18	46	19	30	20	8	54	33	50	*21*	32	24	19	25	31	7	30	14
Home-based work	1	2	0	3	2	0	15	0	1	1	*0*	4	0	1	0	1	0	0	2.5
Teleworking	1	2	1	2	0.5	1	0.5	0	1	1	*0*	5	0	1	1	2	9	2	1.5
Shift-working contracts	44	55	47	43	53	56	39	52	56	65	*30*	59	52	42	51	38	49	78	50
Annual hours contracts	10	4	5	10	6	5	4	11	5	13	*2*	64	11	6	3	14	8	15	9

Source: Cranet-E survey Results (1995/96/97), Centre for European HRM, Cranfield School of Management, UK.

countries such as Switzerland and Norway reaching 73 per cent and 72 per cent respectively. The general observation which can be made here is that in countries where workers are more highly paid there is more room for part-time work (Switzerland, West Germany, Denmark, Norway, Sweden). In countries with lower wages on the average, part-time pay is not easily accepted by employees.

With reference to temporary/casual contracts, Greece shows an average position of 21 per cent with percentages ranging from a lowest of 3 per cent for East Germany and a highest of 55 per cent for Spain. The same is true for fixed-term and shift working contracts where again Greece shows a middle range rate of 21 per cent and 30 per cent respectively.

Finally, home-based work, teleworking and annual hours contracts are very rare among Greek firms in the sample although we know that the first two are quite common among small medium-sized Greek firms. The same holds true for other countries in the survey where the percentage of organisations not using these practices is quite high.

General trends

From the previous discussion and the overall picture from Cranet-E it can be seen that certain forms of flexibility are gaining recognition in Greece among larger companies as opposed to the situation in previous years when the lack of social security benefits, the low pay level and the long hours of work among workers in the flexible deregulated schemes found especially in smaller companies have given a negative image to flexibility. However, the awareness that flexibility does not mean exploitation, and the willingness of the State to provide the legal framework and of social partners to proceed through social concensus, shows that flexibility will gain acceptance. This was made clear during the 'Work and Family' conference held in May 1996 in Athens where, apart from part-time work, the annualisation of working hours seemed to be gaining the approval of Labour Unions. As stressed by Frederick DeRoure (1996), flexibility can win full recognition only if the following rules are followed:

- the rule of free choice (employees should have the choice to work or not in an atypical fashion);
- the reversibility rule (employees should be able to turn to the status they had in the past or adopt another status if they so wish);

- the non-discrimination rule ('flexible' employees should not be subjected to discrimination as regards access to promotion and training);
- the pro-rata rule (social rights should always be at least proportional to the actual time worked).

Unions are well aware of the above and the discussion which is taking place at present between social partners shows that a sound and fair legal framework is the only way to promote flexibility and convince interested parties of the potential benefits.

The work and family reconciliation issues

Family and work issues were discussed during a Symposium held in November 1995 in Athens. The main question was whether new forms of work can help in reconciling family and work and in encouraging women to have children. As mentioned already this is a major problem since birth rates are falling and the population is ageing rapidly.

According to the General Secretary for Equality in order to successfully face this issue, it is important to take the following measures (Pantazi, 1996): (a) develop a satisfactory infrastructure for the care of children and the elderly, (b) promote flexible working time; and (c) change the prevailing models of male and female roles in both family and (paid) work. In this respect, the Greek State has taken a series of measures – which include a 16–week maternity leave, a 3–month parental leave, reduced hours of work for the mothers of young children, increased number of hours during which day-care centres can look after the children of working parents and creation of out-of-school creative occupation centres for children. The General Secretariat of Equality is particularly concerned with need to change the prevailing gender roles, and feels that this can be achieved through the media, through formal education and through programmes of training educators in matters of gender equality.

At present in Greece reconciliation is pursued both in individual and collective ways. Collective ways include the State, associations, educational institutions and official bodies, which are involved in the debate and try to promote awareness. On a individual basis some large Greek organisations apply measures which show a high degree of social responsibility and a serious effort to solve the work–family dilemma. Below are brief examples of 3 of the 11 Greek companies, which were candidates for the European Award 1995 organised by the European Network 'Family and Work'.

1. Elais is a food manufacturing firm which places emphasis on the quality of the family life of its employees. In order to promote that quality, the company has taken measures discouraging overtime and the holding of more than one job – and these include: one additional month's pay per year, additional private insurance, additional retirement programme, loans for acquisition of a home or a car, awards to employees with children that have excelled in their studies.
2. Titan, a large cement company, has a social policy which includes among other things social services, additional health services and covering of health costs, a family planning programme, social and cultural activities involving employees' family members, university scholarships, occupational orientation and summer camps for employees' children.
3. 'Costeas-Gitonas', a private educational institution has adopted measures which try to satisfy family needs which include: keeping the children at school in accordance to the parents' working hours, organisation of seminars for family and workplace relations (for both employees and parents of students), full or half scholarships for the children of employees and parents of students), educational leave granted to employees with allowances that make it possible for them to take their families along, maternity-leave up to one year (paid by the company), a 'compressed' week of 3 or 4 working days, more working hours for more pay, possibility of part-time work, etc.

These examples show that some large Greek organisations are very sensitive to the work – family issue although the first two belong to the manufacturing sector and do not apply flexibility. Flexibility on the other hand is extensively used in the third example, i.e. in the educational institution.

CONCLUSIONS

The role of flexibility in enhancing work and family reconciliation can undoubtedly be very important. If flexibility gains in Greece the legal and social status attained in other European Union countries it will be an appealing alternative for employees in larger firms which offer employment to a large percentage of the population and will enhance

8 Human Resource Development in Foreign Multinational Enterprises: Assessing the Impact of Parent Origin Versus Host Country Context[1]

Olga Tregaskis

INTRODUCTION

An organisation's human resource development (HRD) system is a key mechanism for enabling the achievement of business goals through what has been argued to be one of the few remaining sources of competitive advantage (Pedler *et al.*, 1988) – namely, people. It is also closely linked to national contextual factors. As such, the political and educational system play an important role in determining the types and levels of skills available in the labour market as well as in shaping national values and approaches to training and development issues. National context can therefore be considered a key predictor of organisational HRD practice. However, globalisation has introduced many changes, one of which has been the increasing presence of foreign multinationals (or MNEs) in host countries. Under such conditions, there is a need to compare the role of the host–national context to that of the parent in shaping MNE management practice.

The analysis presented in this chapter tests the relative impact of the host–national context, and the national origin of the parent company in shaping the HRD practices of foreign MNEs operating in Britain. It draws on data collected from European as well as US and Japanese multinationals, thereby considering the cross-national generalisability

This paper was first published in *International Studies of Management and Organization*, 28, 1, (1998)

of previous studies (Adler, 1984; Brewster, 1995) which have tended to focus solely on non-European companies in a non-European context (Werssowetz and Beer, 1985; Greenhalgh *et al.*, 1986; Ishida, 1986; Gleave and Oliver 1990).

The first section reviews, briefly, the evidence and arguments on the role of national context and national origin in shaping organisational practice. This is followed by a more detailed examination of how demands arising from the institutional and cultural contexts of different countries creates nationally divergent organisational approaches to human-resource-development. On the basis of these studies, two research hypotheses are developed and subsequently tested.

THE INFLUENCE OF NATIONAL CONTEXT ON MANAGEMENT PRACTICE

There is considerable evidence that the national context of a firm's operations plays a significant role in shaping organisational practices (Brewster and Hegewisch 1994; Brewster 1995; Ferner, 1997). For example, Sparrow, Schuler and Jackson (1994) identified clusters of countries showing how organisations in different parts of the world operationalise HRM differently as a result of environmental pressures. Muller (1998) examined how the highly regulated institutional arrangements in Germany restricted the freedom of large companies to go their own way on HRM and IR issues.

Cultural studies reveal that the peoples of different countries share values, cognitions and behaviours which differentiate them from other cultures (Hofstede, 1980; Laurent, 1986; Ronen, 1986). 'These differences are also evident in nationally divergent work values (Greenwood, 1971; Redding, 1976; Ronen and Kraut, 1977; Badawy, 1979; Griffeth *et al.* 1980) and managerial attitudes (Laurent, 1986). These facts have implications for the organisational systems which are designed to motivate, reward and develop the people within them (Crozier, 1964; Child, 1981; Welge, 1981; Dimaggio and Powell, 1983; Laurent, 1986)

National legal frameworks also impact on organisations. For example, collective agreements which differ in scope and centralisation across countries define a range of organisational practices (Gustaffson 1990; Wise 1993; Filella and Hegewisch 1994); while Pieper (1990) identified legal differences in education certification, recruitment and dismissal procedures in Europe and the United States that make for significantly different HRM practices in those countries. There is also evidence that specific legislation has led to different training and development practices, as in France where a training levy system is correlated with higher average expenditures on training and development by French organisations, in comparison with UK ones (Tregaskis and Dany, 1996). Moreover, GDP expenditures on labour market development programmes also differ across countries (Brewster, 1995), helping shape the skill levels in the labour markets on which organisations rely; and significant increases in training activity are often linked to legislation, as in the UK health and safety regulations, the Food and Safety Act of 1990 or Financial Services Act of 1988 (Felstead and Green, 1993).

Organisations rely on available labour skills so that the role of national educational systems in providing this is vital (Quack *et al.*, 1995). There is a significant, wide body of research in this area, with some studies focusing on national educational systems. For example, Barsoux and Lawrence (1994) examined the French educational system and its significance in determining and sustaining the *cadre* system. Constable and McCormick (1987) and Handy (1987) found the UK management education system and the traditional focus on experience as opposed to qualifications to have been detrimental to the skill levels of British managers. It has been argued that, as educational systems shape the skills and knowledge of individuals, they in turn shape organisational training systems as a result of their requirements for training and career aspirations (Hoskins and Anderson, 1992). Comparisons of Japanese, US and German educational systems have demonstrated their impact on labour market skill development, individual demand and organisational expectations (Conrad and Pieper, 1990; Gapper, 1992; Shackleton *et al.*, 1995). Other studies have suggested that these systems have a significant impact on national and organisational economic performance (IMS/MSC/NEDO 1985; Worswick 1985; Steedman and Wagner 1987; Jarvis and Prais 1989).

This evidence reveals that the national context represented by people's values as well as by the legislative and educational traditions of a country is an important determinant of organisational HRD practice.

THE INFLUENCE OF THE PARENT ORGANISATION ON MNE MANAGEMENT PRACTICE

Multinational parent companies exert influence over their subsidiaries by introducing home-country practices into host countries, irrespective of local conditions. This is evident in the work of Hedlund and Åman (1984) who looked at Swedish multinationals, of Tsurumi (1986) who studied Japanese companies, and of Stopford and Turner (1985) who argued that US multinationals introduced US-style personnel practices to Britain via their British subsidiaries. Yet, research examining the failure of multinationals in overseas operations would suggest a need to adapt management practices as opposed to imposing them abroad (Gleave and Oliver, 1990).

The degree of control exerted by the parent is one of the primary factors determining the extent of the transference of management practices to the MNE (Harzing, 1999). Egelhoff (1988) provided an extensive review of differences in parent-company control orientations towards their subsidiaries. For one thing, parent companies may adopt formal bureaucratic control structures involving on-site inspections or the control of management processes (Child, 1973; Doz and Pralahad, 1984). Five key mechanisms are often associated with this formal approach (Martinez and Jarillo, 1991):

1. centralisation, i.e. the degree to which decisions are taken by top management (Lawrence and Lorsch, 1967; Pugh *et al.*, 1968; Galbraith, 1973).
2. normalisation in the form of written documentation of policy, job descriptions, and so forth (Simon, 1976).
3. standardisation which generally follows when policy is written down and made into rules or uniform ways of operating (Child, 1972).
4. planning those activities aimed at guiding the functions of unrelated business units – e.g, strategic planning, budgeting and goal setting (March and Simon, 1958; Galbraith and Kazanjian, 1986).
5. output and behavioral control, where output control refers to the evaluation of records or reports submitted to the head office by the subsidiary (Mintzberg, 1979), while behavioral control involves the direct and personal monitoring of employee behaviour.

Less formal mechanisms of control may also be employed. This informal approach has been referred to as 'the cultural model' whereby the organisational culture makes implicit the rules and norms (Balliga and Jeager, 1984). Specific informal methods used to achieve control include direct contacts among managers from different functions or business units in the forms of teams, committees and/or task forces (Lawrence and Lorsch, 1967; Galbraith, 1973) as well as informal communication networks through personal contacts across the organisation, management trips, management transfers and so on. Moreover, individuals are socialised by communicating ways of working (Pfeffer, 1982), through training international and national managers, and by actively managing their career paths and reward mechanisms. Expatriates become a vital tool in this model as they are used to promote the parent company's culture and various characteristics of the parent's national culture (Edstrom and Galbraith 1977; Hedlund and Åman, 1984; Lincoln *et al.* 1986; Tsurumi 1986; Kale and Barnes 1992; Torbiorn 1994).

The national origin of the parent has been found to correlate with different control orientations (Daniels and Arpan, 1972; Child, 1981) and multinational organisational structures (Doz and Prahalad 1984). Ronen (1986) found that US parents tended to control subsidiaries through formalised, standardised and impersonal methods (see also Neghandhi and Welge, 1984). Preference for geographical divisions by US companies was used to allow some element of local autonomy. European parents, in contrast, tended to use personal relationships and the experience of corporate culture to control subsidiary practices. In addition, the preference for product divisions led to tighter centralised parent control. Japanese parents have relied heavily on expatriates placed in key management positions, coupled with the extensive use of training systems to implicitly promote parent-company practice.

Care, however, must be taken not to stereotype from such results. The multinational organisation is dynamic, complex and its subsidiaries heterogenous in character (Ferner, 1994; Quintanilla, 1998). Particular types of control may be appropriate for some subsidiaries but not for others (Martinez and Jarillo 1991), as revealed by debates on the process of internationalisation (Chandler, 1962; Perlmutter, 1965; Vernon, 1966; Stopford and Wells, 1972; Hedlund, 1986; Bartlett and Ghoshal, 1987; Adler and Ghadar 1990). Still, corporate/headquarters control operates as a mechanism for transferring characteristics of the parent national's context to its subsidiaries operating in host countries. Consequently, foreign MNEs are likely to have practices that differ from those of indigenous organisations or host-country multinationals.

Finally, the degree of parent-company influence on subsidiary practices depends on the extent to which these practices affect large proportions of the local labour force, are visible, and/or require a high degree of interaction with locals (Meyer and Rowan, 1977; DiMaggio and Powell, 1983). HR is one of the functional areas that is decentralised most and tends to be least controlled by the parent, when compared with finance, investment or production matters (Peccei and Warner, 1976; Hedlund 1981). However, the HR-function's centralisation tends to differ depending on which occupational group is affected. For example, decisions regarding managerial personnel tend to be centralised, whereas those regarding employees tend to be localised (Negandhi and Welge, 1984).

PATTERNS OF HRD IN JAPAN, THE US AND EUROPE

This section highlights how organisational approaches to HRD vary across countries in relation to various parameters, although it is restricted to those countries where multinational representation in Great Britain is high, namely Japan, US and Europe (German, French and British). The evidence shows us that organisations from different countries have developed processes and structures, reflected in their management practices, that help them operate within contexts often strongly defined by national institutional and cultural demands. However, it is unclear if, in the case of the multinational company, such practices are transferred to overseas subsidiaries.

Commitment to training and development

Japanese organisations place a strong emphasis on HRD, with 69 per cent of them providing off-the-job training (Felstead *et al.*, 1994). This contrasts starkly with the United States where there is a strong culture of employees undertaking training themselves rather than relying on employers to hire and train them. German off-the-job training expenditure is extensive, although it tends to be focused on managerial and professional employees (Lawrence, 1993). On-the-job training is highly regulated under the vocational educational system, and follows specific company plans which in turn are based on state-wide training plans (Conrad and Pieper, 1990). In France, there is a strong focus on the development and retention of the *cadres* or managerial elite, often achieved through highflyer schemes (Bournois and Roussillon, 1993). While the skills of the wider workforce are ignored (Barsoux and Lawrence, 1992). In Britain, recent research on managerial training and development suggests there has been an improvement in employer's financial and strategic commitment to HRD issues during the last 10 years (Thomson *et al.*, 1997). However, the tradition of investment in employee skills by employers, individuals and the state has been extremely weak and is characterised by a low level of apprenticeship (Employment Department, 1994) and managerial training (Constable and McCormick, 1987; Handy, 1987) – which have frequently been linked to criticisms of Britain's lack of competitiveness (IMS/NEDO/MSC, 1985; Steedman and Wagner, 1987).

Preferences for academic or vocational qualifications also differ markedly across the countries. In Japan, academic qualifications are of extreme importance, particularly for new recruits. As such, there is a strong emphasis on young people to do well at school. In the United States, however, the apprenticeship system has virtually collapsed, but it also combines one of the highest levels of degree achievement with the highest levels of educational under-achievement (Gapper, 1992). While a strong emphasis is placed on the MBA degree the quality varies dramatically between and within states. The value of academic qualifications in France is similar to that in Japan, with the gap between salaries, according to the nature of the diploma obtained, increasing considerably throughout an individual's career (Glaude, 1989). In general holding a degree from a *Grande Ecole* or a university is vital for career progression. Germany has a highly developed and respected vocational education and training system (known as the dual system) which combines on-the-job learning in companies with theory taught in vocational schools – the responsibility for vocational education is shared between employers and the state (Randlesome, 1994). There is also a strong emphasis on academic achievement. Great Britain differs from both Germany and France in that the level of qualifications held by the workforce is significantly lower; and its system of recruitment and promotion is more heavily influenced by the level of experience of the candidates as opposed to their qualifications (Handy, 1987).

Government policy

In Japan, government expenditures on training are lower than in most of its US and European counterparts, with employers being the main funders of job-related training. In the United States, intervention is restricted to federal funding of vocational training and of education directed at disadvantaged groups. However, there have been criticisms that employers have treated this funding as wage subsidies. In Europe, both Germany and France have highly regulated training legislation, but this is not the case in Britain. In Germany, training policies and standards are the responsibility of the government not of employers, with regulation of the dual system making it possible for employers to offer apprenticeship training at almost zero cost. Industry-wide collective agreements on wages mean that German companies do not have much of a problem with poaching by other firms that offer higher wages because they do not invest in training. French training is also highly legislated, and state intervention in the field of training is of long standing. Companies with more than 10 employees are legally bound to spend a specified percentage of the annual pay roll on training (1.5 per cent in 1994), of which 30 per cent is usually spent on *cadre* training (Barsoux and Lawrence, 1992). Evidence suggests that this legislation has had a significant impact on increasing training expenditures in French companies (Holden and Livian, 1992; Tregaskis and Dany, 1996). British government policy, during the late 1980s and early 1990s, placed the responsibility for training firmly with the employer and the employee within the context of a deregulated training environment.

Internal labour markets

Organisations can either look to the external labour market and buy in, through recruitment, the HR skills they need, and/or they can develop those skills within the organisation using the HRD system to build an internal organisational labour market.

Japanese organisations use a wide range of HRD tools which are firmly rooted in the notion of lifetime learning (Shimada 1980; Ishida 1986; Wickens 1987; Oliver and Wilkinson 1992) and internally focused labour markets. Research has shown that Japanese employer-led training is correlated positively with high employment stability (OECD, 1993). The extent to which employer-led training has created employment stability or has been made possible by it is difficult to disentangle. In the United States the link between training and labour-market stability is important because US mobility rates are amongst the highest in the OECD so that high mobility rates have been used to explain why US employers are reluctant to invest in training. Great Britain is similar to the United States, while in Germany and France different, traditions and legislation provide a safer environment for internal labour-market investment. For example, German retention of traditional management hierarchies allows career progression, while wage regulation reduces the threat of poaching. In France, regulation makes it more expensive for employers to get rid of people. While strategic demands for redundancy, particularly in times of recession, cannot be ignored, such legislation coupled with controls on training expenditures are likely to encourage a focus on internal labour markets.

Predictors of MNE HRD practice

The evidence suggests that in the case of the multinational organisations, the national context in which a subsidiary operates, and the national origin of its parent are both potential key factors influencing MNE level management practices. To be able to predict more precisely the relative importance of each in determining MNE level management practices we need to consider the nature of the inter-dependency between the parent and specific MNE practices, and the MNE and its local national context. For example, where a parent organisation wants its MNEs to adopt technologies and practices which can be integrated and are congruent with its own – due to strategic, structural or historical reasons – we might expect practices characteristic of the parent's home-country environment to be transferred to the MNE, and reflected in the diversity of organisational practices as a function of the national origin of the parent. In contrast, where the MNEs practices are of less direct significance to the parent and linked to local institutional systems or traditions – such as the educational and training system or labour market conditions – and affect local as opposed to international personnel, we might expect the local national context to be a more important predictor of MNE practice.

To clarify the role of national context and parent's national origin in shaping HRD practices two hypotheses were tested. National environment and the national origin of the parent were – for methodological reasons detailed in the next section – limited to Britain and those MNEs most heavily represented in Britain. The first hypothesis based on the argument that the parent's national origin is the key predictor of MNE practice stated that:

Hypothesis 1: There will be statistically significant differences in the HRD practices of MNEs based in Britain according to the national origin of their parent company (Japanese, US, European).

If however, parent's national origin is not a significant predictor of HRD practice the results will fail to support this hypothesis. As such there may be two explanations for these findings. First, that national context is the more important predictor. Secondly, there is a common or 'best practice' approach to HRD common to multinationals irrespective of their national origin. To assess the influence of host-nation context the following hypothesis was tested:

Hypothesis 2: The HRD practices of both local (British) and foreign (Japanese, US, French and German) MNEs will not statistically significantly differ from those of non-MNEs based in Britain.

If the results reveal significant differences between MNEs and non-MNEs (i.e. indigenous organisations) we would conclude that host-nation context factors fail to explain HRD practice. If the reverse were true then we would expect the HRD practices in all organisations based in Britain to show a high degree of similarity.

METHODOLOGY

To simplify the research design the national context the MNEs operated in was restricted to a single country – namely Great Britain. Data from Cranet-E was used in this analysis. This is a comparative survey of strategic HRM conducted by a collaborative international research network consisting of academics from top European business schools. The data is collected from senior HR specialists in organisations employing 200 or more employees (for a wider discussion of this project, its methodology and contents, see Brewster and Hegewisch, 1994 and Brewster *et al.*, 1996).

Sample

A data was collected in 1995 using a postal survey. The sampling frame consisted of 5988 organisations representing all industrial sectors in the United Kingdom (this includes England, Scotland Wales, and Northern Ireland). This was compiled by a specialist mailing company drawing on the most up-to-date listing of personnel specialists in the United Kingdom. A total of 1178 questionnaires were returned, yielding a response rate of 22 per cent.

For this study, a sub-sample of the UK survey consisting of manufacturing companies based in Britain was drawn for analysis in order to ensure a tighter match between the samples of multinational and indigenous organisations. MNEs were categorised into three groups: (1) a European cluster consisting of French, German and British subsidiaries; (2) a Japanese cluster; and (3) a US cluster all with subsidiaries based in Britain. Indigenous organisations consist of independent single or multiple site organisations based in Great Britain. These criteria give a sample of 260 MNEs and 115 indigenous organisations.

There is a significant difference in the size structure of the two samples (chi-square 0.0158, df 1) as MNEs tended to be larger than indigenous organisations. Altogether, 34 per cent of MNEs employ between 200 and 499 people and 66 per cent employ 500 or more. This compares with 47 per cent of indigenous organisations employing between 200 and 499 and 53 per cent employing 500 or more.

The multinational sample consisted of 151 British organisations, 69 US, 16 French, 14 Japanese and 10 German ones. There were no significant differences in the sizes of European, Japanese and US multinationals (chi-square 0.8654, df 2) so that they can be taken as broadly matched samples.

Defining the HRD indicators

Six indicators of HRD policy and practice were selected for analysis. These indicators and the questionnaire items used to measure them are presented in Table 8.1.

The strategic position of HR is used as an indicator of the emphasis the organisation places on people-related issues. Evidence suggests that where the HR department has a strong strategic position, training and development issues are integrated more effectively with the business concerns of the organisation (Schuler and Jackson 1987; Schuler 1992). Commitment to HRD is measured in terms of an organisation's expenditures as a percentage of the annual salaries and wages bill and the average number of days training employees receive per year. Felstead *et al.* (1994) demonstrate the difficulties that have arisen in attempting to draw comparisons of training expenditures across countries and among organisations. Nevertheless, combined with other indicators of HRD, it provides useful information on organisational commitment to employee development.

Work force data on skill needs, training effectiveness and employee performance were used as indicators of the focus of HR forecasting and planning. This type of information, if utilised correctly, can have a significant impact on the effectiveness of HRD activities in meeting organisational goals. A range of career-development mechanisms were adopted as indicators of individual and career-development opportunities often associated with a focus on internal labour markets. Changes in training-delivery methods of organisations were chosen to reflect a particular style or ethos underlying organisational HRD. For example, a focus on informal training such as Japanese on-the-job training, when compared with formal courses leading to certification, as in France, reflects differences in the types of training programmes emphasised.

Table 8.1 Training and development indicators and questionnaire items

HRD Indicators	*Questionnaire items*
Strategic position of HR	Representation of HR specialist on the board of directors; involvement of human resource specialists in the development of corporate strategy; presence of a written HR strategy; HR function has responsibility for training policy; increasing line-management responsibility for training issues.
Commitment to training	Expenditures on training and development as a percentage of the annual salaries and wages bill; average number of days training received by managerial, professional/technical, clerical and manual employees.
Workforce data:	
Methods of training needs identification	Use of line management; performance appraisals; business plans; training audits; and employee requests to identify training needs.
Methods of evaluating training effectiveness	Formal evaluation immediately after training or some time after training; informal feedback from line management or trainees; and tests.
Use of appraisals	Appraisals used to determine individual needs; for career development; promotion potential; organisational needs; and occupational groups receiving appraisals.
Career-development mechanisms	Use of regular career planning; international experience; succession planning; highflyer schemes; job rotation; assessment centres.
Change in training-delivery methods	Use of internal training staff; line management; external providers; job rotation; external courses; coaching; computer based packages; open learning; mentoring; on-the-job training.
Training and development challenges for the future	People management training; strategy formulation; technology; health and safety; customer service; management of change; quality management.

Similarly, emphasis on distance or self-learning methods as opposed to formal institutional training suggests employee-led versus organisational-led approaches to HRD.

Indicators of future training and development challenges were used to show whether organisations perceive future training demands differently as a partial result of factors associated with country of origin or with national context.

Data analysis

The data used in the analyses were dichotomously coded – with 1 indicating the presence of a particular practice and 0 its absence. The only exceptions were: (1) the data measuring organisational commitment to training – for example, expenditures and average number of training days for different occupational groups – because they were continuous, and (2) the importance of future training and development which was measured on a five-point Likert type scale ranging from 5=very important to 1=not at all important. In the first stage of the analysis the dichotomous data were analysed using the Kruskal–Wallis test to examine differences between the practices of the three types of MNEs (European, US and Japanese). Where differences were found, the standard error of differences between proportions statistic was used to assess where these differences lay (Sparrow *et al.*, 1994). Analysis of variance (ANOVA) was used to test differences among the MNEs, using the continuous data. These statistical methods account for differences in sample sizes, making it possible to assess if differences were a result of real divergence in practice or merely a reflection of unequal sample sizes. Given the large number of tests that were conducted for each variable, the significance level used was increased to 0.001.

In the second stage of the analysis, DFA was used to assess if there were significant differences between the practices of MNEs and British indigenous organisations. DFA is a multivariate technique which makes it possible to discriminate between two or more groups, based on a series of variables. This analysis made it possible to assess whether the differences or similarities found during the first analysis reflected similarity with host-country practices or similarity in multinational approaches. The same variables used in stage 1 of the analysis were used at this second stage.

RESULTS AND DISCUSSION

Hypothesis 1

The results showed significant differences on only three of the 50 variables measured, which would fail to support the argument put forward by the first hypothesis that parent's national origin predicts MNE HRD practice. However, where differences did exist they were found to relate specifically to the use of planned job rotation used more by Japanese MNEs than US or European ones (Kruskal-Wallis chi-square: 10.72; df 2; significance: 0.0001). The complete listing of significant and non-significant results are detailed in Appendix I. Since the emphasis placed on job rotation by Japanese companies is widely referred to in the literature as a mechanism of internal employee development, this finding would be consistent with the argument of country-of-origin factors influencing the practices of subsidiaries. Significant differences were also found in relation to succession planning which is used most by European MNEs (Kruskal-Wallis chi-square: 10.51; df 2; significance 0.0008), and high-flyer schemes also used most by European MNEs (Kruskal-Wallis chi-square: 10.57, df 2, significance 0.0003). A more detailed analysis was conducted on the European sample to establish if any differences emerged as a result of the influence of one particular country within the European cluster and the results revealed that this was in fact the case. Specifically, British MNEs were more likely to use succession planning (Kruskal-Wallis chi-square: 22.93; df 4; significance 0.0001) and French MNEs to resort to highflyer schemes (Kruskal-Wallis chi-square: 19.03; df 4; significance 0.0003). In the case of France, the use of high-flyer schemes may be explained by the societal emphasis on hierarchy and intellectual achievement (Barsoux and Lawrence, 1992); while the use of succession plans by British MNEs emphasises the focus on identifying a core of high-potential staff for development. Training statistics in Britain showing levels of employee training positively correlated with occupational status and previous levels of education and training would support the idea of an emphasis on a small core of well-trained high-potential employees (Employment Department, 1994).

These findings showed that there are some differences in the practices of MNEs according to the parent's national origin; although these are limited. Examination of the differences within the European sample also highlighted the strength of the divergence in parent national contexts which exists and impact on the MNE. However, the results also revealed no differences between the MNEs on over 90 per cent of the practices examined. This suggests either a similarity in MNE practices reflecting the practices of successful companies or a strong similarity between MNE and host-country practices. This was the key question tested through the second hypothesis.

Hypothesis 2

Comparisons made between MNEs and indigenous organisations revealed both differences and similarities. These results suggest that, in some areas of HRD, there is a commonality among MNEs, irrespective of national origin – what some may consider the element of multinational 'best practice'. However, in other areas the similarity in MNE and indigenous practice suggests that the national context of operation is a key factor influencing organisational HRD approaches.

The DFA solution accounted for 25 per cent of the variance in responses. The predictive ability of the solution was high, showing that organisational responses to questionnaire items correctly classified 87 per cent of MNEs and 50 per cent of indigenous organisations. As such, the items were good predictors of organisational type, namely multinational or indigenous. The significant differences in training practices between the two types of organisations are shown in Table 8.2. Appendix I contains the complete set of significant and non-significant results for this analysis.

On the strategic positioning of HR, MNEs scored significantly higher on 'having a written HR strategy', having 'the head of HR on the board (or equivalent)', and having 'HR involvement in the development of corporate strategy from the outset', when compared with indigenous organisations. There was no significant difference between the two types of organisations in terms of who had responsibility for training and development policy. In the majority of cases, this was held by the HR department as opposed to line management. Nor were there any differences in the changes of line-management responsibility for training issues, with both types of organisations indicating increasing line-management responsibility. These findings suggest that MNEs demonstrate a stronger element of strategic integration between HR and business issues – a characteristic often expected when employees are seen as a key strategic resource and investment. If this is the case, our findings imply that indigenous British organisations continue to see employees as a cost and as such tend to exclude HR issues from central strategic decision-making. Alternatively, it may be that the indigenous organisations adopt different or less formal mechanisms of strategic integration than those measured within the confines of this study.

There were no significant differences between levels of expenditures by MNEs and indigenous organisations. This could mean that, while foreign organisations invest heavily in their home country (as is the case in France and Germany), they do not necessarily do the same in host countries, or at least in Britain. This suggests that there is no direct transference of management practices from country to country.

Table 8.2 HRD practices discriminating between MNEs and indigenous organisations

Variables	*MNEs (%) (n=373)*	*Indigenous (%) organisations (n=270)*
Appraisal:		
to determine individual training	92	77
Strategic position of HR		
have a written HR strategy	62	50
head of HR on the board	56	35
HR involved in corporate strategy	50	44
Training need identification		
employee requests	81	67
performance appraisal	80	70
Training effectiveness evaluation		
informal feedback from trainees	81	68
informal feedback from line managers	82	66
Career development mechanisms		
use of assessment centres	26	17
use succession plans	57	27
use international experience	30	04
Increase in training & development delivery methods:		
external courses	31	30
coaching	78	60
computer based packages	73	68
mentoring	64	43
Training & development future challenges:*		
people management	4.77	4.61
health & safety	4.11	4.32
strategy formulation	3.95	3.92

This means these data are continuous, while all other data are categorical (0 or 1).

Summary statistics: Eigen value 0.3229; Canonical correlation 0.4941; Wilks lambda 0.7558, significance 0.0001.

Whether this is due to varying labour market conditions, to a less regulated and legislated training market or to organisational strategies is difficult to estimate. However, it must be acknowledged that organisations operate corporate strategies which may not necessarily coincide with the best interests of the host country. There is also increasing pressure being placed on individuals to take responsibility for their own development. The concept of a lifelong career within a single company is disappearing, and that of 'employability' is becoming a more interesting prospect. Therefore, financial investment may be reduced while training activity, led by the employee, actually increases.

There were no significant differences among the organisations in the use of six out of ten methods of collecting workforce data, suggesting common approaches adopted by both MNEs and indigenous organisations. Where differences were revealed, they showed MNEs to use methods of workforce data collection more than indigenous organisations. The collection of such data in terms of identifying training need and evaluating training effectiveness is a key feature in the effective and efficient utilisation of employees. The data showed a greater tendency for MNEs to use what may be considered 'sophisticated' techniques of training-need identification, such as the analysis of business plans and training audits.

This divergence may be explained in terms of apparent cost because such methods can be more expensive both in terms of time and people resources than the more frequently adopted informal methods of gaining information from line managers and employees themselves. The results also suggest that indigenous organisations operate HRD systems for short-term benefits rather than for long-term goals which require knowledge of training needs and of training effectiveness. Assessing need and evaluating added value are two areas of training and development that have traditionally been poorly handled by companies. However, HR departments are increasingly being asked to demonstrate the value of training to the business, and training-need identification and evaluation can help fulfil this requirement.

In terms of the appraisal system, there was a consistent pattern between the two types of organisations in that appraisals were most common for the managerial and technical/professional staff and least common for the lower occupational levels (namely, clerical and manual staff). However, significant differences between the two organisational types was also evident. MNEs were more likely to use an appraisal system to determine individual training needs, when compared with indigenous organisations. There was no difference in the use of the appraisal system to determine promotion potential, career-development opportunities, and organisational training needs. There was similarity in the relative reasons for the use of appraisals, with identification of individual training needs being the most commonly used approach and identification of organisational training needs being the least common one.

Analysis of the items measuring career-development mechanisms showed that MNEs were more likely to use succession planning, international experience, and assessment centres for the development of employees, compared to indigenous organisations (see Table 8.2). Indigenous organisations may think that it is more cost effective to spend time and resources on recruiting people into the organisation and on developing a core of top management, as opposed to spending a lot of time and money on developing expensive internal-development mechanisms for the wider workforce. No significant difference in the use of career plans, job rotation or highflyer schemes between MNEs and indigenous organisations was evident.

Examination of training-delivery methods showed that MNEs have increased their use of external training courses, coaching, computer-based packages, and mentoring more than indigenous organisations (see Table 8.2). As these data are not absolute but relative, it is not possible to establish if MNEs are doing more in delivering training than indigenous organisations, although the results indicate a move towards more internally focused training by both types of organisation.

No differences were found in the use of the other training-delivery methods. However, some of the largest increases in delivery methods were associated with the more progressive and non-standard mechanisms such as computer-based and open-learning packages. This was coupled with the lowest increases being associated with the use of external-training providers and of line managers. These findings suggest a shift in the nature of training and development from formally structured employer-led programmes to more flexible employee-led and-controlled learning procedures.

Finally, analysis of the future training need items showed some divergence in emphasis between the two types of organisations (see Table 8.2). In particular, indigenous organisations identified health and safety issues as more important than MNEs. This emphasis may reflect the high levels of regulation in the area in Great Britain as well as directives from the European Community. While MNEs are also subject to such changes, these organisations may have greater financial resources to respond to them, making such regulations' impact less important. In contrast, MNEs attached greater importance to people-management issues and to strategy formulation than indigenous organisations, which may reflect the challenges facing MNEs in increasingly competitive markets. People-management and management of change issues were seen as key future training needs by both MNEs and indigenous organisations.

Table 8AI.1 (Cont.)

HR involved in corporate strategy	36	51	51	50*	44*
HR responsible for T&D policy	21	39	31	33	36
Increase in line management responsibility for T&D issues	50	48	44	45	42
Training need identification					
Use project business plans	64	77	74	74	61
Use training audits	64	64	69	67	58
Use line management requests	79	81	83	82	71
Use performance appraisals	79	78	81	80*	70*
Use employee requests	79	77	83	81*	67*
Evaluating training effectiveness					
Use tests	57	41	48	46	31
Use formal evaluation immediately	64	71	81	77	63
Use formal evaluation later	57	59	64	62	46
Use informal line management feedback	79	79	83	81*	68*
Use informal trainee feedback	79	80	84	82*	66*
Career development mechanisms					
Use career plans	7	20	35	29	16
Use assessment centres	29	26	26	26*	17*
Use international experience	14	23	35	30*	4*
Succession planning	29*	43*	65*	57*	27*
Job rotation	64*	10*	25*	23	18
High-flyer schemes	14*	16*	41*	32	17
Increase in training & development Delivery methods:					
Internal training staff	43	46	44	44	39
Line management	43	39	42	42	26
External providers	50	48	53	52	42
On-the-job training	79	49	57	56	48
External trainers	71	55	53	54	51
External courses	29	35	30	31*	30*
Coaching	79	77	79	78*	60*
Computer-based packages	79	75	72	73*	68*
Open learning	86	65	74	72	61
Mentoring	64	52	69	64*	43*
Training & development future challenges:					
People management	4.79	4.74	4.78	4.77*	4.61*
Technology computers	4.29	4.43	4.46	4.44	4.32
Strategy formulation	3.64	3.81	4.03	3.95*	3.92*
Health & safety	4.29	4.09	4.10	4.11*	4.32*

Table 8AI.1 (Cont.)

	Results for Proposition 1			*Results for Proposition 2*	
	Japanese MNEs (n=14)	*US MNEs (n=69)*	*European MNEs (n=177)*	*All MNEs*	*Indigenous organisations*
Customer service	3.07	4.29	4.27	4.21	4.14
Management of change	3.93	4.54	4.62	4.56	4.41
Quality management	4.29	4.22	4.29	4.27	4.32
Appraisals					
For managers	93	94	92	93	78
For professional/technical staff	93	90	89	89	75
For clerical staff	86	81	76	78	66
For manual staff	64	38	45	44	39
To determine individual needs	86	93	93	92*	77*
To determine organisational needs	64	57	63	62	47
To determine promotion potential	71	80	81	80	64
For career development	64	77	83	80	63

* $p < 0.001$

References

Adler, N. (1984) 'Understanding the ways of understanding: cross-cultural management methodology reviewed', *Advances in International Comparative Management*, 1: 31–67.

Adler, N. and Ghadar, F. (1990) 'Strategic human resource management: a global perspective', in Pieper, R. (ed.), pp. 235–60.

Badawy, M. K. (1979) 'Styles of mid eastern managers', *California Management Review*, 22: 51–8.

Balliga, B. R. and Jeager, A. M. (1984) 'Multinational corporations: control systems and delegation issues', *Journal of International Business Studies*, 15(2): 25–40.

Barsoux, J.-L. and Lawrence, P. (1992) *Management in France*, London, Cassell.

Bartlett, C. A. and Ghoshal, S. (1987) 'Managing across borders: new strategic requirements', *Sloan Management Review* 28, summer: 7–17.

Beer, M., Spector, B., Lawrence, P.R., Hills, Q. D. and Walton, R. E. (eds) (1985) *Human Resource Management*: A general Managers Perspective, London, Colier Macmillan.

Bournois, F. and Roussillon, S. (1993) 'The management of 'highflyer' executives in France: the weight of the national culture', *Human Resource Management Journal*, 3(1): 37–56.

Brewster, C. (1995) 'Towards a 'European' Model of Human Resource Management', *Journal of International Business Studies* 26(1): 5–21.
Brewster, C. and Hegewisch, A. (1994) *Policy and Practice in European Human Resource Management*. London, Routledge.
Brewster, C., Tregaskis, O., Hegewisch, A. and Mayne, L. (1996) 'Comparative research in human resource management: a review and an example', *The International Journal of Human Resource Management*, 7(3): 585–604.
Chandler, A. (1962) *Strategy and Structure*, Cambridge, Mass. MIT Press.
Child, J. (1972) 'Organization structures and strategies of control: a replication of the Aston study', *Administrative Science Quarterly*, 17: 163–77.
Child J. (1973) 'Strategies of control and organizational behavior', *Administrative Science Quarterly*, 18: 1–17.
Child, J. (1981) 'Organizational structures, environment and performance: the role of strategic choice', *Sociology* 6: 2–22.
Conrad, P. and Pieper, R. (1990) 'Human resource management in the Federal Republic of Germany', in Pieper, R. (ed.), pp. 107–39.
Constable, J. and McCormick, R. (1987) *The Making of British Managers*, London, British Institute of Management.
Crozier, M. (1964) *The Bureaucratic Phenomenon*, Chicago, IL, University of Chicago Press.
Daniels, J. D. and Arpan, J. (1972) 'Comparative home country influences on management practices abroad', *Academy of Management Journal*, 15: 305–17.
DiMaggio, P. and Powell, W. (1983) 'The iron cage revisited: institutional isomorphism and collective rationality in organizational fields', *American Sociological Review*, 48: 147–60.
Doz, Y. and Prahalad, C. K. (1984) 'Patterns of strategic control within multinational firms', *Journal of International Business Studies*, 15(2): 55–72.
Edstrom, A. and Galbraith, J. (1977) 'Transfer of managers as a coordination and control strategy in multinational organizations', *Administrative Science Quarterly*, 22: 248–68.
Egelhoff, W. G. (1988) *Organizing the Multinational Enterprise: An Information Processing Perspective.* Cambridge, Mass. Ballinger.
Employment Department (1994) *Training Statistics 1994*, London, HMSO.
Felstead, A. and Green, F. (1993) 'Cycles of training? Evidence from the British recession of the early 1990s', *Discussion Papers in Economics*, Leicester, University of Leicester.
Felstead, A., Ashton, D., Green, F. and Sung, J. (1994) *Vocational Education and Training in the Federal Republic of Germany, France, Japan, Singapore, and the United States*, Leicester, Centre for Labour Market Studies.
Ferner, A. (1997) 'Country of origin effects and HRM in multinational companies', *Human Resource Management Journal*, 7(1): 19–37.
Ferner, A (1994) 'Multinational companies and Human Resource Management: An overview of the research issues', *Human Resource Management Journal*, 4(3): 79–102.
Filella, J. and Hegewisch, A. (1994) 'European experiments with pay and benefits policies', in Brewster, C. and Hegewisch, A. (eds), pp. 89–106.
Galbraith, J. R. (1973) *Designing Complex Organizations*, Reading, Mass., Addison-Wesley.

Galbraith, J. R. and Kazanjian R. K. (1986) *Strategy Implementation: Structure, Systems and Process*, 2nd edn edition), West, St Paul, MN.

Gapper, J. (1992) 'The high price of ignorance: American worries over competitiveness have put education and training on the political agenda', *Financial Times*, 17 Aug.

Glaude, F. (1989) 'Salaries et Carriéres des Ingénieurs Diplômés. Un Classement des Grandes Ecoles', *Economies et Statistiques*, 249: 1–12.

Gleave, S. and Oliver, N. (1990) 'Human resource management in Japanese manufacturing companies in the UK: five case studies', *Journal of General Management*, 16(1): 54–68.

Greenhalgh, L., Kersie, R. B. and Glikey, R. W. (1986) 'Rebalancing the workforce at IBM: a case study of redeployment and revitalization', *Organizational Dynamics* 13(1): 30–47.

Griffeth, R. W., Hom, P. W., DeNisi, A. and Kirchner, W. (1980) 'A multivariate multinational comparison of managerial attitudes', Paper presented at the *Fortieth Annual Meeting of the Academy of Management*, Detroit, MI, August.

Guest, D. and Hoque, K. (1995) 'The influence of national ownership on human resource management practices in UK greenfield sites', paper presented at *International Industrial Relations Association HRM Study Group Meeting*. Washington, DC, June.

Gustaffson, L. (1990) 'Promoting flexibility through pay policies – experiences from the Swedish national administration', *Flexible Personnel Management in the Public Services*. Paris, OECD.

Handy, C. (1987) *The Making of Managers: A report on Management Education, Training and Development in the United States, West Germany, France, Japan, and the UK*, London, NEDO.

Harzing, A-W. (1999). *Managing the Multinationals: An International Study of Control Mechanisms*. Elgar: Cheltenham, UK.

Hedlund, G. (1981) 'The role of foreign subsidiaries in strategic decision-making in Swedish multinational corporations', *Strategic Management Journal*, 9: 23–6.

Hedlund, G. (1986) 'The hypermodern MNC – a heterarchy?', *Human Resource Management*, 25(1): 9–35.

Hedlund, G. and Åman, P. (1984) *Managing Relationships with Foreign Subsidiaries – Organization and Control in Swedish MNCs*, Stockholm, Sveriges Mekanforbund.

Hofstede, G. (1980) *Culture's Consequences: International Differences in Work-Related Values*, Beverly Hills, CA, Sage.

Holden, L. and Livian, Y. (1992) 'Does strategic training policy exit? some evidence from ten european countries', *Personnel Review*, 21(1): 12–23.

Hoskins, D.M. and Anderson, N. (1992) *Organisational Change and Innovation – Psychological Perspectives and Practices in Europe*, London, Routledge.

IMS/MSC/NEDO (Institute of Manpower Studies/Manpower Services Commission/ National Economic Development Office) (1985) *Competence and Competition*, London, NEDO.

Ishida, H. (1986). 'Transferability of Japanese human resource management abroad', *Human Resource Management*, 25(1): 103–20.

Jarvis, V. and Prais, S. (1989) 'Two nations of shopkeepers: training for retailing in Britain and France', *National Institute Economic Review*, 128: 58–74.

Kale, S. H. and Barnes, J. W. (1992) 'Understanding the domain of cross-national buyer–seller interactions', *Journal of International Business Studies*, 23(1): 101–32.

Laurent, A. (1986) 'The cross-cultural puzzle of international human resource management', *Human Resource Management*, 25: 91–102.

Lawrence, P. (1993) 'Human resource management in Germany', in Tyson, S., Lawrence, P., Poirson, P., Manzolini, L. and Vicente, C. S. (eds), pp. 25–44.

Lawrence, P. R. and Lorsch, J. W. (1967) *Organization and Environment*, Boston, MA, Harvard Graduate School of Business Administration.

Lincoln, J., Hanada, M. and McBride, M. (1986) 'Organizational structures in Japanese and US manufacturing', *Administrative Science Quarterly*, 31: 223–64.

Macharzina, K. and Staehle, W. H. (eds) (1986) *European Approaches to International Management*, Berlin Walter de Gruyter.

March, J. G. and Simon, H. A. (1958) *Organizations*, New York, Wiley.

Martinez, J. I. and Jarillo, J. C. (1991) 'Coordination demands of international strategies', *Journal of International Business Studies* 22(3): 429–46.

Meyer, J. W. and Rowan, B. (1977) 'Institutionalized organizations: formal structure as myth and ceremony', *American Journal of Sociology*, 83: 343–63.

Mintzberg, H. (1979) *The Structuring of Organisations*, Englewood Cliffs, NJ., Prentice-Hall.

Muller, M. (1998) 'Human Resource and Industrial Relations Practices of UK and US Multinationals in Germany', *The International Journal of Human Resource Management*, 9(4): 732–49.

Negandhi, A. R. and Welge, M. (1984) *Advances in International Comparative Management*, Supplement 1, Greenwich, CT, JAI Press.

OECD (1993) *Employment Outlook*, Paris, OECD.

Oliver, N. and Wilkinson, B. (1992) *The Japanization of British Industry*, London, Blackwell.

Peccei, R. and Warner, M. (1976) 'Decision-making in a multi-national firm', *Journal of General Management*, 1(4): 66–71.

Pedler, M., Boydell, M. and Burgoyne, P. (1988) *The Learning Company*, Sheffield, Manpower Services Commission.

Perlmutter, H. V. (1965) 'L'enterprise Internationale: Trois Conceptions', *Revue Economique et Sociale* 23.

Pfeffer, J. (1982) *Organizations and Organization Theory, Marshfield, MA, Pitman.*

Pieper, R. (ed.) (1990) *Human Resource Management: An International Comparison*, Berlin, Walter de Gruyter.

Pugh, D. S., Hickson, D. J., Hinings, C. R. and Turner, C. (1968) 'Dimensions of organization structure', *Administrative Science Quarterly*, 13(1): 91–114.

Quack ' S., O'Reilly, J. and Hildebrandt, S. (1995) 'Structuring change: training and recruitment in retail banking in Germany, Britain and France', *International Journal of Human Resource Management*, 6(4): 759–94.

Quintanilla, J (1998) 'The Configuration of Human Resource Management Policies and practices in Multinational Subsidiaries', PhD thesis, the University of Warwick.

Randlesome, C. (1994) *The Business Culture in Germany*, Oxford, Butterworth–Heinemann.

Redding, S. G. (1976) 'Some perceptions of psychological needs among managers in South-East Asia', paper presented at the Third International Conference at the *International Association for Cross-Cultural Psychology*, July, Tilburg, Netherlands.

Ronen, S. (1986) *Comparative and Multinational Management*, Chichester, John Wiley.

Ronen, S. and Kraut, A. I. (1977) 'Similarities among Countries based on Employee Work Values and Attitudes', *Columbia Journal of World Business*, 12(2): 89–96.

Schuler, R. S. (1992) 'Strategic human resource management: linking the people with the strategic needs of the business', *Organizational Dynamics*, summer: 18–32.

Schuler, R. S. and Jackson, S. E. (1987) 'Organizational strategy and organizational level as determinants of human resource management practice', *Human Resource Planning*, 10(3): 125–41.

Shackleton, J. R., Clarke, L., Lange, T. and Walsh, S. (1995) *Training for Employment in Western Europe and the United States*, Aldershot, Edward Elgar.

Shimada, H. (1980) *The Japanese Employment System*. Tokyo, Japan Institute of Labor.

Simon, H. (1976) *Administration Behavior*, 3rd edn, New York, Free Press.

Sirota, D. and Greenwood, J. M. (1971) 'Understand your overseas work force', *Harvard Business Review*, 49(1): 53–60.

Sparrow, P., Schuler, R. S. and Jackson, S. E. (1994) 'Convergence or divergence: human resource practices and policies for competitive advantage world-wide', *The International Journal of Human Resource Management*, 5(2): 267–99.

Steedman, H. and Wagner, K. (1987) 'A second look at productivity, machinery and skills in Britain and Germany', *National Institute Economic Review*, Nov.: 84–95.

Stopford, J. M. and Turner, L. (1985) *Britain and the Multinationals*, Chichester, John Wiley.

Stopford, J. M. and Wells, L. T. (1972) *Managing the Multinational Enterprise*, New York, Basic Books.

Thomson, A., Storey, J., Mabey, C., Gray, C., Farmer, E. and Thomson, R. A. (1997) *Portrait of Management Development*, London, Institute of Management.

Torbiörn, I. (1994) 'Operative and strategic use of expatriates in new organizations and market structures', *International Studies of Management and Organization*, 24(3): 5–17.

Tregaskis, O. and Dany, F. (1996) 'A comparison of HRD in France and the UK', *European Journal of Industrial Training*, 20(1): 20–31.

Tsurumi, Y. (1986) 'Japanese and European multinationals in America: a case of flexible corporate systems', in Macharzina, K. and Staehle, W. H. (eds), pp. 23–38.

Tyson S., Lawrence, P., Poirson, P., Manzolini, L- and Venice, C-S. (eds) (1993) *Human Resource Management in Europe*, London, Kogan Page.

Vernon, R. (1966) 'International investment and international trade in the product cycle', *Quarterly Journal of Economics*, 80(2): 190–207.

Welge, M. K. (1981) 'A comparison of managerial structures in German subsidiaries in France, India and the United States', *Management International Review* 21(2): 5–21.

Werssowetz, R. O. and Beer, M. (1985) 'Human resources at Hewlett-Packard', in Beer, *et al.*, (eds), pp. 711–47.

Wickens, P. (1987) *The Road to Nissan.* London, MacMillan.

Wise, L R. (1993) 'Wither solidarity: transitions in Swedish public sector pay policy', *British Journal of Industrial Relations*, 31(1): 73–95.

Worswick, G.D.N. (ed.) (1985) *Education and Economic Performance*, London, Gower.

9 In Search of Management Development in Europe: From Self-fulfilling Prophecies to Organisational Competence

Henrik Holt Larsen

INTRODUCTION

The last decade – with its emphasis on organisational culture, experiential learning, managerial competence, strategic HRM, the learning organisation, etc. – has changed the demands and expectations to management development, as well as the methods and techniques by which these demands and expectations are met. This has a great impact on the role and effectiveness of so-called high-flyer programmes in organisations, as these programmes are anchored in the organisational setting. New developments have appeared in the following areas:

1. The *objective* of management development is being questioned, in particular whether one is training a selected, elitarian group of individuals through high-flyer programmes or stimulating an all-encompassing change in management processes.
2. The *target group* for management development is being challenged, and arguments are put forward that it should be enlarged to include anybody who has a significant impact on managerial processes in the organisation, whether or not the person in question has a formal managerial position. Obviously, this has a direct impact on the use of high-flyer programmes.
3. Development of *job structure*, *information technology* and *organisational characteristics* are all seen as part of (or at least contributing to) management development.
4. The belief in universal managerial practices is being challenged if not replaced by a recognition of the *situational* and *task specific*

This has important implications for the career prospects for the specialists: 'They will be highly valued, but not primarily by their own specialist peers. In the long term, many professional groupings will realise that organisations rather than individuals or each other are their prime clients. When they do so, contribution to core competencies will be the basis for professional esteem and reputation' (Herriot, 1992, p. 55). The complex, knowledge-based organisation with specialists, multispecialists (Clark, 1992, p. 139), project managers, generalist managers, etc. does not work very well together with the classic, universal career track model, which is mainly fueled by corporate loyalty, rather than intrinsic job commitment.

Performing a job exposes the person to a number of problems, choices and experiences, which may or may not eventually increase the person's competence. What determines whether being exposed to a given situation causes learning to occur, depends on the quality of the experience itself. Theories of experiential learning have documented that learning is most likely to occur, when the person is exposed to a demanding task, when the stock of previously acquired experiences do not give the immediate solution to the problem, and when the learning situation has an element of surprise: 'Many of the most disruptive and the most valuable learning experiences share the characteristics of being surprising. We know we have learned something new when we are surprised,' (Sims and McAulay, 1995, p. 13). By stating this, Sims and McAulay implicitly claim that perceived learning is identical to actual learning. This disregards, however, two types of situations nevertheless characterised by learning, the first being an actual change in competencies of the individual, without being recognised by the individual, and the second being 'unpleasant experiences' which, however, provide actual learning.

Also, it should be stressed that learning is not necessarily bound to the job situation: 'In the final analysis, all development is self-development whether it takes place on or off the job, at work or at home, in school or on vacation' (Moulton and Fickel, 1993, p. 18).

Classic management development does to a certain extent provide the opportunities for experiential learning, as fast-track programmes often involve job rotation and special assignment. The problem with some of these jobs or tasks is, however, that they often are *designed* for trainees and other fast-track participants. As a result of this, they often have an 'artificial' character, involving a lot of investigation, report writing and being an 'observer' of what goes on, rather than being 'thrown in at the deep end' and do the 'dirty job' oneself.

The effectiveness of (quite often unexpected) experiential learning processes, combined with the *de facto* difficulties in planning carefully management development processes anyway, are explaining why so much achievement of managerial competence happens incidentally. This is confirmed by recent research. Thus, Mumford *et al.* (1989) did a study on 144 directors from over 40 acknowledged blue chip companies. This study showed that 'most directors learned accidentally and through unstructured experiences. Few had career objectives and a plan to help them achieve them' (Here quoted from Clark, 1992, p. 60).

The need for an alternative model of management development

The above analysis of the traditional model of management development demonstrates the need for a different concept, which takes into account the business community of today (with an increasing share of knowledge organisations), which bridges the gap between personal growth and organisational learning, which diminishes the disadvantages of fast-track programmes, which opens up for non-managerial career development (of professionals, specialists and other highly competent employees), and which incorporates experiential learning as a supplement to formal training. This is the topic of the following section.

MANAGEMENT DEVELOPMENT AS KNOWLEDGE CREATION – AN INTEGRATED MODEL OF MANAGERIAL COMPETENCE

Strategic management development

In management development, there is a need for securing an integration of business strategy, HR strategy and management development. Many classic high-flyer programmes have been comprehensive and secured an intensive development of the participants, but they have been out of tune with the strategic profile of the organisation. This is a serious attack on the effectiveness of management development programmes as well as the entire philosophy behind them. *If* management development has to be taken seriously, it has to deal with authentic managerial processes. *If* the focus is on experiential learning, there is a vast overlap between learning and working. *If* management development has to encompass key people in the organisation, they should be involved in tasks of strategic importance. And *if* management development is also aiming at giving people a feel for whether they belong in the organisation in the long run, they should know what the organisation stands for. So, in short, investing in management development means opening up for using the company vision, mission, overall objectives and corporate strategy as facilitators for the management learning process. This is what Burgoyne (1988) calls 'Stage 6': 'Management development processes enhance the nature and the quality of corporate policy formulation and they are also used to implement these enhanced policies' (here quoted from Storey, 1994, p. 372).

Defining the organisational 'scene' as an interactive component in management also means that the organisational *culture* becomes of vital importance. As Schein stated: 'Leaders create cultures, but cultures, in turn, create their next generation of leaders' (1985, p. 313). Management development means being introduced to the organisational culture, being socialised into it, being able to operate – successfully – within it, being able to 'carry it' as a role model, and rewarding, respectively punishing organisational behaviour which is concordant with or conflicts with the culture. However, at the same time as one should be able to operate – safely – within the present culture, one should be able to initiate an adjustment of this culture to changing contextual conditions. This aspect of organisational culture has not been sufficiently considered in traditional management development.

Experiential managerial learning

It has been stated above that realistic management development implies that the distinction between learning and working dissapears. Hence, management development should build on our present theoretical knowledge of experiential or action learning. The concept of 'action learning' is in itself not new, as it goes back to some of Revans' early work (1982). It is 'an approach to the development of people in organizations which takes the task as the vehicle for learning. It is based on the premise that there is no learning without action and no sober and deliberate action without learning.' (Pedler, 1991, p. xxii, here quoted from Storey, 1994, p. 375). This fairly rigorous statement has almost (unwillingly?) got a Skinnerian flavour, although no reference is made to the reinforcement potential of the actual performance. Mumford (1994), who has been mentioned previously and is one of the pioneers in experiential learning, analyses how socalled real-time management experience can be used in learning. And Margerison (1994) links action learning and excellence in management development. In this chapter, experiential managerial learning will be defined as the (deliberate or incidental) process by which an individual (either a managerial or a non-managerial employee) develops competencies of a managerial nature by being exposed to – and acting in relation to – managerial tasks. These learning incidents are facilitated by a synergetic relationship between (1) action and reflection of the individual; and (2) individual and organisational development. Hence the individual managerial learning takes place within – and is influenced by – a given organisational context, is (from the outset) an inductive learning process, but is reinforced by its organisational contextualisation and conceptual generalisation.

On-the-job and other experiential type methods of management development have for decades been regarded as important means of management development, but there is an increasing need to incorporate and benefit from the last decade's intensive development of the theory of learning and knowledge creation. An example of this is the knowledge creation theory by Nonaka (1994).

Management development as a learning creation process

Although we have explicitly used the term 'knowledge organisation', all organisations are in fact 'knowledge organisations'. Knowledge work is sometimes defined as work performed by socalled 'knowledge workers'. However, this creates an artificial distinction between 'knowledge workers' and 'non-knowledge workers'. The latter category is rather meaningless, as it is hard to imagine any work not requiring the use of knowledge. It is more appropriate (at an operational level, at least) to maintain that there is a varying *degree* of knowledge intensity in any given task, job and organisation.

Management development is a result of (and benefiting from) organisational knowledge creation, but is in turn also contributing to this process. This is a crucial aspect of Nonaka's theory about learning creation, which is a very innovative perspective on management development, among others because it is reflecting the increasing predominance in society of knowledge and knowledge-intensive organisations.

According to Nonaka, 'organizational knowledge creation . . . should be understood in terms of a process that "organizationally" amplifies the knowledge creation by individuals, and crystallizes it as a part of the knowledge network of organization' (1994, p. 17). This amplification and crystallisation process happens through informal communities of social interaction within the organisation, interaction between the organisation and its surroundings (customers, suppliers, competitors, etc.), and by integrating the informal social interaction with the formal strategy development processes of the organisation. In other words, management development which is a joint individual and organisational development process, is nurtured through individual and organisational knowledge creation. And this knowledge creation occurs through informal, intra-and inter-organisational networking as well as by incorporating informal social interaction in formal strategic processes. Hence, Nonaka's theory incorporates several of the arguments in this section: the strategic outspring, emphasis on experiential learning, the inter-relationship between the individual and the organisation, etc. And, somewhat surprisingly, the actual means of management development have got traits in common with some of the standard management development methods like job rotation, participation in inter-departmental or inter-organisational projects, fast track programme, etc.

Nonaka makes a distinction between 'explicit' and 'tacit' knowledge. An important characteristic by management development is the fact that an essential part of it is acquiring 'tacit knowledge'. 'Tacit knowledge is deeply rooted in action, commitment, and involvement in a specific context' (Nonaka, 1994, p. 16), and this is exactly what management development is all about. By the same token, however, it makes it difficult to monitor management development, as well as evaluating the effect of it. As Polanyi puts it: 'We can know more than we can tell' (1966, p. 4, here quoted from Nonaka, 1994, p. 16).

The intention by including Nonaka's theory of knowledge creation in this chapter is not to claim, that he has found the universal solution to the management development problems and paradoxes described in this chapter. However, his theory is a valuable supplement to the existing theory of management development, which for the most part dates back to an industrial society with mainly hierarchical, bureaucratic organisations. Nonaka's theory takes us a little step into the knowledge (creation) era.

Concluding remarks

Here we have listed the actual (and to a certain extent future) demands on the management development and high-flyer phenomena. Also, we have outlined what might eventually be components in a comprehensive model of management development in knowledge-intensive organisations.

This model is not per definition superior to the classic model of high-flyer programmes and supposed to replace these entirely. Probably, some kind of balance between the two will provide the best picture of management development. Herriot (1992, pp. 67–8) has in a very explicit way described this balance:

- We're valuing change and development, but we're also valuing steady loyalty and organisational experience
- We're encouraging individual stars, but also cross-functional collaboration
- We're valuing local initiatives, but also nurturing core organisation-wide competencies
- We're concerned with individually based rewards and careers, but we value collaborative teamwork.

Another interesting perspective on management development is by asking the fundamental, although important question: Are there any financial consequences of doing one or the other thing in the management development area? Tyson *et al.* (1994) have done a survey trying to identify the profile of financially successful companies. Their results show:

> All the organisations in our sample regarded employee and management development as a most important contributor to business strategy achievement. The quality of management was frequently seen as providing competitive advantages over other companies, and much attention was therefore devoted to the identification of potential and the systems to make management development happen in the way the company wanted. Systems were seen as extremely important in this regard: appraisal, succession planning and personal development plans, were all mentioned, along with formal delivery mechanisms for development, using outside providers, and counselling and coaching from within. Management development and business development were said to go hand in hand. Young high flying managers were regarded as the seed corn of the company: to be preserved, developed and encouraged.
>
> Tyson *et al.*, 1994, p. 21.

As one can see, the organisations are 'picking' some ingredients from the classic management development model (identification of potential, high flying managers, etc.), but also include some of the characteristics of the new model (strategic emphasis and the belief that business development and management development go hand in hand). Tyson *et al.* also stress the need for 'developing the whole range of skills and abilities at all levels in the (1994, p. 21) organization'. In other words, what they call a 'learning partnership' must be established.

MANAGEMENT DEVELOPMENT IN EUROPE – A QUANTITATIVE STUDY

In this section we will utilise Cranet-E to illustrate national differences in management development. The purpose of this is twofold: first to relate management development (in particular high-flyer policy and practices) to other HRM methods and, secondly, to illustrate national differences in the use of management development programmes. The intention is not to interpret these differences from a national culture perspective, but to illustrate the relationship between management development and other HRM procedures in different national settings.

Cranet-E comprises almost 5000 private and public organisations with more than 200 employees in 15 European countries. The same questionnaire has been used in all countries, and the data presented below all stem from the most recent survey, undertaken in 1995. This survey comprised 14 countries. In Tables 9.1–9.12, the countries are named by their national code (UK, F, E, NL, etc.). Separate data are presented for East-and West-Germany (D(e) and D(w), respectively), despite the political unification of what was earlier two independent countries.

The first question we will look at is the *prevalence of high-flyer policies* in Europe. Included in the survey is a question whether the organisation has a high-flyer policy. These data are presented in Table 9.1.

Table 9.1 shows that most of the countries fall into one out of two categories. In eight countries, approximately 20–30 per cent. of all organisations have a written high-flyer policy. In five other countries, the percentage is much lower, typically in the range of 10 per cent. Hence, less than a third of all companies in the 14 countries have a written high-flyer policy. However, if one adds to this the respondents with an 'unwritten' policy, up to two-thirds of all organisations in

Table 9.1 Percentage of organisations with a 'high-flyer' policy

Country	*OZ*	*B*	*BL*	*CH*	*CY*	*CZ*	*D(w)*	*D(e)*	*DK*	*E*	*F*	*FN*	*G*	*H*	*I*	*IRL*	*N*	*NL*	*PL*	*S*	*T*	*UK*
Yes, written	15	27	19	27	18	23	26	10	16	22	24	5	43	7	10	20	ni	21	7	31	24	12
Yes, unwritten	15	28	35	28	34	28	27	26	18	41	34	15	31	44	32	17	ni	19	20	25	46	23
No	62	39	26	41	34	40	42	50	65	29	36	76	23	30	34	51	ni	55	63	40	18	61
Don't know	5	5	7	1	0	2	2	6	0.5	0	3	1	3	6	7	7	ni	2	9	1	2	1

Note: ni = question not included
Source: Cranet-E.

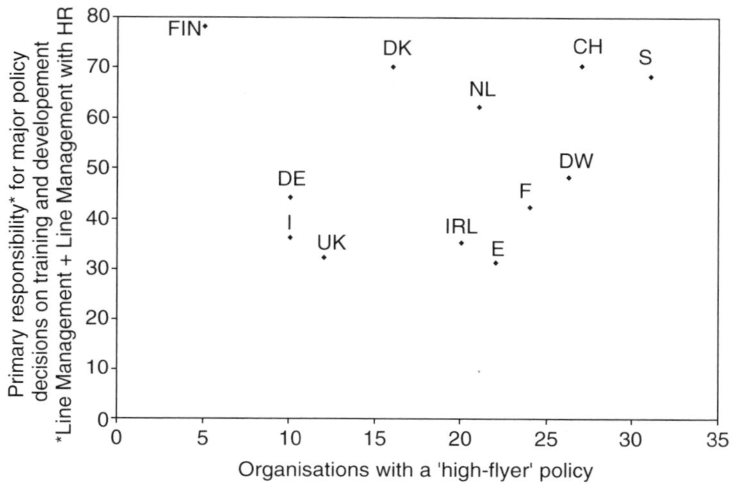

Figure 9.4 Percentage of organisations with a high-flyer policy and line manager responsibility for training and development
* Line manager responsibility for training and development is obtained by adding the two rows 'Line Management' and 'Line mngt with HR', see Appendix 9.12

This corresponds with the general trend, supported by survey data, but not reproduced here, that there is an increasing focus on internal training courses, relative to external courses. This usually means a more pronounced use of internal instructors, among whom can easily be line managers. In particular, line managers play an important role in internal training courses when there is a need to clarify and discuss the corporate strategy and the specific work plans deducted from this.

In conclusion, line managers are to an increasing extent involved in the development of HR. They carry a major responsibility for training and development, they are involved in coaching and mentoring, and they are used for training the employees. Not surprisingly, then is people management and supervision considered as an important training area over the next three years, see Table 9.7.

The Cranet-E data show that it is in no way becoming easier to be a line manager. In most European countries, *managerial jobs* have (over the last 3 years) become *wider/more flexible* (see Table 9.8).

Table 9.2 Percentage of organisations with a change in responsibility of line management for training and development over the last 3 years

Country	*OZ*	*B*	*BL*	*CH*	*CY*	*CZ*	*D(w)*	*D(e)*	*DK*	*E*	*F*	*FN*	*G*	*H*	*I*	*IRL*	*N*	*NL*	*PL*	*S*	*T*	*UK*
Increased	50	35	38	45	40	23	30	12	34	38	56	50	38	19	24	52	49	59	27	63	39	48
Same	41	57	49	49	55	63	64	82	55	49	40	47	55	62	61	44	46	38	61	35	50	46
Decreased	6	6	8	5	0	8	4	4	8	8	2	3	5	11	10	4	3	1	7	1	5	4

Source: Cranet-E.

Table 9.3 Percentage of organisations where there has been a change in the use of coaching over the last three years

Country	*OZ*	*B*	*BL*	*CH*	*CY*	*CZ*	*D(w)*	*D(e)*	*DK*	*E*	*F*	*FN*	*G*	*H*	*I*	*IRL*	*N*	*NL*	*PL*	*S*	*T*	*UK*
Increased	35	29	24	37	16	5	25	7	25	17	13	21	15	17	9	28	27	41	12	32	21	35
Same	36	41	17	26	24	8	28	22	44	18	12	30	37	8	20	36	51	46	51	59	24	38
Decreased	3	2	3	1	3	0	2	2	1	2	0	3	1	5	3	1	1	1	3	1	0	2
Not used	17	21	28	29	29	62	28	36	20	43	62	33	32	47	31	19	11	6	31	4	19	19

Source: Cranet-E.

Table 9.4 Percentage of organisations where there has been a change in the use of mentoring over the last 3 years

Country	*OZ*	*B*	*BL*	*CH*	*CY*	*CZ*	*D(w)*	*D(e)*	*DK*	*E*	*F*	*FN*	*G*	*H*	*I*	*IRL*	*N*	*NL*	*PL*	*S*	*T*	*UK*
Increased	35	17	10	10	40	2	12	8	28	7	7	4	5	11	31	21	5	10	17	31	26	34
Same	32	24	32	16	40	5	27	28	56	21	8	13	13	17	37	19	15	22	47	38	25	27
Decreased	3	2	7	2	0	0	2	2	1	3	2	0	64	4	7	0	1	2	4	1	3	2
Not used	24	51	30	57	16	68	40	33	6	50	72	62	19	47	3	44	63	57	29	26	15	33

Source: Cranet-E.

Table 9.5 Percentage of organisations where there has been a change in the use of on-the-job training over the last 3 years

Country	*OZ*	*B*	*BL*	*CH*	*CY*	*CZ*	*D(w)*	*D(e)*	*DK*	*E*	*F*	*FN*	*G*	*H*	*I*	*IRL*	*N*	*NL*	*PL*	*S*	*T*	*UK*
Increased	51	46	17	54	47	25	40	22	42	43	32	61	27	23	49	47	35	38	24	69	46	48
Same	43	43	30	41	37	47	41	43	42	40	52	34	55	48	25	47	54	44	63	29	31	48
Decreased	1	0	13	1	5	4	1	1	0	2	7	1	3	13	3	1	2	2	2	0	5	1
Not used	5	6	18	1	3	10	7	13	7	5	4	0	5	3	7	0	2	8	8	0	1	0.5

Source: Cranet-E.

Table 9.6 Percentage of organisations where there has been a change in the use of line managers over the last 3 years

Country	*OZ*	*B*	*BL*	*CH*	*CY*	*CZ*	*D(w)*	*D(e)*	*DK*	*E*	*F*	*FN*	*G*	*H*	*I*	*IRL*	*N*	*NL*	*PL*	*S*	*T*	*UK*
Increased	33	29	11	47	24	16	25	9	27	21	40	23	20	14	22	44	37	34	18	25	37	44
Same	47	42	48	48	42	42	58	55	55	38	45	62	44	45	36	41	51	42	46	63	36	45
Decreased	6	4	8	2	3	5	2	2	2	4	4	5	7	9	5	1	3	3	3	2	8	3
Not used	5	19	11	3	16	20	6	12	9	22	6	2	17	17	9	4	2	15	31	8	4	5

Source: Cranet-E.

Table 9.7 Percentage of organisations considering people management and supervision, as a training area, to be important to them over the next 3 years?

Country	*OZ*	*B*	*BL*	*CH*	*CY*	*CZ*	*D(w)*	*D(e)*	*DK*	*E*	*F*	*FN*	*G*	*H*	*I*	*IRL*	*N*	*NL*	*PL*	*S*	*T*	*UK*
Very	87	34	49	75	66	58	60	39	53	53	64	71	43	51	46	77	65	29	43	91	60	79
Quite	10	40	30	22	29	30	32	33	34	34	29	24	28	25	22	19	27	41	36	9	32	15
Average	1	20	8	3	3	7	4	18	9	8	4	4	15	14	12	2	5	22	13	0	5	4
Not very		3	6	1	0	1	2	3	1	2	1	0	5	1	5	0	1	5	2	0	0	1
Not at all		1		0	0	1	0	0	1	0	0	0	0	1	2	0	0	1	4	0	0	0

Source: Cranet-E.

Table 9.8 Percentage of organisations where there has been a major change in the specification of managerial jobs over the last 3 years

Country	*OZ*	*B*	*BL*	*CH*	*CY*	*CZ*	*D(w)*	*D(e)*	*DK*	*E*	*F*	*FN*	*G*	*H*	*I*	*IRL*	*N*	*NL*	*PL*	*S*	*T*	*UK*
Jobs made more specific	23	20	26	20	32	27	11	17	37	18	21	25	45	30	37	20	16	16	33	12	25	19
No major change	19	32	42	35	37	22	19	27	25	35	30	29	31	18	29	29	37	22	26	29	32	25
Jobs made wider/more flexible	56	52	21	42	11	51	66	55	38	30	43	45	21	43	22	43	37	52	50	57	22	58
Don't know	2	3	9	2	0	1	4	1	4	2	1	4	5	1	0	1	2	2	2	1	1	1

Source: Cranet-E.

In conclusion, this analysis of the Cranet-E data from the 1995 survey has shown, that high-flyer policies are widely used by European organisations, with great variations, however, from one country to the other. Also, high-flyer policies are only to a moderate extent linked to (not to speak of integrated with) corporate strategy and appraisal systems used to determine promotion potential and career development.

The analysis has also showed that line managers are increasing involved in training and development of the employees – as coaches or mentors, and as instructors in organisational training. This enlarged HR responsibility may be one of the factors explaining why managerial jobs have become wider/more flexible over the last years. More tasks (in particular the HR responsibility) are being assigned to line managers, an example of which is the involvement in high-flyer programmes.

CONCLUSION – IMPLICATIONS FOR MANAGERS AND RESEARCH

In this section, we will summarise the discussion of management development from the previous sections as well as outline the implications for practitioners and future research.

Management development: what is it for?

It has been an important conclusion in this chapter that management development should not solely be seen as a career development process for a small number of high-flyers. Instead, it should be regarded as an organisational, experientially based learning process. This learning process *integrates individual and organisational competence development*. The organisation develops core competencies, which constitute the strategic, competitive advantage of the organisation. (In addition, the management of organisational competencies is in itself a competitive advantage.) The individual develops managerial skills, knowledge, attitudes and commitment, which facilitates the person's participation in managerial processes. (This is not necessarily the same as holding a formal managerial position in the organisation.)

The key element in the organisational learning process is *knowledge creation*. Learning is heavily influenced by the organisational culture in the sense that socialisation to the culture is in itself a learning process, as well as the culture can be a powerful barrier for experimentation, questioning basic values, etc. Managers (and other influencial persons in the organisation) have a strong influence on creating, moulding and changing the culture, at the same time as they are themselves 'victims' of the culture.

HR directors, being responsible for management development, should consider the organisation as a learning ground and stimulate knowledge creation. They can do this *not* just by running a training department, but being part of the top management team. Creating learning opportunities means developing the organisation and vice versa. Individual learning, job design, organisation development, strategic and vision management merge in an integrated competence development process. There should be a predominant contextual focus, so that extra-organisational (including international) factors are taken into consideration.

Management development: for whom?

The target group for management development in a knowledge-intensive organisation is not only high-potential managerial candidates, but everybody who play (or could eventually come to play) a significant role in the competence development of the organisation. Obviously, people who have an impact on managerial processes and outcomes in the organisation, are obvious candidates for management development activities. However, as the core competence of the organisation has strategic significance for the survival of the organisation, all employees involved in knowledge creation should be included as well.

For the HR director, this means that fast-track programmes for management candidates should be supplemented by a whole range of other development activities (see below) for other groups of employees. In addition to this, it should be remembered that the use of fast-track programmes is somewhat problematic in the first place. Hence, such systems may eventually be abandoned in total and replaced by more flexible, less elitist and more psychologically 'digestible' career development models. Such models should cater for individual differences in career orientation, actual competence and development potential.

Management development: how?

'Learning by working' and 'working by learning' are the key vehicles for management development. Types of experiential learning processes are: challenging, varied tasks, special assignments, job rotation, membership of cross-organisational teams, involvement with extra-organisational stakeholders, etc. All these have in common the learning potential which can be released by considering them as not just 'ways of getting the work done' but also catalysts for competence development. It is of fundamental importance, however, that action and reflection go hand in hand, and that learning occurs by the synergy between the two.

The HR director has in a sense only limited impact on the experiential management development, as most of it takes place on the job or close to the job. This is why the line managers get a crucial role. They become 'strategic learning managers', as they are (through job design and allocation of tasks to the individual employees) automatically, albeit indirectly creating the learning possibilities. They become a strategic apex, because performance and knowledge creation has to be coordinated with (and extracted from) the overall strategy of the organisation.

In addition, line managers have – and get to an increasing extent – the responsibility for developing the HR in their unit. Cranet-E (Brewster and Hegewisch, 1994) shows that line managers have during the last years got an increasing responsibility for HR. This is a logical consequence of the fact that human resources in a knowledge-intensive or service-providing organisation are not only a production factor but also the 'product' themselves.

Hence, the demands on the line managers are comprehensive. Often, line managers are not equipped to hold career discussions with the subordinates and quite of few of them don't feel it is their responsibility anyway. There seems to be a vast need for clarifying the role of the line manager as well as the division of labour between the line manager and the HRM manager. Also needed is a reward structure for line managers which supports the role expectations to them.

Implications for future research

Although we have outlined an overall model for managerial knowledge creation in organisations, there still are a number of loopholes which could be filled by future research.

First, although there has been a considerable increase in the study of organisational learning processes, we are still far from being able to portray the organisation as a learning entity. In the present chapter, we have mainly drawn on one theoretical model, i.e. that of Nonaka. However, to fully understand the knowledge creation processes in the organisation, we need further research in this area

Secondly, the chapter has dealt quite extensively with managerial tasks and roles with special emphasis on the line manager tasks. Although we have come a long way, our understanding of the dynamics of managerial processes (which is not the same as the behavioral patterns of 'managers') is limited. In particular, we need to know more about the strategic role of line managers, as well as the future role of middle managers.

As it was stressed in an earlier section, high-flyer programmes are a popular, albeit controversial and problematic method of management development. Considering how intensively high-flyer programmes are used for career development (and vacancy filling) are used, we need to know more about the impact of these programmes.

Finally, although this chapter has attempted to stress the *process* aspect of learning, we are still tempted to talk about knowledge, rather than knowing or learning, we talk about organisations rather than organising, we talk about structures rather than processes, and we talk about flyers rather than flying. This is probably indicative for the field of management development, but no excuse for it.

APPENDIX TABLES

Part IV
Industrial Relations

10 Evaluating Change in European Industrial Relations: Research Evidence on Trends at Organisational Level

Michael Morley, Chris Brewster, Patrick Gunnigle and Wolfgang Mayrhofer

INTRODUCTION

As far back as 1960, Kerr *et al.* argued that there was a logic to industrialism which would lead to greater convergence, with, in particular, technological and economic forces bringing about greater similarities in industrial relations systems. This debate on the transformation of the industrial relations systems of different countries in response to the internationalisation of markets, technological innovations and increased workforce diversity has been the focus of much research in industrial relations in the last decade (Locke *et al.*, 1995). In Europe in particular, according to Gunnigle and Roche (1995), the analysis of industrial relations practices and policies has never been so closely tied to an appreciation of commercial, national and international political pressures. The challenges to traditional or established industrial relations arise from such major forces as intensified international competition, changes to the structure of product and service markets, European integration and new approaches to the management of manufacturing technologies. However, the response to these pressures is not the same in every country. Rather, according to Locke *et al.*, (1995, p. 158) employment relations 'are shaped in systematic and predictable ways by institutions which filter these external pressures and the [decisions] of the key actors. Patterns of adjustment in countries that have a history of strong centralised industrial relations institutions tend to follow an incremental, negotiated pattern and aim to achieve results that balance the interests of different social groups and economic interests'. In other countries, they argue that the 'adjustment has tended to be unilateral with unions and their traditional institutional supports and political allies put on the defensive'. Lansbury has argued that even though 'all European countries are experiencing intensified pressures to adapt their traditional industrial relations practices in response to increased global competition and changing technologies.... Most European countries are uncertain about the precise nature of the industrial relations system they should be seeking to establish and which will be appropriate in decades to come' (Lansbury, 1995, p. 47–8).

It is clear that the last decade witnessed large-scale change in the social, political, legal and economic climate of many European countries, resulting in changes in the nature of the relationship between governments, employers and trade unions. While the consen sus emerging from the analysis of the possible ramifications for industrial relations appears to suggest that there is something new in European industrial relations in the 1990s, there continues to be considerable disagreement over the nature and extent of the current transformation. Thus in Europe, as in the United States, the 1980s saw major challenges to the established institutions of industrial relations (Hyman, 1994). The social and economic environment became increas ingly hostile to unionism and to many traditional union prac tices and policies (Blanchflower and Freeman, 1992) and many of the gains made by the labour movement were reversed in the 1980s (Baglioni, 1990). It has been argued that that there has been an explosive divergence in industrial relations with different strands of development moving away from each other in different directions, rather than an implosive convergence towards one central best practice (Streeck, 1988) and the potentially convergence-encouraging process of Social Dialogue has, for its part, produced little apart from working parties (Baldry, 1994). Other commentaries have focused on the increased adoption of HRM approaches which, following US usage, are seen as anti-union (Beaumont, 1992; Cradden, 1992).

By contrast, it has been pointed out that even though there has been a concerted effort to individualise the employment relationship, the thesis relating to the withering away of trade union influence in Europe is not supported (Brewster *et al.*, 1994); that individual and collective approaches to the management of this relationship are not necessarily alternatives and can and do co-exist (Storey and Sisson, 1993) and that the assumption in much of the literature that HRM intrinsically involves anti-unionism is unwarranted (Brewster, 1995).

This chapter examines these debates in the light of new evidence on some of these trends. It investigates a number of key aspects of industrial relations at the level of the employing organisation as a means of evaluating developments in the nature and conduct of industrial relations. In particular, it examines:

- levels of trade union membership in organisations across Europe;
- the extent and nature of trade union recognition;
- trade union influence; and
- the locus of policy determination in industrial relations.

CHANGE, DIVERGENCE AND CONVERGENCE IN EUROPEAN INDUSTRIAL RELATIONS

In the last decade or so the context and consequently the nature of industrial relations in Europe has undergone major changes: 'All countries, though not all precisely at the same time, faced the need to overcome recession and simultaneously preserve or improve the efficiency of their economies. While Government policy makers were concerned principally with recouping lost output, curing inflation and trimming budget deficits, private firms engaged in sweeping complicated industrial restructuring, designed chiefly to improve competitiveness through technological innovation, new, more advanced products, and new standards for the utilisation of labour' (Baglioni, 1990, p. 10). Similarly, Bridgford and Stirling (1991, p. 17) point out that: 'Structural shifts in labour markets, movements of capital into different sectors and the alterations of patterns of ownership have taken place' and, they argue, have taken place alongside the introduction of new managerial strategies.

At least three sets of economic influence have exerted pressure on industrial relations in the developed industrial countries from the 1970s (Turner and Morley, 1995). First, macroeconomic forces that determine wage and price changes are increasingly effected by expanding global competition in product markets; secondly, the structure of financial markets – the market for corporate control and access to capital – is increasingly emphasising short term returns to capital over long-term development, particularly in the US and the UK, but now spreading even to countries like Germany, which have different ownership patterns; finally, technological change, primarily production function influences, has changed the optimum scale and nature of production (Mitchell and Saidi, 1992). The inter-relationship between technological developments and increased competition is viewed by some academic commentators as rendering traditional mass production systems and its supporting institutions redundant (Piore and Sabel, 1984; Marshall, 1992) – though it is worth pointing out that there are many instances where they survive substantially unchanged. Although changes in technology such as the development of information technology and robotics generally provided the possibility of new ways of working, Marshall argues that it was competition which made new arrangements essential for the economic survival of firms. Along with the twin forces of competition and technology (and partly as a result), consumer demand for high quality customised products increased, fragmenting the traditional mass markets of standardised products. While the standardised mass production system was production driven, the present competitive environment is largely consumer driven. The altered economic conditions of the 1980s and 1990s, Mar shall claims, do not just change the 'magnitude' of the requirements for economic success but also alter the necessary structures and policies. These new structures and policies centre on developing three key factors at firm level: product quality, productivity and labour flexibility.

According to Piore and Sabel (1984), these developments herald a new industrial revolution and a major restructuring of capitalism. The economic viability of firms depends on their ability to restructure to withstand increased global competition and the fragmentation of mass markets. In the 1970s and 1980s both firms and national economies that were capable of offering more diverse and customised products fared better than more traditional producers of standardised mass products. Firms that are flexible enough to engage in small-batch or customised production can command higher profit margins and are less vulnerable in their market position. Alternatively, traditional producers of standardised mass products faced greater competition from low cost economies in developing countries particularly in the area of labour costs. Labour intensive industries, such as textiles, are especially vulnerable to this type of competition. In general, Piore and Sabel (1984) argue, firms who compete in standardised mass markets must be able to reduce wages and operation costs in order to survive. Whereas firms involved in producing for discrete or specialised market segments are able to give employees significant benefits in the form of enhanced employment security and high wage levels (Tailby and Whitson, 1989).

The argument should not be confined to the (shrinking) production sector. Very similar developments can be adduced in the service sector too; and pressures on the public sector are forcing substantial change there.

These shifts in the European industrial relations environment during the 1980s were associated with changes in labour markets: 'The composition of employment shifted from traditionally highly unionised to non-union sectors and workers and collectivist ideologies lost favour for individualist ones' in advanced OECD countries (Blanchflower and Freeman, 1992, p. 57). This approach placed the emphasis on dealing with individual employees and included what are often termed HRM techniques such as elaborate communications mechanisms, career development, employee involvement initiatives and performance related pay. It was an approach in which employers sought new systems of work organisation, employment contracts and working time arrangements to provide the flexibility necessary to adjust to the competitive conditions of the 1980s (Kern and Schuhmann, 1990; Rubery and Wilkson, 1994) and to the fragmentation of mass markets. This holds regardless of whether a firm is competing on the basis of low costs or product or service innovation and quality: indeed, similar arguments can be advanced for the public service sector. With either strategy, labour flexibility is essential, albeit in different forms. Firms may also attempt to reduce their labour costs, or make their use of labour more cost-effective, through the increased use of peripheral employees; they may treat their HR as a potentially creative resource for adding value in the production process. Once again, very similar arguments can be advanced for the public sector, where restricted budgets are also putting similar pressures on managements.

Management capacity to pursue strategies aimed at increasing labour flexibility and productivity increased in the 1980s as unemployment steadily increased and as trade union membership declined in some economies (Müller-Jentsch, 1987). Thus managements have had the opportunity to define the nature and conditions of the employment relationship to a greater extent than previously. As Hyman (1994, p. 38) put it: 'It is certainly true that in a number of the countries of Western Europe, the 1980s and the 1990s have seen an abrupt loss of trade union membership and influence, and a new assertiveness on the part of management. This has been connected to a questioning of traditional forms of regulation external to the firm, whether by law or by sectoral collective agreements.'

These changes have occurred internationally; certainly in the developed countries and particularly in Europe. The effect has been to reactivate the debate about 'convergence'. Described as an 'old debate' (Locke *et al.*, 1995, p. 159), it argues that the effects of increasing internationalisation in general, and the role of the European Union in particular, will eventually give rise to an increasing similarity of industrial relations, at least in Europe. Due *et al.* (1991, p. 88) suggest that it is reasonable to postulate the existence of trends towards convergence in European industrial relations and in the industrial systems prevailing in the individual member states, primarily because there are 'new' actors in European industrial relations: 'Actors have arrived who, via their actions and status, consciously strive to create convergence in industrial relations across the boundaries of member states . . . we now have actors who, far from being intent solely on promoting national interests, act solely on the basis of supranational considerations. . . . An actor oriented analysis which pays due attention to EC cooperation will inevitably concentrate on convergence trends deriving from the supranational character of the actors.' This convergence, they argue will emerge in parallel to the convergence trends implicit in technology transfer, market developments and other forms of cooperation.

Hyman (1994, p. 2) sets out a set of common trends in the environment of European industrial relations which have loosened the hold of established institutions and country differences. Among the trends he identifies are the sectoral and occupational restructuring of employment; a harsher labour market with the return of mass unemployment; intensified global competition; a fiscal crisis of public employment; and a political shift to the right in much of western Europe.

However, despite the shifts that have occurred in the context of industrial relations, it is widely recognised that industrial relations in Europe differs significantly from country to country and that the extent and nature of change varies considerably. Due *et al.* (1991, p. 91), who we have already quoted as noting the rationale for convergence, also point out that 'the trend towards convergence in European labour markets does not appear to have been very prevalent. Most of today's member states have thus been members of the Community for 20–30 years, sharing in many fields the same market and technological base, without producing any general homogenisation of industrial relations'. Hyman (1994, p. 2) notes that it is an uncontentious proposition that 'in most European countries it is possible to speak of national industrial relations systems, in the sense of institutional arrangements shaped by legislative frameworks, historical traditions, accumulated vested interests and learned patterns of behaviour'. While such systems 'have appeared increasingly precarious as a result of the challenges emerging in the 1970s and intensifying in the 1980s there remains significant variations in experience between and within countries' (Hyman, 1994, p. 5). A variety of reasons have been advanced for the differences that exist: referring to country size (Poole, 1986); economic concentration (Stephans, 1990) or directly to political factors (Przeworski and Spague, 1986).

Excellent papers by Visser (1992) and Bean and Holden (1992) have tested levels of unionisation as one variable in industrial relations and found that full explanation requires attention to an extensive complex of factors. Visser found that although union membership is subject to variation, countries tend not to change relative to one another, so that the rank ordering of countries' membership levels tend to stay the same. Brewster *et al.* (1994, p. 6) point to the fact that industrial relations is contextually bound, existing within a cultural, social, structural and most importantly of all, a political web, or, as one assessment put it: 'critical variables such as culture, ideology and the degree of centralisation of collective bargaining institutions restrict the responses of individual actors to similar changes in their external environments' (Locke *et al.*, 1995, p. 139).

This national divergence points to a number of important issues. Key questions concern the extent to which governments recognise trade unions as social partners, and the way in which trade unions are organised to relate to governments. It is arguable however that this is not a simple correlation. Unions are indeed 'out in the political cold' in some countries, but are still seen as relevant by conservative governments in nearly all European states. Therefore, beyond the current political landscape the question of trade union recognition at national level is likely also to be determined by more deep rooted factors like, for example, tradition, images of justice or cultural elements. Thus, it has been argued that in many European countries conservatism has a strong 'social catholic' element which includes an acceptance of clear collective rights (Brewster *et al.*, 1994). What operates successfully in one country may not be appropriate for another and, while importation of specific features of one system may occur, a blanket approach to the transposition of complete industrial relations systems onto pre-existing ones appears limited.

In Europe specifically, Gospel (1992, p. 488) highlighted the fact that laws and directives are not sufficient in themselves to bring about significant change: 'They will only be important if there is a willingness to use them and institutions to implement them. This refers in particular to awareness and capabilities on the part of employees and trade unions. Here it is true that at the European level there are significant institutional gaps in this respect, as is evidenced by the difficulty of developing the social dialogue. At the level of the individual countries there are also gaps, with weak union movements in some member states.'

THE CHALLENGE OF CONTEMPORARY DEVELOPMENTS IN EUROPEAN INDUSTRIAL RELATIONS: HRM AND THE INDIVIDUALISATION OF THE EMPLOYMENT RELATIONSHIP

Arising out of the inherent conflict of interests in the employment relationship and the indeterminate nature of labour effort, management will constantly seek to exert control over the labour process in the interests of the firm's owners (Turner and Morley, 1995). HRM is often seen as a key contemporary feature of this attempt. Relevant to our discussions here are two interconnected aspects of the concept that impinge directly upon the relationship between managements and trade unions: whether HRM should be conceived of as inimicable to industrial relations; and whether HRM is intrinsically linked with the individualisation of the employment relationship in a way that threatens the existence of collective relationships.

The distinction between the fields of study of HRM and industrial relations has been heightened, primarily because of their perceived incompatibility. HRM has variously been referred to as a subject which reflects an attempt to redefine both the meaning of work and the way individual employees relate to their employers, a subject which involves a synthesis of elements from international business, organisation behaviour, personnel management and industrial relations, or as an approach which refers to the policies, procedures and processes involved in the management of people (Legge, 1989). Above all, the focus of HRM on the individual, and its general unwillingness to acknowledge the existence of distinct interests within the workplace, has created a picture of simple common interest among managers and the managed, an interest supposedly centred solely on the organisation's success in the marketplace (Storey and Sisson, 1993;

Blyton and Turnbull, 1994). This is both too narrow and too simplistic an account of the labour management process, reflecting a managerial ideology rather than an objective summary of organisational reality.

However, there is controversy in this area of meaning. Several contributors have identified a number of inconsistencies and contradictions in HRM (see, for example; Legge, 1989; Blyton and Turnbull, 1994). Turner and Morley (1995) argue that the terms HRM and industrial relations, both being concerned with the management of labour in one form or another, can be taken together to mean the management of labour and that the differences are more a result of the perspective and hierarchical position of the observer than any inherent difference in the substance of the observed phenomena. Thus HRM and traditional industrial relations could potentially be regarded as 'options within options' which are not necessarily incompatible, but which may exist simply as two items in a very long shopping list. Indeed Storey and Sisson (1993, p. 2) argue that more and more there is a contemporary blurring of the boundaries between the two. While this may run contrary to the US experience in this whole area, there may well be a European dimension to this debate which is worthy of much greater exploration. As Brewster (1995, p. 16) argues: 'Developing the (HRM) concept to take account of the more limited autonomy (or greater support) of organisational managers in Europe, and including the external factors within a different model of the concept of HRM, has a value beyond the presentation of simple diagrams.'

Europe has a tradition of collectivism and consensus building and trade unions have a social legitimacy in Europe on a much grander scale than in the US. Brewster and Hegewisch (1994) argue that despite many internally distinctive features, Europe has a coherence of its own, and a distinctiveness from other major blocks. This is particularly true in the HRM area relating to decentralisation and devolvement, pay flexibility, employee investment, industrial relations, employee communications, flexible working patterns and the development of European Union social policy. Hence, an argument can be developed that in Europe at least the two concepts may not be in opposition, they may be different perspectives on the same process (Brewster, 1995).

In support of this argument, Lansbury (1995) suggests that the experiences of European countries in regard to the relationship between bargaining and HRM appear to differ from that of the USA 'Unions and collective bargaining are retained partly as a result of the legal framework, partly due to high levels of unionisation, and partly as a feature of the social democratic version of HRM at a macro level'

(Lansbury, 1995, p. 49). However, the standing of, and the prospects for, the HRM concept are arguably still uncertain, even though, as Storey (1995) points out, it seems to promise the set of guidelines which so many managers have been so desperately seeking. What is clear is that the successful integration of HRM with collective bargaining and more traditional approaches to industrial relations is ultimately dependent on employers co-operating with union representatives, and unions adopting a less adversarial approach, so that a type of mutual commitment can be worked out (Kochan and Dyer, 1994; Brewster, 1995; Lansbury, 1995).

Individualising the employment relationship is often seen as a key feature of HRM. The contemporary literature identifies an increased management emphasis on the development of an individualist orientation in management–employee interactions as one of the most important developments in industrial relations in the past decade (Beaumont, 1985; Kochan *et al.*, 1986; Guest, 1987; Storey, 1989, 1992; Bacon and Storey, 1993). The most popular manifestations of individualism identified in the literature incorporate the areas of performance appraisal; performance related pay; communications; job design and a diminished role for employee representative bodies, particularly trade unions. The core issue in the literature addressing the assumed inherent tensions between collectivism and individualism is whether they are alternatives or whether they might co-exist at establishment level. In this respect Storey and Sisson (1993) argue that: 'the mid to late 1990s are likely to witness a new agenda. . . . The consequence of these changes is that the handling of both collective and individual issues (in unison) is likely to be the essential management requirement during the forthcoming period'.

Using the data collected through Cranet-E, we explore some of these issues.

Trade union membership

Across Europe, it is apparent that there are substantial differences in the extent to which employees belong to trade unions. While there are problems with comparing these figures across countries because of differences in definitions, in meaning and indeed in how the data are collected (Visser, 1990; Blanchflower and Freeman, 1992) which make small percentage differences of limited value, nevertheless, the data is in general instructive. In the hostile environment of recent years that we have been describing, unions in many developed countries have

of every 10 in the Netherlands, 9 in Denmark and continues to be almost universal in Norway. In Spain, trade union recognition would appear to be on the increase, rising from 61 per cent in 1990 to a high of 84 per cent in 1995.

Trade union influence

Assessing union influence is an altogether more complex task. Unlike membership or recognition, influence is largely perceptual (if two parties believe one is influential, then that one will be influential, regardless of how an objective observer of the 'power balance' might assess the position). Furthermore, any discussion will be affected by national cultures and expectations. In the survey, no attempt was made to measure any absolute standards of influence. It was decided that the most reliable data would be obtained from estimates of the change of influence within each organisation on a simple increased-same-decreased scale. This section, therefore, is presented with these caveats.

HR directors were asked whether they thought the influence of trade unions on their organisation had increased, decreased or remained the same over the last 3 years.

Perhaps the most significant finding here is that 'no change' is the most frequent response in all countries. Where there are changes, increases and decreases in influence are reported by significant numbers of different organisations in all countries. General trends are not to be confused with universality.

Otherwise the results show that a fifth of the organisations in the Latin countries report an increase in trade union influence in the last 3 years: in Spain this is almost matched by the organisations reporting a decrease in influence, but in France and Italy it is almost twice as many organisations as report a decrease. More than a quarter of organisations in Norway report an increase in union influence and very few report a decrease. The UK, Ireland, the Netherlands and Turkey stand out as having far more organisations reporting a decrease in union influence than report an increase.

In the UK, around 50 per cent of all organisations reported union influence declining in the first 3 rounds of the survey. By 1995 'no change' had become more common than 'decrease' as a response to this figure, with 35 per cent of organisations reporting decreased union influence. In Sweden, a majority of respondents (73 per cent) report no change in union influence over the least 3 years, while the number reporting a decrease in influence has dropped from 29 per cent in 1992

Table 10.6 Trade union influence

Country	*CH*	*D(w)*	*D(e)*	*DK*	*E*	*F*	*FIN*	*I*	*IRL*	*N*	*NL*	*S*	*T*	*UK*
Increased	7	13	12	15	23	21	13	20	6	27	11	8	5	4
Same	78	68	70	63	57	67	71	68	65	67	4	73	47	55
Decreased	10	18	15	20	18	11	15	12	25	5	41	17	26	35

Table 10.7 Trade union influence: 4-year comparisons (% organisations)

	Germany				*Spain*				*France*				*Sweden*				*UK*			
	1990	*1991*	*1992*	*1995*	*1990*	*1991*	*1992*	*1995*	*1990*	*1991*	*1992*	*1995*	*1990*	*1991*	*1992*	*1995*	*1990*	*1991*	*1992*	*1995*
Increased	26	25	23	13	38	44	33	23	9	7	8	21	25	29	11	8	6	4	4	4
Same	67	65	67	68	49	44	54	57	46	47	51	67	66	59	61	73	45	44	42	55
Decreased	7	10	9	18	13	12	14	18	46	46	41	11	10	21	29	17	49	52	54	35

to 17 per cent in 1995. In Germany, there has been a drop in the numbers reporting an increase (from 26 per cent in 1990 to 13 per cent in 1995) and a corresponding rise in those reporting a decrease in influence (from 7 per cent in 1990 to 18 per cent in 1995). The percentage reporting 'no change' remains constant at approximately 67 per cent. The trend is somewhat similar in Spain. The 1995 survey results reveal a fall off in the numbers reporting an increase in union influence and a slight rise in those reporting decreased influence for the union movement. There is a marginal rise in the 'no change' category. Finally, in France union influence would appear to be levelling off or indeed on the increase. Our data suggest that it is certainly not decreasing. The number of organisations reporting a decrease in union influence has dropped from 46 per cent in 1990 to 11 per cent in 1995.

Industrial relations policy determination and implementation

Our research also addressed the issue of where organisational policies on industrial relations are mainly determined (international headquarters; national headquarters; subsidiary; site) and with whom does primary responsibility lie for major policy decisions on industrial relations (line management or HR department).

Our evidence indicates clearly that where the respondent is part of a large group, industrial relations policies are most typically determined at national headquarters level. This is the case for all countries (though in the UK, Ireland and Finland almost as many organisations determine industrial relations policy at site/establishment level, as do so at national level).

This area remains a key concern for managements. Asked to identify the major HRM or Personnel challenges for the next 3 years the rather broader categorisation of 'employee relations' ranked as one of the first three priorities in all countries except Denmark, the Netherlands and Sweden.

It is also an area where the specialist departments are least likely to share responsibility for policy with line managers.

Of the six aspects of personnel work explored (pay and benefits, recruitment and selection, training and development, industrial relations, health and safety and workforce expansion/reduction) industrial relations was the one most likely to be held as the sole responsibility of the HR department in all countries except Spain, France, the Netherlands and Turkey – and in those countries it was the second most likely to be held as solely HR department responsibility. It is also

Table 10.8 Where policy decisions on industrial relations are mainly determined (% organisations)

Country	*CH*	*D(w)*	*D(e)*	*DK*	*E*	*F*	*FIN*	*I*	*IRL*	*N*	*NL*	*S*	*T*	*UK*
International HQ	9	8	3	1	0	5	1	7	3	1	7	1	3	3
National HQ	55	60	43	47	63	43	45	57	41	64	51	43	65	36
Subsidiary	31	23	39	36	19	25	12	7	14	20	27	34	5	25
Site/establishment	6	8	16	16	18	27	43	29	41	15	15	23	28	35

Table 10.9 Primary responsibility for major policy decisions on industrial relations (% organisations)

Country	*CH*	*D(w)*	*D(e)*	*DK*	*E*	*F*	*FIN*	*I*	*IRL*	*N*	*NL*	*S*	*T*	*UK*
Line management	6	13	18	23	9	4	17	27	5	6	12	7	32	3
Line management with HR	19	16	27	23	13	13	31	15	21	12	39	21	14	20
HR dept. with line management	25	34	31	27	32	38	33	29	50	42	33	47	22	48
HR dept.	46	34	24	22	33	45	18	22	22	38	14	24	24	24

noticeable in this regard that this is the area where fewest organisations in most countries have extended line management responsibility recently.

DISCUSSION

The new empirical data presented in this chapter leads us to support the view that there are elements of both convergence and divergence at work in European industrial relations; but overall our evidence indicates that we are still a long way from any coherent move towards convergence. Our evidence is of course limited by the form in which it was collected. It is an international survey which aimed at obtaining substantial numbers of responses across a variety of different countries. Questioning was, therefore, restricted. In particular, our data is, as we have indicated, drawn from senior personnel/HR practitioners at the top level of often complex organisations. There would seem to be no obvious reason why their answers to the survey questions should not be well informed, and evidence from Chief Executive Officers in Switzerland of whom we asked the same questions, and from comparative surveys of work place representatives and managers (Bielenski *et al.*, 1992) seem to confirm that, faced with factual questions, different parties will give similar responses. The questions on trade union influence, as we have pointed out, are not factual.

Even given these limitations, it is nonetheless a substantial and rich source of information, filling a gap at the level of international comparisons between organisational practices. A key finding from the survey is the reinforcement that national differences remain more significant than sector or size dimensions

On the issue of trade-union membership within Europe, there has been some fall off, but perhaps what is more significant is the degree of continuity over the last decade. In relation to trade union recognition, the data reveals that in most European countries, and despite such large membership differences, 7 out of every 10 employers, across most sectors recognise trade unions. Of course, the figures are unable to reveal whether these organisations have reduced the range of issues that they bargain over, or have withdrawn recognition for some groups of staff. Nevertheless, in the absence of other comparative information on these topics, the finding about the extent of union recognition should give pause to those who too glibly assert the 'trade-union decline' argument.

With respect to trade union influence, this research suggests that in most European states, a majority of organisations have seen no change in influence over the last 3 years, a finding which is again at variance with the 'withering away of union influence' thesis. The form of evidence that we have here is more questionable than that in the other areas. Measures of influence are more susceptible to individual respondent interpretation than questions about numbers or the existence of recognition. Since influence is a perceptual concept the views expressed by HR or personnel directors are important and the changes over time, or lack of change, are significant. We may need to be particularly careful about drawing international comparisons here, however.

Industrial relations remains an important subject for HR and personnel departments, and policy in these areas is usually retained by the national headquarters. At whatever level, responsibility for IR policy is normally shared between personnel/HR departments and line management, though this is the area where the specialists are most likely to have full responsibility for policy. Finally on the subject of employee communication/consultation, a large increase has taken place in the use of direct verbal and direct written mechanisms, potentially reflecting the necessity to increase employee commitment in order to achieve organisational success. This increase, however, runs in parallel with the collective channels, thus supporting the argument that the two are not incompatible (see next chapter).

FURTHER RESEARCH

Our survey cannot address the differing connotations that issues such as trade unionism itself, membership, recognition and influence have across different countries. Thus we have had to take as read the fact that, for instance, trade unions in Scandinavia typically adopt a much wider role involving a close involvement in social security and other systems well beyond the workplace. Similarly, the importance of union membership varies with the relevance of other, sometimes legally defined, means of employee representation within the workplace: recognition may be carefully defined in law or, as in the UK, simply *de facto*; and influence can be exercised at a range of levels from individual, work group, through a variety of collective bargaining arrangements. These differing connotations simply serve to reinforce the importance of country level distinctions and the distance that we remain from any convergence of European industrial relations.

Further research will also have to take more account of recent developments not fully considered yet. A prominent example is the growing pressure on individualised arrangements on the state and organisational level concerning the management of labour. Coming from such different sources as, for example, increasing economic pressure through heightened competition and less appreciation for collective mechanisms in an individualised 'post-modern' society, this pressure leads to various interesting phenomena. In Germany, for example, the economic and labour market situation at the moment sometimes 'makes strange bedfellows'. In a recent labour conflict, the traditional borderline between employers' federations and plant management on the one side and trade unions and works councils on the other side could only be maintained with difficulty. Instead of traditional contradictions new alliances emerged. Plant management and works councils jointly tried to avoid costly power struggles, whereas the associations on both sides took a more rigorous and basic stance. Such phenomena may not be singular, but reflect a broader development in industrialised countries leading to a more complex power distribution which in turn influences bargaining processes, etc. at all levels of industrial relations. If this is so (and there seems to be some evidence for that), future research efforts will not only face an even more complicated situation in this field but will also be more important.

References

Abromeit, H. and Blanke, B. (eds) (1987) *Arbeitsmarkt, Arbeits beziehungen und Politik iu den Soer Jahren*, Opladen, West dentscher, Verlag.

Baglioni, G. and Crouch, C. (eds) (1990) *European Industrial Relations: the Challenge of Flexibility*, London Sage.

Bacon, N. and Storey, J. (1993) 'Individualization of the employment relationship and the implications for trade unions', *Employee Relations*, 15(1): 5–17.

Baglioni, G., (1990) 'Industrial relations in Europe in the 1980s', in Baglioni, G. and Crouch, C. (eds), pp. 1–42.

Baldry, C. (1994) 'Convergence in Europe: a matter of perspective', *Industrial Relations Journal*, 25(2): 96–110.

Bean, R. and Holden, L. (1992) 'Cross national differences in trade union membership in OECD countries', *Industrial Relations Journal*, 23(1): 52–9.

Beaumont, P. (1985) 'New plant work practices', *Personnel Review*, 14(5): 15–19.

Beaumont, P. (1992) 'The US human resource management literature: a review', in Salaman, G. (ed.), pp. 20–37.

Bielenski, H., Alaluf, M., Atkinson, J., Bellini, R., Castillo, J.J., Donati, P., Graverson, G., Huygen, F. and Wickham J. (1992) 'New forms of work and activity: a survey of experiences at establishment level in eight European countries', European Foundation for the Improvement of Working & Living Conditions, *Working Paper*, Dublin.

Blanchflower, D. and Freeman, R. (1992) 'Unionism in the United States and other advanced OECD countries', *Industrial Relations*, 31(1): 56–80.

Blyton, P. and Turnbull, P. (1994) *Dynamics of Employee Relations*, London, Macmillan.

Brewster, C. (1995) 'Towards a European model of human resource management', *Journal of International Business Studies*, 1–18.

Brewster, C. and Hegewich, A. (1994) *Policy and Practice in European Human Resource Management: The Price Waterhouse Cranfield Survey*, London, Routledge.

Brewster, C., Gunnigle, P. and Morley, M. (1994) 'Continuity and change in European industrial relations: evidence from a 14 country survey', *Personnel Review* 23(3).

Bridgford, J. and Stirling, J. (1991) 'Britain in a social Europe: industrial relations and 1992', *Industrial Relations Journal*, 22(4): 263–73.

Cradden, T. (1992) 'Trade unionism and HRM: the incompatibles?', *Irish Business and Administrative Research Journal*, 13: 24–36.

Due, J., Madsen, J. and Jensen, C. (1991) 'The social dimension: convergence or diversification of industrial relations in the single European market?', *Industrial Relations Journal*, 22(2): 85–103.

Ferner, A. and Hyman, R. (1992) *Industrial Relations in the New Europe*, London, Blackwell.

Gospel, H. (1992) 'The single European market and industrial relations: an introduction', *British Journal of Industrial Relations*, 30(4): 483–94.

Guest, D. (1987) 'Human resource management and industrial relations', *Journal of Management Studies*, 24(5): 503–21.

Gunnigle, P. and Roche, W. (1995) *New Challenges to Irish Industrial Relations*, Dublin, Oak Tree Press.

Hyman, R. (1994) 'Industrial relations in Western Europe: an era of ambiguity?', *Industrial Relations*, 33(1): 1–24.

Kern, H. and Schumann, M. (1990) *Das Ende der Arbeitsteilung?*, 4th edn, München, C.H. Beck.

Kerr, C., Dunlop, J., Harbison, F. and Myers, C. (1960) *Industrialism and Industrial Man*, Cambridge, Mass., Harvard University Press.

Kochan, T. and Dyer, L. (1994) 'A model of organisational change in the context of union–management relations', *Journal of Applied Behavioural Science*, XII Spring: 59–78.

Kochan, T., Katz, H. and McKersie, R. (1986) *The Transformation of American Industrial Relations*, New York, Basic Books.

Lansbury, R. (1995) 'Workplace Europe: new forms of bargaining and participation', *Technology, Work and Employment*, 10(1): 47–55.

Legge, K. (1989) 'Human resource management: a critical analysis', in Storey, J. (ed.), *New Perspectives on Human Resource Management*, London, Routledge,

Locke, R., Kochan, T. and Piore, M. (1995) 'Reconceptualizing comparative industrial relations: lessons from international research', *International Labour Review*, 134(2): 139–63.
Marshall, R. (1992) 'Work organisation, unions and economic performance', in Mishel, L. and Voos, P. (eds).
Mishel, L. and Voos, P. (eds) (1992) *Unions and Economic Competitiveness*, New York, ME Sharpe.
Mitchell, J. and Saidi, M. (1991) 'International pressures on industrial relations: macroeconomics and social concertation', in Treu, T. (ed.).
Müller-Jentsch, W. (1987) 'Eine neue Topographie der Arbeit – Organisationspolitische Herausforderungen für die Gewerkschaften', in Abromeit, H. and Blanke, B. (eds.).
OECD (1994) *Employment Outlook*. Paris, OECD, p. 173.
Piore, M. and Sabel, C. (1984) *The Second Industrial Divide: Prospects for Prosperity*, New York, Basic Books.
Poole, M. (1986) *Industrial Relations: Origins and Patterns of National Diversity*, London, RKP.
Przeworski, A. and Spague, J. (1986) *Paper Stones: A History of Editorial Socialism*, Chicago, University of Chicago Press.
Rubery, J. and Wilkinson, F. (eds) (1994) 'Introduction', *Employer Strategy and the Labour Market*, Oxford, Oxford University Press.
Salaman, G. (ed.) (1992) *Human Resource strategies*, London, Open University, Sage.
Stephans, J. (1990) 'Explaining cross – national differences in union strength in bargaining and welfare', paper read to the *XII World Congress of Sociology*, Madrid, 9–13 July.
Storey, J. (1992) *Developments in the Management of Human Resources*, Blackwell, Oxford.
Storey, J (1995) *Human Resource Management: A Critical Text*, London, Routledge.
Storey, J. (ed.) (1989) *New Perspectives on Human Resource Management*, London, Routledge.
Storey, J. and Sisson, K. (1993) *Managing Human Resources and Industrial Relations*, Buckingham, Open University Press.
Streeck, W. (1988) *Change in Industrial Relations: Strategy and Structure, Proceedings of an International Symposium of New Systems in Industrial Relations*, Tokyo, Japan Institute of Labour.
Tailby, S. and Whitson, C. (eds) (1989) 'Industrial relations and restructuring', *Manufacturing Change: Industrial Relations and Restructuring*, Blackwell, Oxford.
Treu, T. (ed.) (1991) *Participation in Public Policy Making: The Role of Trade Unions and Employer Associations*, Berlin, Walter de Gruyter.
Turner, T. and Morley, M. (1995) *Industrial Relations and the New Order: Case Studies in Conflict and Co-Operation*, Dublin, Oak Tree Press.
Visser, J. (1990) 'Trends in union membership', *Employment Outlook 1991*, Paris, OECD.
Visser, J. (1992) 'Union organisation: why countries differ', paper read to the *IX World Congress of the IIRA*, Sydney.

11 Communication, Consultation and the HRM Debate

Wolfgang Mayrhofer, Chris Brewster, Michael Morley and Patrick Gunnigle

INTRODUCTION

Early discussions of management gave little emphasis to communication. Although it was implicit in the management function of command and the structural principle of hierarchy, Luthans (1992) argues that the early theorists never fully appreciated its significance or fully developed or integrated it into management. More recently, since the concept first came to prominence in the early 1980s, communication and consultation with employees has held a central place in the discussion and practice of human resource management. The European Union's Work Councils Directive has brought the debate on communication and consultation into even sharper focus. It requires the establishment of employee work councils in organisations with 1000 employees or more in any member state and with 150 employees or more in each of at least two member states. As we write, the European Commission is exploring the notion of national works councils being made mandatory in all countries of the EU. Today, the popular literature promulgates the notion that in the high performance organisation, information is a tool, not a privilege. The overarching philosophy is that everyone in the organisation must have access to the maximum amount of information that is reasonable for them to assimilate, understand and utilise.

A good deal of research has focused on the delegation of decision-making and increasing access to information for individuals at lower levels in the organisation (Blau and Alba, 1982; Bowen and Lawler, 1992). In a debate on the role and significance of communication in today's business environment, Smyth (1995) argues that the role of internal communications in an organisation is no longer limited to merely providing information to employees; rather, in the present business environment, it has a role to play in defining and improving the relationship between employers and employees and in helping in the management of strategic, structural, technological and process changes within the organisation. Of greater significance, Smyth's research identifies eight practical roles which the communication function will likely perform in leading edge organisations, namely acting as: the cultural conscience of the organisation, the communication planner, the communicator of decisions, the facilitator of re-visioning, the provider of the big picture context, the facilitator of real-time listening, the integrator of the internal culture and the external brand, and the facilitator of consultation, involvement and empowerment. Thus, it has been argued that by using effective consultation methods, the quality of management decisions is likely to be enhanced and once a decision is made in this way, there is a greater chance of gaining commitment and co-operation from employees (Kanter, 1989; Spreitzer, 1995; Keane, 1996; Vernon, 1996). Other organisations will seek to involve employees in decision-making and problem-solving to streamline management and offer the 'new/knowledge worker' a sense of involvement and motivation (Redmond *et al.*, 1993; Pivec and Robbins, 1996) while others (e.g. Davis, 1997; Sisson, 1997) suggest that an economic dividend accrues from good information and consultation practices: the knowledge of the organisation resides in the individuals and groups that make it up. That knowledge is rarely tapped to any significant degree – unlocking that repository can bring an organisation huge competitive advantages.

Partly because of the dominance of US thinking about the topic and the use of non-union companies as exemplars of good practice, there has been a tendency to associate the concept of HRM with the individualisation of communication and a move away from, or even antagonism towards, the concept of industrial relations – communication and consultation which is collective and particularly that which is trade union based. The non-union implication sits uneasily with the history and circumstances of Europe (Brewster, 1999), even though there is increasing acceptance in European organisations of the value of the HRM concept. This chapter examines the current situation in Europe regarding communication and consultation. It draws upon the Cranet-E evidence to examine the extent of communication and consultation that takes place in organisations in the various European countries and the extent to which that is individual or collective.

The final part of the chapter uses, but goes beyond, this data to examine whether competitive pressures are likely to force European organisations to increasingly individualise their communication and consultation or, alternatively, are the historical, institutional and situational constraints so extensive that organisations in Europe will be unable to adopt a fully operational (individualised) model of HRM? This is more than an academic and conceptual question because it has profound implications for the strategy and future development of organisations. The chapter concludes that the alternatives posited in the current models are inadequate to capture the reality of European organisations; that Europe (and perhaps other parts of the world) needs a conception of HRM which can encompass a positive collective relationship with employees and trade unions; that there are cases and evidence which suggests that there are already signs of the development of such a concept of HRM; and that, indeed, there may be positive advantages to such an approach.

COMMUNICATION, CONSULTATION AND HRM

Some of the key questions in HRM are about communication and consultation with the workforce within the organisation. Effective communication, it could be argued, is at the heart of effective human resource management. There is now clear evidence that organisations across Europe are going beyond trite statements about their employees being their major asset to developing and increasing the amount of communication and consultation in which they involve those employees (Brewster *et al.*, 1994b). However, because of the inherent conflict of interests in the employment relationship and the indeterminate nature of labour effort, management will constantly seek to exert control over the labour process in the interests of the firm's owners. Thus the introduction of some consultation mechanisms are designed principally to integrate employees into the organisation, but are not designed to challenge the basic authority structure of the entrprise (Marchington *et al.*, 1992; Blyton and Turnbull, 1994). But, as Andresky (1986, p. 81) warns 'if an organisation chooses to have a consultative committee as a means of boosting employee productivity, it must not be treated like a puppet union'.

Much of the writing on HRM builds on the 'Harvard' school of work on HRM which, in its seminal text, argued that the centre of management's task lay in, 'balancing and, where possible, integrating the interests of the many stakeholders of the enterprise' (Beer *et al.*, 1985, p. 11) – and they argued, further, that the employees are the most important stakeholders and as such expect a voice in decisions that affect them (Gonring, 1991). As a consequence employee communication and consultation are often seen as a central element of HRM.

The importance of communications in organisations is not confined to the area of HRM. For management, as well as organisational, theorists communication is the key element and theoretical construct, respectively, for describing and explaining organisational phenomena. In his classic study Mintzberg (1975) showed that communication in its various forms is one of the key tasks of the job of managers. From a different point of view, Weick states that 'interpersonal communication is the essence of organization because it creates structures that affect what else gets said and done by whom' (Weick, 1989, p. 97) Even more significant is communication in the conceptualisation of organisations made by sociological systems theory. Luhmann argues that communications are the basic elements of social systems. In particular, it is argued that the (latent) structures that form and guide communications are relevant if one is interested in the behaviour of organisations (Luhmann, 1987).

In the international realm, communication has a central place, too. 'All international business activity involves communication. Within the international and global business environment, activities such as exchanging information and ideas, decision making, negotiating, motivating, and leading are all based on the ability of managers from one culture to communicate successfully with managers and employees from other cultures' (Adler, 1991, p. 64) Literature on international HRM stresses that cross-border communication happens constantly in multinational companies. This includes communications between expatriates and host country members as well as between employees of various offices in different countries (Dowling *et al.*, 1994; Briscoe, 1995).

Trade-union recognition and influence is closely linked to the European practice of employee involvement (Table 11.1).

Employers have to deal with workplace (and often wider) works councils wherever the employees request it in Germany (for companies with five or more employees), Italy and Portugal. In Greece the unions can insist on the establishment of a works council where the organisation is larger than 20 employees; there have to be 35 or more employees in the Netherlands; 50 or more in Spain and France and 100 in Belgium. In the UK, the new Labour Government's espousal of the Social Chapter means that much of the recent legislation in this area will come into force in that country too now, but even before then

Table 11.1 Incidence of statutory works councils/statutory board-level employee representation in the 12 member states

Country	*Statutory works councils*	*Statutory board-level employee representation*
Belgium	•	–
Denmark	–	•
Germany	•	•
France	•	•
Greece	•	•*
Ireland	–	•*
Italy	–	–
Luxembourg	•	•
Netherlands	•	•
Portugal	•	•*
Spain	•	–
UK	–	–

• In Existence
– Not present
•* Confined to state enterprises
Source: EFILWC (1990), p. 5.

employers were still required to consult their employees on a number of issues. Where unions are recognised, under the terms of the Employment Protection Consolidation Act 1978, the Trade Union Reform and Employment Rights Act 1993 and the Health and Safety at Work Act 1974, they must be consulted with on relevant matters. In the case of redundancies, as a result of a European Court of Justice ruling in 1994 which forced the then Government to introduce the Collective Redundancies and Transfer of Undertakings Regulations 1995, UK employers are obliged to consult with 'workforce representatives', even where there is no recognised union (see Aikin and Mill, 1994; Vernon, 1996).

Throughout Europe, various forms of works council (conceived of by the European Commission, according to Naudin (1997), as a first step towards a more labour-friendly Europe) have differing degrees of power: but most would shock US managers brought up on theories of 'management's right to manage'. In Germany and the Netherlands, for example, employee representatives can resort to the courts to prevent, or to delay, managerial decisions in areas like recruitment, termination, or changing working practices which in the United States would be areas for considerable managerial prerogative.

Beyond the workplace, legislation in countries such as the Netherlands, Denmark and, most famously, Germany requires organisations to have two-tier management boards, with employees having the right to be represented on the more senior Supervisory Board. Employee representation can, depending on country, size and sector, range up to 50 per cent of the Board. These arrangements give considerable (legally backed) power to the employee representatives and, unlike consultation in the US, for example, they tend to supplement rather than supplant the union position. In relatively highly unionised countries it is unsurprising that many of the representatives of the workforce are, in practice, trade union officials. In Germany, as one instance, four-fifths of them are union representatives.

Furthermore, many of the largest companies in Europe are now covered by the same European legislation: the European Works Councils Directive. There is, within the Directive, scope for differing arrangements, but again it can be seen as, and was designed to be, another pressure towards increasing communication and consultation. There has been an interest in consultative processes and in raising the level of social dialogue within organisations throughout Europe ever since the Vredeling proposals of the 1970s (Weston and Martinez-Lucio, 1997). It is estimated that in excess of 1200 firms operating throughout the EU are affected by the legislation (TUC, 1995). Some view this as the re-emergence of the European industrial relations convergence thesis once again (Streek, 1987; Teague, 1993; Locket *et al.*, 1995), which when combined with the globalisation of capital and an increased interest in corporate affairs among employees results in an increased consciousness among employee representatives in 'new forms of transnational engagement, no matter how precarious and embryonic' (Weston and Martinez-Lucio, 1997, p. 767). Marginson and Sisson (1998) have coined the term 'virtual collective bargaining' to emphasise the limited nature of these international effects. Others view the European works council initiative with some concern. For example Ramsay (1997, p. 314) suggests that though they offer a channel for seeking to match the internationalisation and mobility of capital, they face many of the same problems as national or workplace bodies. In particular his concern is with 'the capacity of this arrangement to achieve greater influence for employees over management decisions in a form which seek to break out of the national systems straitjacket, and so confront an intensifying apparent challenge to industrial democracy from the internationalisation of capital'. He concludes, revealing his UK confrontational approach, that while a wide range of outcomes is possible:

'at present the balance of probabilities suggests that management will be able to contain most European Works Councils and engage in at least successful damage limitation' (Ramsay, 1997, p. 320). Hage (1996), warns of the danger of abstracting institutions from their social settings and meanings and suggests that a blanket approach may lead to an elision of the varied ways in which such arrangements really act and are acted upon by people at workplace level, while Stoop (1994) highlights the major obstacles which limit the development of a common international culture in this area.

Replacing industrial relations by HRM?

As has already been pointed out, there is no serious doubt about the importance of communication for management and HRM. Many, however, have argued that the form of communication involved will necessarily be anti-union. Above all, the focus of HRM on the individual, and its general unwillingness to acknowledge the existence of distinct interests within the workplace, has created a picture of simple common interest among managers and the managed, an interest supposedly centred solely on the organisation's success in the marketplace (Blyton and Turnbull, 1993; Storey and Sisson, 1993). There is an assumption in much of the literature that HRM policies are in some way linked to attempts to replace traditional industrial relations bargaining over work issues, or at least to more limited opportunities for trade unions to exercise their functions. This is the conclusion of Storey's (1992) broad study of the impact of HRM in the UK; and of Kochan *et al.* (1986) and Fiorito *et al.* (1987) in the US. A leading British trade union official writes of: 'the experience of many unionists that human resource management is associated with derecognition and a systematic attempt to undermine the union role' (Monks, 1994, p. 45).

Storey (1992) identified 25 'constituent elements' of 'HRM recipes': including, notably for the discussion here, a 'desire to marginalise shop stewards' (Storey and Sisson, 1993, p. 16). Mahoney and Deckop (1986) argued that among the key characteristics of HRM was a move from 'a collective, negotiating focus to a more general approach to more direct communication with employees'. In a similar way, Beaumont identifies 'major items typically mentioned' in the US literature as part of HRM: including a high degree of participation of individuals in task related decisions and sophisticated arrangements of internal communication (Beaumont, 1992).

Guest believes that industrial relations is based on a system of collective bargaining which has as its objective the reconciliation of the differing interests of managements and employees; HRM is a managerial philosophy which aims to replace the collective relationship with an individualised one in which management will either deny the existence of separate employee interests or subordinate them to those of management (Guest, 1987, 1990). It has been pointed out that studies of HRM in the United States have tended to take place in the non-union sector (Beaumont, 1992). A constant thread in research programmes in the US has been the link between HRM practices and non-unionism (see, e.g. Kochan *et al.*, 1984, 1986). 'In the US a number of... academics have argued that HRM [the concept and the practice] is anti-union and anti-collective bargaining' (Beaumont, 1991, p. 300).

In contrast, other researchers – particularly in Europe – have found that the adoption of HRM techniques has little separate and specific impact on trade unionism in the UK (Beaumont and Harris, 1989), in Ireland (Roche and Turner, 1994), or in Germany (Fischer and Weitbrecht, 1995). Referring to Millward's work on the British Workplace Industrial Relations Survey a trade union leader remarked: 'The conclusion is that there is no correlation between human resource management and anti-unionism' (Monks, 1994, p. 42). Any thesis relating to the withering away of trade-union influence in Europe is not supported by the evidence (Brewster *et al.*, 1994a; Morley *et al.*, 1996). Individual and collective approaches to the management of this relationship are not necessarily alternatives and can and do co-exist (Storey and Sisson, 1993) and it has been argued that the assumption in much of the literature that HRM intrinsically involves anti-unionism is unwarranted, based upon a particular (US-style) vision of HRM (Brewster, 1995b).

Hence, the key question that is linked with this debate is: will individual(ised) communication take over from more collectivist or union communication? Part of the answer is a matter of empirical analysis, and we make a contribution to that below using empirical data from various European countries. Another part of the answer, however, concerns the problem of identifying a consistent definition for HRM. The confusion surrounding the concept of HRM has been pointed out on many occasions (see, as examples, Conrad and Pieper, 1990; Boxall, 1992; Guest, 1992; Storey 1992; Goss, 1994). Conceptually, a range of definitions of HRM is possible: from an almost etymological analysis at one end to a clearly normative perspective at the other (Brewster, 1994). For the purposes of this chapter it is only important to note that while there is this dichotomy of interpretation about whether HRM is or is not intrinsically anti-union, there is no doubt at all that the literature implies or states that communication and consultation is at the heart of HRM.

Individualised communication in Europe

Given the popular notion spread in the scientific and practitioner oriented literature, individualised communication should be an important element of organisational practices. Indeed, our data are very clear on that point: communications to individuals is extensive and is increasing.

When analysing the communication patterns of organisations one can (at least analytically) distinguish between two intertwined aspects, often called downwards and upwards communication.

Downward communication indicates that the intended flow of direction of information is from management to the employees. With regard to the information channel used one can see in our data that the use of direct ways of communications has increased. Across Europe, the Cranet-E survey finds that direct verbal communication is increasing in between 32 per cent (Italy) and 63 per cent (Sweden and the UK) of organisations with a European average of 53 per cent. Only 2 per cent of organisations across Europe are using less direct verbal communication. A similar picture arises from the evidence on direct written communication to employees. Of course, with computerisation, HR information systems and mail-merge techniques it becomes much easier for managers to write 'individually' to all staff involved in a particular change: and the opportunity is being taken. Between 30 per cent (Norway) and 64 per cent (Netherlands), with a European average of 50 per cent, of organisations have increased their use of direct written communication, 37 per cent of organisations have increased their use of electronic communication with employee's and 47 per cent have increased their use of team briefings. In all these cases, almost no organisations have decreased their use of communication mechanisms (Table 11.2).

Overall, one can see a definite increase in the use of various methods of communication employed by organisations. (Figure 11.1).

The writers on HRM who are advising employers that the commitment of their employees is vital to success in the future, and that the way to achieve that commitment is through increasing communication, can take comfort from these figures. Of course, when the question is

Table 11.2 Percentage of organisations reporting a change in the use of direct verbal or written methods to communicate major issues to employees during the last 3 years

Country	*B*	*CH*	*D (w)*	*D (e)*	*DK*	*E*	*F*	*FIN*	*I*	*IRL*	*N*	*NL*	*S*	*T*	*UK*
Direct verbal															
Increased	52	53	59	36	51	40	45	57	32	55	38	51	63	43	63
Same	40	43	40	61	44	45	44	37	39	38	54	39	34	31	32
Decreased	2	1	1	1	1	3	2	3	5	1	3	3	2	3	1
Not used	3	1	1	0	0	5	3	1	0	0	0	3	1	2	1
Direct Written															
Increased	55	60	34	26	48	49	55	48	36	51	30	64	44	34	62
Same	39	37	60	67	46	40	37	49	37	40	58	34	52	41	34
Decreased	1	2	4	1	3	3	2	1	3	1	5	1	2	1	1
Not used	3	0	1	3	1	5	4	0	0	1	1	1	1	2	0

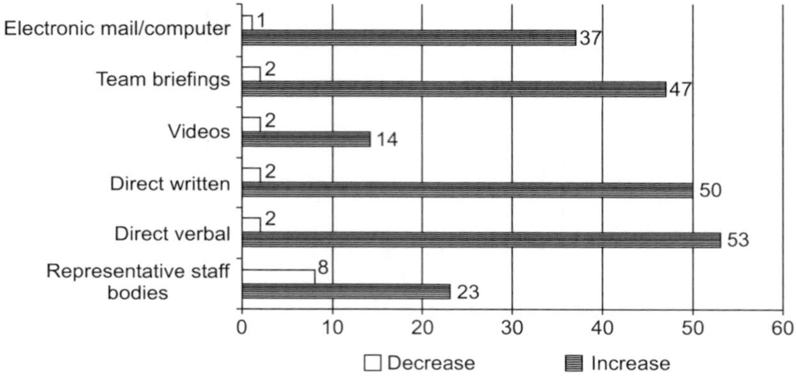

Figure 11.1 European averages of percentage of organisations reporting an increase/decrease in the use of various methods

asked of senior personnel practitioners (as it is in the Cranet-E survey) it is possible that they are exaggerating the extent of the improvement in communication: there may be an element of 'wishful thinking' here. However, the figures are so large and so consistent, that it seems likely that they reflect some kind of reality. We are encouraged in this view by the fact that in other respects the Cranet-E data does indicate that respondents are likely to report that their organisations are not following the received wisdom.Furthermore, the only other major cross-national survey which covers communication, and which drew data from employees as well as employers, confirms the findings (Sisson, 1997). It would seem that the fact is that organisations are communicating more with their employees.

With regard to what is communicated through these channels, this varies from case to case. Two areas of central interest for management and employees are information on organisational strategy and information on organisational finances.

In Europe, at least 9 out of every 10 organisations formally brief their managers about the organisation's strategy and financial results. However, there is a marked 'slope' in the provision of information below the managerial level. The further down the organisation one goes the less likely employees are to be given this information. Thus, information on strategy is provided for manual workers by 12 per cent of organisations in West Germany and 57 per cent in Finland. Other countries have figures between these two with half having less

Table 11.3 Briefing of different groups of employees

Country	*B*	*CH*	*D(w)*	*D(e)*	*DK*	*E*	*F*	*FIN*	*I*	*IRL*	*N*	*NL*	*S*	*T*	*UK*
Strategy															
Management	97	98	92	91	95	97	95	97	88	97	96	99	98	83	95
Professional/ technical	66	48	41	50	60	69	50	86	76	72	75	83	58	57	72
Clerical	46	22	21	27	49	26	32	62	41	54	62	42	61	29	49
Manual	40	21	12	19	36	20	25	57	34	43	55	40	52	21	41
Financial performance															
Management	97	92	96	93	96	90	95	93	80	94	95	98	96	68	96
Professional/ technical	70	79	76	76	74	68	77	92	49	65	76	80	68	27	78
Clerical	56	57	67	64	68	33	65	90	27	52	70	47	76	12	61
Manual	50	54	54	47	51	25	50	86	15	42	66	43	67	11	52

Table 11.4 Percentage of organisations reporting a change in number of employees communicating their views through more individualised ways of communication

Country	*B*	*CH*	*D(w)*	*D(e)*	*DK*	*E*	*F*	*FIN*	*I*	*IRL*	*N*	*NL*	*S*	*T*	*UK*
Through immediate superior															
Increased	26	44	24	18	23	29	36	24	22	36	28	39	34	37	31
Same	59	54	73	76	72	64	60	72	58	58	67	58	65	47	66
Decreased	6	0	1	2	3	0	1	1	0	1	2	1	0	2	1
Not used	6	0	1	1	2	1	1	0	0	0	0	0	0	0	0
Direct to senior management															
Increased	29	39	22	12	26	19	25	35	22	38	20	32	27	20	34
Same	55	50	62	62	66	47	60	57	58	49	64	50	65	37	58
Decreased	2	3	4	11	5	5	3	4	0	2	13	10	5	10	2
Not used	12	4	9	9	2	17	7	0	0	3	2	4	2	5	3
Through quality circles															
Increased	23	27	30	13	11	26	13	24	14	13	10	13	17	29	17
Same	16	18	20	18	16	11	18	21	20	10	21	10	21	15	13
Decreased	4	3	1	2	1	2	5	2	3	1	2	3	2	3	2
Not used	49	42	42	53	64	40	55	41	7	51	60	68	53	15	58

than a quarter of organisations informing manual workers about strategy. A very similar picture occurs in terms of financial information, though here the slope indicating the difference in providing information to different groups of employees is not so steep. The financial performance of the organisation thus is made known to employees to a greater extent than this is the case in the area of strategy. In nearly two thirds of the countries 50 per cent or more of the organisations also brief manual workers, being the least informed group within the organisation, about financial performance. Table 11.3 shows the briefing patterns for various employee groups across the European countries analysed in this study in the area of strategy and financial performance.

The other part of organisational communication, upward communication, is being use to feed information from the employees to the management. Again, we can differentiate between various communication channels especially relevant for the question of individualistic or collectivist oriented communication.

Communications via direct access to senior management, the immediate superior or quality circles can be regarded as expression of an individualisation of communication between employees and management, leaving more institutionalised means aside. The use of communication to the immediate superior, in particular, and also direct communication with senior management, has increased. Between 18 per cent (East Germany) and 44 per cent (Switzerland) of the organisations report an increase in using the immediate superior as a means of communicating employees' views to the management. The same trend can be seen in the case of direct communication between employees and senior management, whereas the increase in the area of quality circles is not at the same level. Table 11.4 gives a detailed overview.

Collective communication in Europe

The increases in individual communication might be manifestations of organisations following a pattern seemingly prescribed by concepts of HRM in terms of replacing collective modes of communication and trade unions with more individualised communications. To analyse this at organisational level, we examine various aspects of collective communication.

Communication through representative bodies continues to be a growth area in most European countries. The increase in direct ways of individualised downward communication does not necessarily mean that the use of more collective oriented communication channels

Table 11.5 Percentage of organisations reporting a change in the use of representative staff bodies to communicate major issues to employees during the last 3 years

Country	*B*	*CH*	*D(w)*	*D(e)*	*DK*	*E*	*F*	*FIN*	*I*	*IRL*	*N*	*NL*	*S*	*T*	*UK*
Increased	18	24	22	19	36	20	20	39	19	13	43	27	18	23	12
Same	59	44	66	73	53	58	62	54	58	57	50	58	67	37	45
Decreased	4	4	2	2	2	5	7	4	5	7	2	1	9	2	16
Not used	15	17	8	4	6	7	7	1	0	8	2	8	4	8	17

Table 11.6 Percentage of organisations reporting a change in number of employees communicating their views through more collectivist ways of communication

Country	*B*	*CH*	*D(w)*	*D(e)*	*DK*	*E*	*F*	*FIN*	*I*	*IRL*	*N*	*NL*	*S*	*T*	*UK*
Trade unions/works councils															
Increased	26	10	17	21	25	19	14	14	20	16	35	30	11	14	11
Same	59	43	65	66	60	55	65	57	61	53	59	59	71	41	47
Decreased	6	6	8	5	7	13	17	19	3	11	3	5	16	3	16
Not used	6	29	7	2	6	6	2	5	0	10	1	2	0.5	11	21
Regular workforce meetings															
Increased	33	26	8	4	33	34	30	37	36	32	23	32	42	24	34
Same	40	42	81	72	59	35	44	57	32	37	55	46	54	28	40
Decreased	3	4	4	10	1	4	6	1	3	2	6	5	2	4	3
Not used	18	21	5	9	4	16	16	2	2	15	13	11	1	12	19
Suggestion schemes															
Increased	11	19	33	10	8	12	10	19	7	14	5	10	20	34	19
Same	16	30	38	24	31	17	12	44	19	28	34	27	52	26	23
Decreased	8	19	8	7	8	5	4	19	2	4	7	16	17	1	8
Not used	58	24	18	46	47	47	67	15	9	36	47	40	8	10	42

will decrease. Indeed, the data show that in addition to the growth of direct communication in a downward way, the use of representative bodies has increased too. Between 12 per cent (UK) and 43 per cent (Norway) of the organisations say that there was an increase of this way of communication. A decreasing use of this channel is, with the exception of the UK (16 per cent), indicated by only 9 per cent or less of the organisations. Table 11.5 shows the results for the various countries.

More collectivist ways are also used in upward communication within organisations. The use of trade unions and works councils, regular workforce meetings, and suggestion schemes can be regarded as communication channels that are less individualised and more open or bound to institutionalised actors. Besides the increase in these areas, one also can observe in some countries like the UK or Sweden the decrease in the importance of trade unions/works councils and suggestion schemes is higher than the increase. Similarly, compared with the more individualised communication channels, the increases are clearly smaller (Table 11.6).

In support of the 'up-grading thesis' on joint committees (Terry, 1986; Marchington and Parker, 1990), apart from Italy, Ireland and the UK, our data reveal that every country in Europe has three-quarters or more of its organisations with more than 200 employees having a joint consultative or works committee. Nine out of every ten of these have existed for more then 3 years – except in Italy, Ireland and the UK where about a third of such committees have been established more recently. In other words, the countries which have had fewer such consultative arrangements are rapidly creating them. In all countries, the most common response to a question about changes in the use of such committees is that there has been no change in the last three years. Where there has been a change, the number of organisations increasing their use of consultative bodies for communicating major issues to employees outweighs the number reducing their use in every country except the UK. On average 23 per cent of all organisations across Europe are increasing their use of representative channels of communication and only 8 per cent are decreasing their use.

DISCUSSION

Overall therefore our data point to a new balance between individualised and collective communication which, when viewed against the backdrop of a partially changing, though largely stable, trade union role (as highlighted in Chapter 10), might suggest the need for a modified concept of HRM.

First, in Europe at least the evidence is that both individual and representational communication are growing. The considerable moves that have been made by many employers in Europe to expand the degree of information given to the workforce irrespective of legal requirements is clear. This reflects a central theme of standard concepts of HRM – the requirement to generate significant workforce commitment and to respond to technological advances and globalisation which have prompted the decentralisation of decision-making and compelled changes in employer–employee relationships (Pivec and Robbins, 1996). However it is noticeable that this provision of information to the workforce still includes a substantial number of organisations who are expanding their use of the formalised employee representation or trade union channels.

At the supra-national level it is clear that the European Union is committed to maintaining the role of employers and trade unions. These are referred to, in instructive European Union terminology, as the 'social partners'. On the subject of employee communication/consultation, a large increase has taken place in the use of direct verbal and direct written mechanisms, potentially reflecting the necessity to increase employee commitment in order to achieve organisational success. This increase, however, runs in parallel with the collective channels, thus supporting the argument that the two are not incompatible.

Thirdly in the new century organisations in Europe will still be working with trade unions even as individual communication grows. We need a conception of HRM that can encompass that. There has been substantial criticism of the importation of US theory (Cox and Cooper, 1985; Thurley and Wirdenius, 1991). In the context of HRM specifically, Europeans are increasingly critical of the various versions of the 'closed' HRM models. Looking at the UK, Guest sees 'signs that . . . the American model is losing its appeal as attention focuses to a greater extent on developments in Europe' (Guest, 1990, p. 377) and the same author is elsewhere sceptical of the feasibility of transferring the model to Britain.

The inapplicability of autonomy-based models of HRM in Europe has also been noted in Germany. 'An international comparison of HR practices clearly indicates that the basic functions of HR management are given different weights in different countries and that they are carried out differently' (Gaugler, 1988, p. 26). Another German surveying European personnel management, similarly concluded that:,'a single universal model of HRM does not exist' (Pieper, 1990, p. 11). Critiques of any simplistic attempts to 'universalise' the US models have also come from France (see, e.g. Bournois 1991a, b). European authors have argued that 'we are in culturally different contexts' and, 'Rather than copy solutions which result from other cultural traditions, we should consider the state of mind that presided in the search for responses adapted to the culture' (Albert, 1989, p. 75; translation in Brewster and Bournois, 1991).

A 'European' model of HRM was therefore proposed, and subsequently refined (Brewster and Bournois, 1991; Brewster, 1993, 1995b). This re-emphasised the influence of such factors as culture, ownership structures, the role of the state and trade union organisation. Clearly the European evidence suggests that managements can see the unions, for example, as social partners with a positive role to play in HRM. The manifest success of many European firms which adopt that approach shows that the, explicit or implicit, anti-unionism of approaches to HRM based on a 'US style' conception does not fit the European culture. Significantly, even in the UK, where there has been considerable antagonism between trade unions and 'management' the unions, on their side, are now beginning to look more favourably upon management as a topic. In the last 3 years Cranfield School of Management has set up a Centre of Trade Union Management supported by the Trades Union Congress and some of the largest unions in the country as well as some of the smaller ones. The Centre is working with the senior officials of these organisations to help them think through their own management issues in much the same way that a management school would work with any other organisation. This work is increasingly involving the Scandinavian and other European unions.

We see a danger of accepting too readily the bases of HRM developed in the United States as non- or anti-union in that it sets up industrial relations and HRM as opposing and irreconcilable camps. Such a view puts industrial relations (as trade union studies) onto a narrow and ultimately dead-end path. And as has been indicated, this is far from the reality of practice in most European countries. Indeed an acceptance that influential trade unionism and HRM can go hand in hand is being increasingly reported from Europe (Marchington and Parker, 1990; Sisson, 1993; Storey and Sisson, 1993; Purcell and Ahlstrand, 1994) It is also being proposed, if not found, in the USA (see Kochan *et al.*, 1986).

We have based our arguments in this chapter on Europe, the area we know and where we have evidence of current practice. We have made no attempt to generalise our claims but, going beyond our evidence here and drawing on impressionistic evidence from elsewhere, we believe that the theme of this chapter may have value in many other parts of the world. Outside the USA (and even within it?) the concept of HRM has to be developed to include communication and consultation through collective channels, including trade union channels, if it is to meet the tests of practicality and utility.

References

Adler, N. (1991) *International Dimensions of Organizational Behavior*, 2nd edn, Boston, Mass, Kent.

Aikin, O. and Mill, C. (1994) 'No escape from consultation', *People Management*, 26(10): 54–8.

Albert, F. J. (1989) *Les ressources humaines, atout stratégique*, Editions l'harmattan.

Andresky, J. (1986) 'Just a puppet?: outflanking union organizers with management-sponsored "workers" committees', *Forbes* 137(5): 80–2.

Beaumont, P. B. (1991) 'Trade unions and HRM', *Industrial Relations Journal*, 22(4): 300–8.

Beaumont, P. B. (1992) 'The US human resource management literature: a review', in Salaman, G. (ed.), pp. 20–37.

Beaumont, P. B. and Harris, R. (1989) 'The North–South divide in Britain: the case of trade union recognition', *Oxford Bulletin of Economics & Statistics* 51.

Beer, M., Lawrence, P. R., Mills, Q. N. and Walton, R. E. (1985) *Human Resource Management*, New York, Free Press.

Blau, J. and Alba, R. (1982) 'Empowering nets of participation', *Administrative Science Quarterly*, 27: 363–79.

Blyton, P. and Turnbull, P. (1993) *Dynamics of Employee Relations*, London, Macmillan.

Bournois, F. (1991a) 'Gestion des RH en Europe: données comparées', *Revue Française de Gestion*, 3,4,5: 68–83.

Bournois, F. (1991b) 'Gestion stratégique des ressources humaines: comparaisons internationales', *Actes du collogue de l'Association Française de gestion des ressources humaines*, Cergy.

Bowen, D. and Lawler, E. (1992) 'The empowerment of service workers: what, why, how and when?', *Sloan Management Review*, 33: 31–9.

Boxall, P. F. (1992) 'Strategic human resource management: beginnings of a new theoretical sophistication?', *Human Resource Management Journal*, 2,3: 60–79.

Brewster, C. (1993) 'Developing a "European" model of human resource management', *International Journal of Human Resource Management*, 4(4): 765–84.

Brewster, C. (1994) 'HRM: the European dimension', in Storey, J. (ed.), pp. 309–31.

Brewster, C. (1995a) 'Industrial relations and human resource management', *Industrielle Beziehungen* 2(4): 395–413.

Brewster, C. (1995b) 'Towards a European model of human resource management', *Journal of International Business Studies*, 26(1): 1–21.

Brewster, C. (1999) 'Different paradigms in strategic HRM: questions raised by comparative research' in Wright, P. *et al.*, pp. 213–38.

Brewster, C. and Bournois, F. (1991) 'A European perspective on human resource management', *Personnel Review*, 20(6): 4–13.

Brewster, C. and Hegewisch, A. (1994) *Policy and Practice in European Human Resource Management*, London, Routledge.

Brewster, C., Gunnigle, P. and Morley, M. (1994a) 'Continuity and change in European industrial relations: evidence from a 14 country survey', *Personnel Review*, 23(3): 4–20.

Brewster, C., Hegewisch, A., Mayne, L. and Tregaskis, O. (1994b) 'Employee communication and participation', in Brewster, C. and Hegewisch, A. (eds), pp. 154–67.

Briscoe, D. R. (1995) *International Human Resource Management*, Englewood Cliffs, NJ, Prentice Hall.

Conrad, P. and Pieper, R. (1990) 'HRM in the Federal Republic of Germany', in Pieper, R. (ed.), pp. 109–39.

Cox, C. and Cooper, G. (1985) 'The irrelevance of American organisational sciences to the UK and Europe', *Journal of General Management*, 11(2): 27–34.

Davis, T. (1997) 'Open-book management: its promise and pitfalls', *Organizational Dynamics*, 25(3): 6–21.

Dowling, P. J., Schuler, R. S. and Welch, D. E. (1994) *International Dimensions of Human Resource Management*, Belmont, Cal., Wadsworth.

EFILWC (Gold, M. and Hall, M.) (1990) *Legal Regulation and the Practice of Employee Participation in the European Community*, Dublin, European Foundation for the Improvement of Living and Working Conditions working paper EF/WP/90/41/EN.

Fiorito, J., Lowman, C. and Nelson, F. (1987) 'The impact of human resource policies on union organising', *Industrial Relations*, 26.

Fischer, S. and Weitbrecht, H. (1995) 'Individualism and collectivism: two dimensions of human resource', *Industrielle Beziehungen* 2(4): 367–94.

Gaugler, E. (1988) 'HR management: an international comparison', *Personnel:* 24–30.

Gonring, P. (1991) 'Communication makes employee involvement work', *Public Relations Journal*, 47(11): 40–3.

Goss, D. (1994) *Principles of Human Resource Management*, London, Routledge.

Guest, D. (1987) 'Human resource management and industrial relations', *Journal of Management Studies* 24(5): 503–21.

Guest, D. (1990) 'Human resource management and the American dream', *Journal of Management Studies* 27(4): 377–97.

Guest, D. (1992) 'Right enough to be dangerously wrong: an analysis of the In Search of Excellence', in Salaman, G. (ed.), pp. 5–19.

Hage, A. (1996) 'Trade union identity and workplace representation: do works councils make a difference?: some problems of cross-national comparisons in workplace industrial relations, unpublished mimeo', *Industrial Relations Research Unit*, Coventry, University of Warwick.

Jublin, F., Putnam, L. and Roberts, K. (eds) (1989) *Handbook of Organisational Communication: An Interdisciplinary Perspective*, Calif., Sage.

Kanter, R. M. (1989) 'The new managerial work', *Harvard Business Review*, 66: 85–92.

Keane, P. (1996) 'Two-way communication fosters greater committment', *HRMagazine*, 41(10): 50–3.

Kochan, T. A. and Dyer, L. (1992) 'Managing Transformational Change: The Role of Human Resource Professionals', Sloan working paper 3420–92–BPS, MIT, Mass.

Kochan, T. A., Katz, H. C. and McKersie, R. B. (1986) *The Transformation of American Industrial Relations*, New York, Basic Books.

Kochan, T. A., McKersie, R. B. and Capelli, P. (1984) 'Strategic choice and industrial relations theory', *Industrial Relations*, 23: 16–39.

Lansbury, R. (1995) 'Workplace Europe: new forms of bargaining & participation', *Technology, Work & Employment*, 10(1): 47–55.

Locke, R., Kochan, T. and Piore, M. (1995) 'Reconceptualizing comparative industrial relations: lessons from international research', *International Labour Review*, 134(2): 139–63.

Luhmann, N. (1987) *Soziale Systeme*, Frankfurt, Suhrkamp.

Luthans, F. (1992) *Organizational Behaviour*, New York, McGraw-Hill.

Mahoney, T. and Deckop, J. R. (1986) 'Evolution of concept and practice in personnel administration/human resource management', *Journal of Management*, 12(2): 223–41.

Marchington, M., Goodman, J. Wilkinson, A. and Ackers, P. (1992) 'New developments in employee involvement', *Research Series 2.*, Sheffield, Employment Department.

Marchington, M. and Parker, P. (1990) *Changing Patterns of Employee Relations*, London, Harvester Wheatsheaf.

Marginson P and Sisson, K. (1998) 'European collective bargaining: a virtual prospect?', *Journal of Common Market Studies*, 36(4): 505–28

Mintzberg, H. (1975) 'The managers' job: folklore and fact', *Harvard Business Review*, 7,8: 49–61.

Monks, J. (1994) 'The trade union response to HRM: fraud or opportunity?', *Personnel Management*, 9: 42–7.

Morley, M., C. Brewster, P. Gunnigle and W. Mayrhofer (1996) 'Evaluating change in European industrial relations: research evidence on trends at organisational level', *International Journal of Human Resource Management*, 7(3): 640–57.

Naudin, T. (1997) 'Why Renault's rationalisation should not be a fait accompli: Renault undermines European works councils with planned closure of automobile plant in Belgium', *The European*, 10: 18.

Pieper, R. (ed.) (1990) *Human Resource Management: An International Comparison*, Berlin, Walter de Gruyter.

Pivec, M. and Robbins, H. (1996) 'Employee involvement remains controversial', *HRM Magazine*, 41(11): 145–6.

Purcell, J. and Ahlstrand, B. (1994) *Human Resource Management in the Multi-Divisional Firm*, Oxford, OUP.

Ramsay, H. (1997), 'Fool's gold?: European works councils and workplace democracy', *Industrial Relations Journal*, 28(4): 314–24.

Redmond, M., Mumford,M. and Teach, R. (1993) 'Putting creativity to work: effects of leader behaviour on subordinate creativity', *Organizational Behaviour and Human Decision Processes*, 55: 120–51.

Roche, W. and Turner, T. (1994) 'Testing alternative models of human resource policy effects on trade union recognition in the Republic of Ireland', *International Journal of Human Resource Management*, 5(3): 721–55.

Salaman, G. (ed.) (1991) *Human Resource Strategies*, Buckingham, The Open University.

Sisson, K. (1993) 'In search of HRM', *British Journal of Industrial Relations* 31(2).

Sisson, K. (1997) 'New forms of work organisation: can Europe realise its potential?', Results of a survey of direct employee participation in Europe, Dublin, European Foundation for the Improvement of Living and Working Conditions.

Smyth, J. (1995) 'Harvesting the office grapevine: internal communication', *People Management*, 1(18): 24–8.

Spreitzer, G. (1995) 'Psychological empowerment in the workplace: dimensions, measurement and validation', *Academy of Management Journal* 38(5): 1442–66.

Stoop, S. (1994) *The European Works Council: One Step Forward*, ed FNV Centrum Ondernemingsraden.

Storey, J. (1992) *Developments in the Management of Human Resources*, Oxford, Blackwell.

Storey, J. (ed.) (1994) *Human Resource Management: A Critical Text*, London, Routledge.

Storey, J. and Sisson, K. (1993) *Managing Human Resources & Industrial Relations*, Buckingham, Open University Press.

Streek, W. (1987) 'The uncertainties of management in the management of uncertainty', *Work, Employment and Society*, 1(3).

Teague, P. (1993) 'Between convergence and divergence: possibilities for a European community system of labour market regulation', *International Labour Review*, 132(3): 391–406.

Terry, M. (1986) 'How do we know if shop stewards are getting weaker?', *British Journal of Industrial Relations*, 24(2): 169–80.

Thurley, K. and Wirdenius, H. (1991) 'Will management become "European?": strategic choices for organisations', *European Management Journal*, 9(2): 127–34.

TUC (1995) *A Trade Unionist's Guide to European Works Councils*, London, TUC.

Vernon, A. (1996) 'Opening the floor for fruitful debate: consultation with employee representatives in collective redundancies and business transfers', *People Management*, 2(13/6): 40–2.

Weick, K. E. (1989) 'Theorizing about organizational communication', in Jablin, F., Putnam, L. and Roberts, K. (eds), pp. 97–122.

Weston, S. and Martinez-Lucio, M. (1997) 'Trade Unions, management and European works councils: Opening Pandora's box?', *The International Journal of Human Resource Management*, 8(6): 764–79.

Wright, P., Dyer, L., Boudreau, J. and Milkovich, G. (eds) (1999) *Research in Personnel and HRM*, Greenwich, Conn.

Part V

Human Resource Management in Central Europe and the Pacific Rim

12 Human Resource Policies in European Organisations: An Analysis of Country and Company-specific Antecedents

Wolfgang Weber, Rüdiger Kabst and Christopher Gramley

The aim of this contribution is the analysis of HR policies in European organisations. It will pursue the question of whether organisation-specific variables have a major influence on the formulation of HR policies or whether country-specific circumstances bear more responsibility.

A first step in this direction will outline the convergence–divergence discussion, which mainly takes place with the European integration in mind. The conceptual framework of Brewster and Bournois (1991) and Brewster and Hegewisch (1994) provide the basis for the analysis of HR policies in the European context. The explanatory value of country-and company-specific antecedents will be empirically tested by utilising the data from *Cranet-E.*

CONVERGENCE VERSUS DIVERGENCE OF HRM

The increasing tendency towards a global marketplace makes researchers as well as practitioners wonder whether identical company practices will result from this. Adler (1997: 60) asks in this line of thought: 'Are organisations becoming more similar worldwide or are they maintaining their cultural dissimilarities? Is the world gradually creating one way of doing business or is the world maintaining a set of distinct markets defined by equally distinct national boundaries, each with its own culturally distinct approach to business?'. Reviewing the extensive literature devoted to the convergence–divergence discussion (cf. e.g. Schreyögg *et al.*, 1995, pp. 40–1), the question raised seems more than justified, and a common understanding far from attained.

The proponents of the convergence thesis maintain that efficient management approaches are universally accepted. Thus technological and systematic conditions determine the efficiency of the application of management systems (Neghandi, 1979; Kerr, 1983). Kidger (1991, p. 153) assumes 'that differences that might arise from differing beliefs and value orientations of national context are superseded by the logic of technology'. According to this line of argument only antecedents that are specific to the organisation explain the existence of HR policies, while country-specific influences can be neglected.

The advocates of the divergence thesis argue that the national and, in particular, the cultural and institutional frame of reference strongly influence behavior. Thus the universal application of management practices in whatever form must be ruled out (Laurent, 1983; Adler and Jelinek, 1986). As a result country-specific features should be of major explanatory value for the existence of HR policies, whereas antecedents specific to organisations would be of minor significance.

Even this short sketch shows how insufficient a polarised discussion is when it takes place between two extreme positions. It is not astonishing that there is an ever growing number of contributions relative to the convergence–divergence discussion (Child, 1981; Due *et al.*, 1991; Jensen *et al.*, 1995; Sparrow *et al.*, 1994; Walsh, 1995; Adler, 1997). And yet, to date this intensive discussion has not been able to establish a generally accepted explanatory pattern. Certainly, the divergence thesis is not well suited to explaining the emergence of certain transnational management practices, such as, for example, decentralisation (Schreyögg *et al.*, 1995, p. 41). In spite of the continued existence of national differences, Kabst *et al.* (1996, p. 634) discern a uniform influence of the lean-management concept on in-company training in European organisations. Grahl and Teague (1991, p. 67) doubt the validity of the divergence thesis determines the industrial relations agenda across Europe despite the differences in national systems. On the other hand, the integrative shift that has accompanied the European Union does not necessarily lead to convergence. Baldry (1994, p. 67) notes that a unified transnational influence or European legislation does not necessarily induce convergence, as different national contexts can lead to diverging interpretations in organisations. Wunderer (1984,

p. 506) observes that labour – as a factor of production – needs a more specific orientation towards values, traditions, behavioral patterns, and culture than other factors. Consequently it is subject to globalization to a lesser extent. When investigating Japanese, Swiss, and American conglomerates, Hilb (1985) found a great number of universally applied management practices. On the other hand, he also came across management practices that were not transferable. Child (1981) analysed the literature on international comparative management practices and found that work analysing the macro level (e.g. the organisational structure) tended to support the convergence thesis, while the studies analysing the micro level (in particular the behaviour of members of organisation) tended towards the divergence thesis (cf. e.g. Weber *et al.*, 1998). Referring to Child's analysis, Adler (1997, p. 60) concludes that 'organisations worldwide are growing more similar, while the behavior of people within organisations is maintaining its cultural uniqueness'. De Cieri (1996, pp. 159–60) notes in this line of thought: 'Convergence would be expected to facilitate international transferability of management style and practice, and MNEs are justifiably viewed as a considerable force for convergence. The amount and pace of convergence will, however, vary according to the relative power of the opposing forces for divergence. Micro-level factors, such as beliefs, norms, culture, and values, are often cited as forces for divergence. . . . There is also evidence to suggest there are both converging and diverging macro-level factors.'

Following the convergence–divergence discussion this chapter will shed some light on the determinants of HR policies, asking whether country-specific antecedents dominate HR policies or whether unified HR patterns can be discerned.

THE CONCEPTUAL FRAMEWORK FOR THE ANALYSIS OF HR POLICIES IN THE EUROPEAN CONTEXT

In order to be able to contribute to the explanatory value of country- versus organisation-specific antecedents, the determining factors of HR policies cited in the literature have to be identified in a first step. On the basis of this, a conceptual framework for the analysis will be outlined. A great number of researchers have set themselves the goal of identifying key variables for the analysis of HR policies or strategies (cf. e.g. Fombrun 1982; Tichy *et al.*, 1982; Ackermann and Wührer, 1984; Dyer, 1984; Schuler and Jackson, 1987; Boxall, 1992; Elšik 1992;

Schuler, 1992; Brewster, 1993; Brewster, 1994; Hendry, 1994; Sisson and Timperley, 1994). These contributions primarily differ in the relative weight attributed to endogenous and exogenous factors. While, for example, Hendry (1994, p. 114) stresses the importance of the exogenous dimensions (the socio-cultural and legal context, and political and economic risks), Schuler and Jackson (1987) and Ackermann and Wührer (1984) emphasise the influence of endogenous factors (e.g. corporate strategy). Brewster (1993, 1994) can be counted among those researchers who give almost equal importance to endogenous and exogenous factors. From the great range of factors cited, national context, organisational structure, and corporate strategy can be isolated as of particular importance in most concepts. Thus Wunderer (1992, pp. 3–4, 19–20) has developed a concept which supports firm-specific decision-making. It is based on the six dimensions he found to influence the underlying strategic orientation of international HRM: (1) the industrial sector involved, the product programme, and market strategy; (2) culture-specific values, the legal framework, economic and social setting, and corporate culture; (3) company structure and size; (4) management goals, views, and attitudes; (5) the orientation of the employees; and (6) the extent of the company's international orientation. Schuler *et al.* (1993, p. 423) present an integrative concept for international HRM, which analyses the complexity of the interaction between endogenous (e.g. country-specific factors) and exogenous (e.g. the organisational structure and strategy) factors. Devanna *et al.* (1984, p. 35) develop a taxonomy of: 'environmental pressures, organisational strategies and matching HR practices'. Schreyögg *et al.* (1995, pp. 17–18) present a concept for the analysis of HRM in the European context that explains complexity in an input–output model. The HRM function is subdivided into four interdependent functions: recruitment and selection, training and development, compensation, and integration, all of whose manifestations may differ according to country and company.

The basis for the present investigation is the conceptual framework for the analysis of HRM developed by Brewster and Bournois (1991) and Brewster and Hegewisch (1994, p. 6). It not only integrates the above mentioned endogenous and exogenous factors and their influence on HR policies and thus on HR practices but, the approach is also adapted to the specific European context, like the input-output model (Schreyögg *et al.*, 1995). The respective national culture, sector, size, structure, and corporate culture, and the corporate and HR strategy influence the conduct and success of HR practices.

Brewster and Hegewisch (1994, p. 6) comment on their conceptual frame for the analysis of European HR policy as follows: 'The model shows that business strategy, HR strategy and HR practice are located within the external environment of national context, power systems, legislation, education, employee representation and other issues. The model places HRM within the national context. By allowing for a greater input into HRM from the environment in which the organisation is located this approach enables to link HRM more clearly with international contextual variations.'

Based on the conceptual framework developed by Brewster and Bournois (1991) and Brewster and Hegewisch (1994), the analysis will contrast the influence of the *national context*, on the one hand, and of the organisation-specific factors of *sector*, organisational size (*number of employees*), and *corporate strategy*, on the other.

The dependent variable is not merely the existence of an HR policy; it has been further differentiated into several HR functions: pay and benefits, training and development, recruitment and selection, employee communication, equal opportunity/diversity, management principles, and 'high-fliers'. The examination of these HR functions allows a differentiated insight into the question as to which HR functions are primarily influenced by national context or organisational

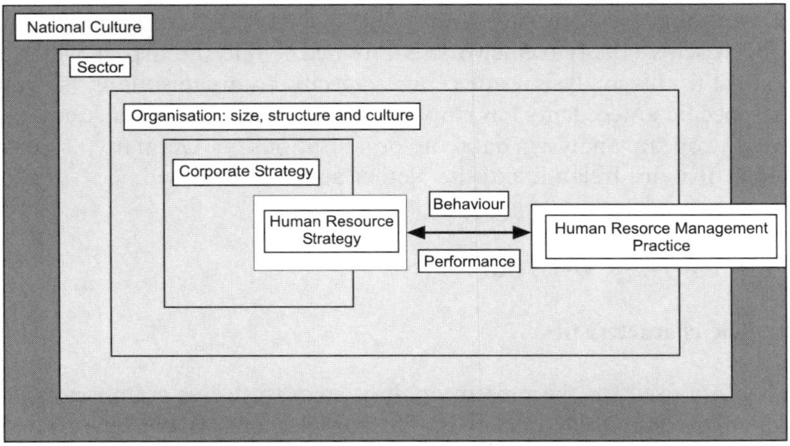

Figure 12.1 Conceptual frame for the analysis of HR policies in the European context
Source: Brewster and Bournois (1991): 6.

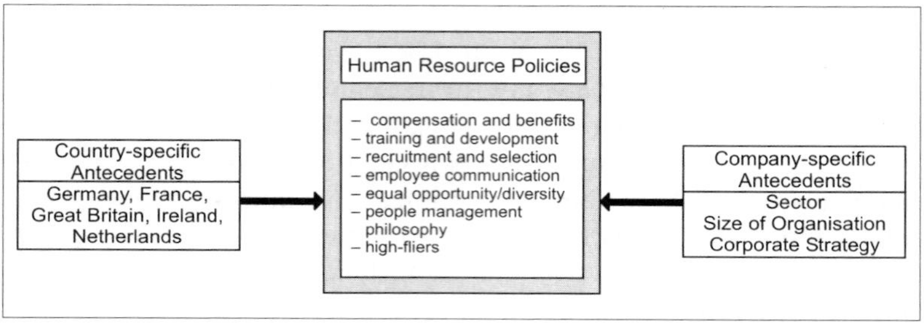

Figure 12.2 Conceptual framework for the analysis of country-and organisation-specific influences on HR policies in the European context

factors. Schreyögg *et al.* (1995, p. 21–2) confirm the exigency of a differentiated analysis of HR functions: 'If one looks at HRM from a functional point of view, there is not much difference between companies and countries. Obviously, all firms in developed industrial countries recruit, develop, organise, deploy, try to influence, assess, and discharge employees. However, there will be some differences in the relative importance of a particular function, contingent upon business traditions, legislation, the educational system, and the labour market.... Since the personnel function is highly contextual, shifts in the external environment will complicate and affect the function.' For the present analysis Brewster and Bournois' (1991) and Brewster and Hegewisch's (1994) framework is retained, while the aspect which is central to this analysis – antecedents specific to organisations vs country-specific antecedents – is emphasized. In order to allow a comparative European analysis, data on organisations in Germany, France, Great Britain, Ireland, and the Netherlands are analysed.

EMPIRICAL ANALYSIS

Sample characteristics

The data used for the present analysis stem from five countries, all of which participate in Cranet-E. The sample consists of organisations from Germany (D), France (F), and Great Britain (GB) as representatives of the larger European countries. The Netherlands (NL) and Ireland (IRL) represent the smaller European nations. The data is from

the explanatory value of the service sector has to be interpreted with much care.
It can be said that there are no significant country-specific differences in the formulation of policies on training and development.

Table 12.5 Influencing factors of HR policies for recruitment and selection

Variables	*Direction*	*Chi-square improvement*	*Significance*
Company-specific antecedents			
corporate strategy	+	58.8	0.0000***
number of employees	+	21.5	0.0000***
service sector	+	ns	0.1230
public sector	+	15.6	0.0007***
Country-specific antecedents			
France	+	ns	0.1206
GB	+	51.6	0.0000***
Ireland	+	5.4	0.0218*
Netherlands	+	26.4	0.0000***
Model chi-square	179.772		
p-value	0.0000		
n	2750		
Proportion of correct classifications	87.75%		

* $p < 0.05$; ** $p < 0.01$; *** $p < 0.001$ (two-tailed).

Not only do corporate strategy and the company size exercise a significant influence on the existence of a policy on recruitment and selection, Great Britain, the Netherlands, and Ireland all have significantly higher probabilities of explicitly formulating such a policy. When the economic sectors are taken into consideration, there is a

Table 12.6 Influencing factors of HR policies for employee communication

Variables	*Direction*	*Chi-square improvement*	*Significance*
Company-specific antecedents			
corporate strategy	+	96.6	0.0000***
number of employees	+	7.8	0.0028**
service sector	+	ns	0.2682
public sector	–	7.2	0.0067**

Table 12.6 (Cont.)

Variables	*Direction*	*Chi-square improvement*	*Significance*
Country-specific antecedents			
France	+	ns	0.4206
GB	+	14.4	0.0000***
Ireland	+	11.3	0.0000***
Netherlands	+	9.1	0.0004***
Model chi-square	146.274		
p-value	0.0000		
n	2718		
Proportion of correct classifications	73.51		

* $p < 0.05$; ** $p < 0.01$; *** $p < 0.001$ (two-tailed).

higher probability of the public, as compared top the industrial sector, having a policy on recruitment and selection.

The existence of an employee communication policy is most strongly influenced by corporate strategy. The company size is another variable with a significant, though much lower degree of influence. Public sector organisations have a lower probability of formulating employee communication policies.

Table 12.7 Influencing factors of HR policies for equal opportunity/diversity

Variables	*Direction*	*Chi-square improvement*	*Significance*
Company-specific antecedents			
corporate strategy	+	56.6	0.0000***
number of employees	+	55.7	0.0000***
service sector	+	ns	0.5122
public sector	+	44.2	0.0000***
Country-specific antecedents			
France	+	ns	0.6913
GB	+	576.0	0.0000***
Ireland	+	93.6	0.0000***
Netherlands	+	122.3	0.0000***
Model chi-square	948.733		
p-value	0.0000		
n	2688		
Proportion of correct classifications	80.13%		

* $p < 0.05$; ** $p < 0.01$; *** $p < 0.001$ (two-tailed).

In Great Britain, Ireland, and the Netherlands the probability of the existence of such a policy is slightly higher than in Germany.

Compared to Germany, the probability for an explicit policy on equal opportunities is significantly higher in Great Britain, the Netherlands, and Ireland. In the latter two, however, with a lower explanatory value. National context seems to have a considerable influence on the question of equal opportunity/diversity.

Both the corporate strategy and the company size are of significant influence on the existence of such a policy. Compared to the country-specific differences, however, these effects are much less influential.

Public sector institutions are more likely to formulate equal opportunity policies than companies from the industrial sector.

Table 12.8 Influencing factors of HR policies for people management philosophy

Variables	*Direction*	*Chi-square improvement*	*Significance*
Company-specific antecedents			
corporate strategy	+	122.6	0.0000***
number of employees	+	32.1	0.0000***
service sector	+	ns	0.2543
public sector	–	12.8	0.0001***
Country-specific antecedents			
France	–	13.3	0.0000***
GB	–	46.8	0.0000***
Ireland	–	11.0	0.0009***
Netherlands	+	ns	0.2267
Model chi-square	238.600		
p-value	0.0000		
n	2688		
Proportion of correct classifications	69.46%		

* $p < 0.05$; ** $p < 0.01$; *** $p < 0.001$ (two-tailed).

The main factor contributing to the presence of a policy on people management philosophy is corporate strategy. The number of employees has a small positive effect; activity in the public sector a low negative influence on the probability of the existence of such a policy. The implication is that the public sector companies have fewer people management philosophies than organisations in the industrial sector.

Country-specific differences cannot be neglected. Especially British, but also French and Irish organisations, have significantly fewer people management philosophies than German ones.

Table 12.9 Influencing factors of HR policies for high-fliers

Variables	*Direction*	*Chi-square improvement*	*Significance*
ompany-specific antecedents			
corporate strategy	+	39.9	0.0000***
number of employees	+	98.9	0.0000***
service sector	–	33.6	0.0000***
public sector	–	119.3	0.0000***
Country-specific antecedents			
France	+	ns	0.6802
GB	–	49.3	0.0000***
Ireland	–	7.1	0.0011**
Netherlands	–	7.5	0.0063**
Model chi-square	355.554		
p-value	0.0000		
n	2635		
Proportion of correct classifications	67.21%		

* $p < 0.05$; ** $p < 0.01$; *** $p < 0.001$ (two-tailed).

Public sector institutions have a greatly weaker probability of formulating a policy on high fliers; and service sector companies a somewhat weaker one. The presence of such a policy increases proportionately in organisations as the number of employees rises, and it correlates well with the presence of a corporate strategy. The national context is important not only in Great Britain, but also the Netherlands and Ireland have a significantly lower probability of a policy on high fliers as compared to Germany, the reference category.

DISCUSSION

The question of whether company-specific variables exercise a unified influence on the European companies surveyed, or whether general country-specific conditions lead to a divergence in the formulation of HR policies, cannot be given a universal answer. Each of the HR policies considered has its own pattern of significant antecedents with diverging explanatory value. Statements can only be made with reference to the individual HR areas.

Table 12.10 Direction and explanatory value (chi-square improvement) of the significant correlation between organisation-and country-specific antecedents and HR policies.

	Pay and benefits	*Training and development*	*Recruitment and selection*	*Employee communication*	*Equal opportunity/ diversity*	*People management philosophy*	*High-fliers*
corporate strategy	+80.5	+83.4	+58.8	+96.6	+56.6	+122.6	+39.9
number of employees	+12.5	+35.8	+21.5	+7.8	+55.7	+32.1	+98.9
service sector	ns	−3.8	ns	ns	ns	ns	−33.6
public sector	−4.7	+10.1	+15.6	−7.2	+44.2	−12.8	−119.3
France	+10.3	ns	ns	ns	ns	−13.3	ns
GB	ns	ns	+51.6	+14.4	+576.0	−46.8	−49.3
Ireland	+4.1	ns	+5.4	+11.3	+93.6	−11.0	−7.1
Netherlands	+12.4	ns	+26.8	+9.1	+122.3	ns	−7.5

Corporate strategy has a positive influence on the existence of HR policies. It is the main explanatory factor with the exception of policies on equal opportunities and high-fliers. Company size is another independent variable which exercises a positive influence on all of the HR policies. Compared to the industrial sector, participation in the service sector has a negative influence on the presence of policies on training and development and high-fliers, the only HR policies about which significant statements can be made. While the public sector diverges from the industrial sector over the whole range of HR policies, the direction of divergence and the explanatory value differ considerably from policy to policy. The public sector has a significantly negative value in regard to the formulation of policies on high fliers.

National context does not possess any significant explanatory value for the formulation of policies for training and development. Concerning the formulation of policies on pay and benefits, recruitment and selection, employee communication, and in particular, equal opportunity/diversity, the results show that outside of Germany there is a higher probability of the presence of such HR policies. For policies on people management philosophy and high fliers, on the other hand, country-specific differences lead to lower probabilities for the existence of these policies outside of Germany. In the question of equal opportunity/diversity Great Britain stands out with its above average relevance. In British companies, as is true in Dutch and Irish organisations, there is a much higher probability of the formulation of equal opportunity policies.

In summary, it can be said that corporate strategy and size of organisation (number of employees) in particular, have a significantly positive influence on all HR policies. Corporate strategy can be interpreted as the main explanatory variable if equal opportunities/diversity and high fliers are disregarded. Divergence between the economic sectors exists above all between the industrial sector and the public sector, with the latter diverging in both directions. Country-specific influences do not appear in HR training and development, whereas for the other HR policies a significant, however, in most cases comparably lower improvement in the explanatory value can be seen. Country-specific variables clearly outweigh company-specific variables only in the area of equal opportunity policy. It is not surprising that country-specific difference are of special importance in the question of equal opportunities, as national culture and legislation strongly influence this HR function.

Figure 12.4 is an attempt to systematise the HR policies according to the dominant antecedents (country vs. company-specific) measured by the explanatory value. A classification outside of the intersection does

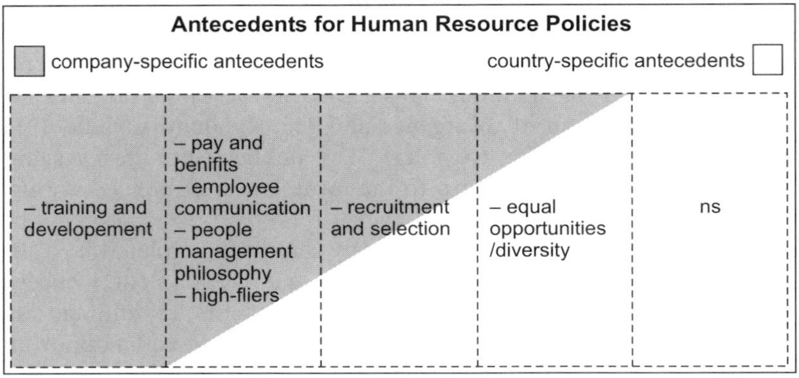

Figure 12.4 Classification of the HR policies according to the dominant antecedents

not mean that other influences can be excluded, but that these other (above considered) influences are of minor significance for the explanation of the dependent variable.

CONCLUSION

The major insight of this contribution is that in the European context HR policies cannot be explained by polarising the discusion and by focussing exclusively on organisation-specific or country-specific antecedents. Results also show that organisation-specific antecedents exercise the dominant influence. This holds true especially for training and development and to a lesser extent also for pay and benefits, employee communication, people management philosophy, and high fliers. Policies on recruitment and selection are decisively influenced by antecedents from both categories. The very high explanatory value of national context for the existence of policies on equal opportunity/diversity is not surprising.

Following Child (1981), De Cieri (1996) and Adler (1997) these results confirm the thesis that organisations have a tendency toward convergence, while the differences in the behaviour of the organisation members continue to exist. Whereas the socio-cultural influences shape the question of equal opportunities and its effect on the behaviour of the organisation members, the other HRM areas reveal much more unified practices.

An interpretation of the convergence–divergence paradigm as a continuum seems appropriate, taking into account that the various HRM areas need to be considered in a differentiated fashion.

References

Ackermann, K. F. and Wührer, G. (1984) *Personalstrategien in deutschen Groaunternehmen – Ergebnisse einer empirischen Untersuchung*, Stuttgart.

Adler, N. J. (1997) *International Dimensions of Organizational Behavior*, 3rd edn, Cincinnati.

Adler, N. J. and Jelinek, M. (1986) 'Is "Organisation Culture" Culture Bound', *Human Resource Management*, 25: 73–90.

Backhaus, K., Erichson, B., Plinke, W. and Weiber, R. (1996) *Multivariate Analysemethoden: Eine anwendungsorientierte Einführung*, 8th edn, Berlin, New York.

Baldry, C. (1994) 'Convergence in Europe – a matter of perspective?', *Industrial Relations Journal*, 25(2): 96–109.

Bortz, J. (1993) *Statistik für Sozialwissenschaftler*, 4th edn, Berlin, New York.

Boxall, P. F. (1992) 'Strategic human resource management: beginnings of a New theoretical sophication?', *Human Resource Management Journal*, 2(3): 60–79.

Brewster, C. (1993) 'Developing a "European" model of human resource management', *The International Journal of Human Resource Management*, 4(4): 765–84.

Brewster, C. (1994) 'The integration of human resource management and corporate strategy', in Brewster, C. and Hegewisch, A. (eds), pp. 22–35.

Brewster, C. and Bournois, F. (1991) 'A European perspective on human resource management', *Personnel Review*, 20(6): 4–13.

Brewster, C. and Hegewisch, A. (1994) 'Human resource management in Europe: issues and opportunities', in Brewster, C. and Hegewisch, A. (eds.), pp. 1–21.

Brewster, C. and Tyson, S. (eds) (1991) *International Comparison in Human Resource Management*, London.

Bühl, A. and Zöfel, P. (1994) *SPSS für Windows Version 6: Praxisorientierte Einführung in die moderne Datenanalyse*. Bonn et al.

Child, J. (1981) 'Culture, contingency and capitalism in the cross-national study of organizations', in Cummings, L. L. and Staw, B. M. (eds), pp. 303–56.

Coenenberg, A. G., Funk, J. and Djarrahzadeh, M. (eds) (1992) *Internationalisierung als Herausforderung für des Personalmanagement, Stuttgart.*

Cummings, L. L. and Staw, B. M. (eds) *Research in Organizational Behavior*. Vol. 3, Greenwich.

De Cieri, H. (1996) *The Social Dimension of the European Union: Implications for Strategic International Human Resource Management in Australian Multinational Enterprises*. Dissertation, University of Tasmania (Australia).

Devanna, M. A., Fombrun, C. J. and Tichy, N. M. (1984) 'A framework for strategic human resource management', in Fombrun, C. J. *et al.*, pp. 33–51.

Due, J., Madsen, J. S. and Jensen, C. S. (1991) 'The social dimension: convergence or diversification of IR in the single European market?', *Industrial Relations Journal*, 22(2): 85–102.

Dyer, L. (1984) 'Studying human resource strategy: an approach and an agenda', *Industrial Relations* 23(2): 156–69.

Eckstein, P. P. (1997) *Angewandte Statistik mit SPSS: Praktische Einführung für Wirtschaftswissenschaftler*, Wiesbaden.

Elšik, W. (1992) *Strategisches Personalmanagement: Konzeptionen und Konsequenzen*, München, Mering.

Fombrun, C. J. (1982) 'Environmental trends create new pressures on human resources', *Journal of Business Strategy*, 3(1): 61–9.

Fombrun, C. J., Tichy, N. M. and Devanna, M. A. (eds) (1984) *Strategic Human Resource Management*, New York.

Grahl, J. and Teague, P. (1991) 'Industrial relations trajectories and European human resource management', in Brewster, C. and Tyson, S. (eds), pp. 67–91.

Hanel, U. (1996) *Ergebnisbericht 1995: The Cranfield Network on European Human Resource Management* Technische Universität Dresden, Lehrstuhl für Betriebswirtschaftslehre, insbes, Personalwirtschaft, Dresden.

Hendry, C. (1994) *Human Resource Strategies for International Growth*, London, New York.

Hilb, M. (1985) *Personalpolitik für Multinationale Unternehmen*, Zürich.

Jensen, C. S., Madsen, J. S. and Due, J. (1995) 'A role for a pan-European trade union movement?: possibilities in European irregulation', *Industrial Relations Journal*, 26(1): 4–18.

Kabst, R., Larsen, H. H. and Bramming, P. (1996) 'How do lean management organizations behave regarding training and development?', *The International Journal of Human Resource Management*, 7(3): 618–39.

Kerr, C. (1983) *The Future of Industrial Societies – Convergence or Continuing Diversity?*, Cambridge.

Kidger, P. (1991) 'The emergence of international human resource management', *International Journal of Human Resource Management*, 2(2): 149–63.

Lammers, C. J. and Aickson, D. J. (eds) (1979) *Organisations Alike and Unlike*, London.

Laurent, A. (1983) 'The cultural diversity of Western concepts of management', *International Studies of Management and Organisation*, 13: 73–96.

Neghandi, A. (1979) 'Convergence in organisational Practices: an empirical study of industrial enterprises in developing countries', Lammers, C. J. and Hickson, D. J. (eds), pp. 323–45.

Schreyögg, G., Oechsler, W. A. and Wächter, H. (1995) *Managing in a European Context: Human Resources, Corporate Culture: Industrial Relations*, Wiesbaden.

Schuler, R. S. and Jackson, S. E. (1987) 'Linking competitive strategies with human resource management practices', *Academy of Management Executive*, 1(3): 209–13.

Schuler, R. S., Dowling, P. J. and De Cieri, H. (1993) 'An integrative framework of strategic international human resource management', *Journal of Management*, 19(2): 419–59.

Schuler, R. S. (1992) 'Strategic human resource management: linking the people with the strategic needs of the business', *Organisational Dynamics*, summer: 18–32.

Sisson, K. (ed.) (1994) *Personnel Management: A Comprehensive Guide to Theory and Practice in Britain*, 2nd edn, Oxford.

Sisson, K. and Timperley, S. (1994) 'From manpower planning to strategic human resource management?', in Sisson, K. (ed.), pp. 153–84.

Sparrow, P., Schuler, R. S. and Jackson, S. E. (1994) 'Convergence or divergence: human resource practices and policies for competitive advantage worldwide', *The International Journal of Human Resource Management*, 5(2): 267–99.

Tichy, N. M., Fombrun, C. J. and Devanna, M. A. (1982) 'Strategic human resource management', *Sloan Management Review*, 23(2): 47–60.

Walsh, J. (1995) 'Convergence or divergence?: Corporatism and the dynamics of European wage bargaining', *International Review of Applied Economics*, 9(2): 169–91.

Weber, W. and Kabst, R. (1996) *Personalwesen im europäischen Vergleich – Ergebnisbericht 1995* (The Cranfield Project on International Strategic Human Resource Management). Universität Paderborn, Lehrstuhl für Betriebswirtschaftlehre, insbes. Personalwirtschaft, Paderborn.

Weber, W., Festing, M., Dowling, P. and Schuler, R. (1998) *Internationales Personalmanagement*, Wiesbaden.
Wonnacott, T. H. and Wonnacott, R. J. (1981) *Regression: A Second Course in Statistics*, New York/Chichester/Brisbone/Toronto.
Wunderer, R. (1984) 'Strategische Personalarbeit – arbeitslos?', *Zeitschrift für Führung und Organisation*, 10: 506–10.
Wunderer, R. (1992) 'Internationalisierung als Herausforderung für das Personalmanagement', in Coenenberg, A. G., Funk, J. and Djarrahzadeh, M. (eds), pp. 1–25.

13 Human Resource Management in Bulgaria: Hot Problems during the Transition to a Market Economy

Elizabeth Vatchkova

INTRODUCTION

This chapter examines some of the key challenges faced by Bulgarian organisations in the HRM area during the transition from a centralised planned economy to a market one. It therefore offers an analysis of the changing nature of HRM which is accompanying the other major social and economic changes characteristic of Bulgaria.

Companies in Bulgaria which have been under transition for 7 years, have been forced to understand, launch and execute the real rules of the global market. Most of the companies had to be transformed urgently in order to meet two general requirements: (1) the force of the international markets and competitors; and (2) the internal process of privatisation. Individuals have had to adapt a new, quite different reality, and have had to jettison, the economic and social security provided for under socialism.

The transition to a market economy in Bulgaria is taking place under conditions of continuous economic, political and social crisis. Its sharpening in January–February 1997 resulted in the decision to introduce a currency board as a tool for limiting and neutralising the destructive tendencies in the economy of the country. In the last 7 years Bulgaria has been characterised by:

1. *A decrease in GDP*: In 1996 it was 10.9 per cent less than the GDP of the previous year. The registered decrease is the greatest for all the years of transition and contributes considerably to the total decrease of 22.9 per cent since 1990. Measured solely on this index, Bulgaria

stays behind all other countries in transition and it is the only one among them that recorded a decrease in GDP in 1996.

2. *High inflation rates:* The unstable acceleration and slowing down of the inflation rates through the period 1990–96 reached an all time high of 700 per cent in 1997, at the beginning of which the country entered into an inflationary spiral. Inflation in Bulgaria is higher than in the other countries in transition for the last 2 years. Despite expectations to the contrary, inflation remains high. From the beginning of the year up to August the inflation rate was 578 per cent.
3. *Increase in unemployment:* Falls in the numbers employed reached their highest values in 1993 and continue at around 14 per cent. The introduction of the currency board brought with it a new wave of unemployment. People have been let go from organisations facing financial crises and from liquidated inefficient enterprises, the speed of whose closures is governed by obligations to the international financial institutions. Workers are laid off because of the extremely dangerous working conditions in some branches of production. Other factors include an increased labour supply and a reduction in unemployment insurance benefits, cuts in insurance payments for graduates and a tightening in the control on the price of labour.
4. *Decrease in living standards and a worsening of the quality of life of the Bulgarian citizen:* As a whole, the conditions for reproduction and realisation of HR have worsened during the transition period. The real income per capita has reduced 65.6 per cent for the period 1990–96. According to information of the Institute for Social Research, 21 per cent of the households were below the social minimum in 1992, compared to 85 per cent in the middle of 1997. In June 1997 the cost of living is 4.5 times higher than the minimum wage. Statistical data highlight that food expenses represent more than half of all the individual likely expenses.

HRM in the organisations is being carried out in very complicated conditions and in a highly dynamic macroenvironment:

- Organisations are facing continous change, as a result of amendments to the legislation and regulation of business activities, changes of ownership, activities, markets, and changes in the conditions and regime of work.
- Currently, there is an aggravated motivation climate as a consequence of job cuts, forced outages, irregular payments, and cuts in the social programmes.

- There have also been changes in the managerial staff of the enterprises, often caused by political problems and non-consideration of the education criteria, of experience in the field and quality of performance.
- Recent years have witnessed an increased number of conflicts among staff and intensified distrust in the institutions.
- There is an insufficiency and absence of management preparation for accepting and implementing the changes in the organisations, lack of flexibility, domination of bureaucratic and administrative approaches in company management.

Overall therefore, HRM in Bulgaria in the transitional period is being carried out in difficult conditions.

In a search for adequate managerial approaches in the complicated conditions of the transition in Bulgaria, a representative survey of the state of human resource management in the organisations under the methodology of Cranfield–Price Waterhouse was conducted in 1996 when Bulgaria joined Cranet-E. The main goal of this survey is, on the basis of comparison with the trends, approaches and methods, of HRM in the developed European countries, to reveal the potential opportunities and prospectives for improvement of HRM in the Bulgarian organisations.

MAIN FINDINGS

Structure of HRM

The studying of the Subject of HRM in the Bulgarian organisations shows, that in their managerial structure *the position of the HRM department/manager has not been appraised.* Although the organisations that have a HRM department/manager are prevalent (72 per cent of the respondents), in comparison with the other European organisations (Executive Report, 1995), excluding Finland, the share of Bulgarian organisations where a HRM function does not exist is the biggest. *During the last three years the dynamics of these units have remained low.* A majority have not changed their numbers and staff qualifications, although those surveyed themselves do point out that big changes that have taken place in the organisations.

An analysis of HRM, its position in the company and its activity shows some positive trends concerning the structure of these units:

- The relative share of the women employed in HRM departments in Bulgaria is greater than in most European countries.
- There is a high percentage of professionals operating in the field.
- Comparatively, a great number of Bulgarian organisations systematically evaluate the performance of the personnel department. HRM activities are an object of higher interest in the enterprises where they exist.

The main responsibility for the decisions on personnel management in 60 per cent of the Bulgarian organisations rests with the chief executives, followed by the administrative directors – 22 per cent and the production directors – 5 per cent. The participation of the line managers in HRM follows the European trend, and is increasing. Almost 50 per cent of the surveyed organisations state, that line managers are mainly responsible for taking the decisions associated with: pay and benefits – in 48 per cent of the surveyed organisations, industrial relations – 42 per cent, training and development of the staff – 49 per cent, workforce expansion/reduction – 38 per cent, recruitment and selection – 33 per cent, and health and safety – 27 per cent.

In Bulgaria the line managers carry much more responsibility for decision-making in the whole spectrum of problems connected with HRM, compared with the ones in the rest of the European countries. The increase of their responsibilities in the last years is also highly significant.

The strengthening of the strategic aspects of management, typical of Western European economies, is proving difficult in Bulgaria – only 25 per cent of respondents have written corporate strategies, and 22 per cent non-written.

The low level of application of corporate missions and strategies in Bulgarian organisations management is a fact that can be explained by a range of circumstances. The unpredictable, sometimes illogical events at the present era are factors that do not contribute to the 'strategic tuning' of managerial teams. The lack of governmental strategy for transition towards a market economy, for structural reform and of priorities for its fulfilment, as well as the sharp changes of the legal regulation of business explain the disinclination for formulating missions and strategies.

Another explanation for the lack of strategic approaches and techniques in managerial practice relates to the pace of altitudinal change. According to Boeva's (1997) research the main characteristics of the

Bulgarian management pattern in the conditions of market transition are the following:

- the prelevance of short-run, operative management;
- a production- rather than a market-oriented management;
- the dominance of centralised management at the expense of the decentralised;
- the low popularity of team work;
- a rejection of planning in the early years of transition;
- a nihilistic attitude towards knowledge as a source for management.

Other causes for the low level of strategic management and the limited participation of the experts in HRM in the development of strategies relate to a lack of managerial self-confidence and the prevalence of a sense of temporary participation in the managerial team. The interviews held with experts in HRM clarify, to a great extent, the causes of their lack of motivation for participation in formulation of strategies. The experts in HRM consider themselves the most risky group when there is downsizing.

Many of the firms, which do not have written corporate strategies, nevertheless, have HR strategies or policies for separate parts of it. Popular among them are policies relating to: pay and benefits, the training and development of the staff, recruitment and selection of the staff and communications between the employees.

A positive tendency in the management of Bulgarian enterprises is the relatively high popularity of written strategies for HR – they exist in 31 per cent of the surveyed organisations (in 38 per cent they are non-written). Written strategies for HR are developed in Bulgaria as frequently as in the French firms and more often than in the enterprises in Eastern German provinces (21 per cent), Hungary (26 per cent), Western German provinces (25 per cent) and Italy (27 per cent).

Another positive tendency relates to the development of organisational policies for separate aspects of activities relating to: payment and benefits (75 per cent); training and development of personnel (58 per cent), recruitment and selection (56 per cent), employee communications (46 per cent), equal opportunities (18 per cent), philosophy of people management (18 per cent) and 'high-fliers' (19 per cent).

A third positive tendency is that more than half of the Bulgarian organisations which have strategies in the area of HRM report that they are translated into work programmes, with fixed deadlines for completing the events.

The head of the personnel/HRM function has a place on the main board of directors in only 32 per cent of cases – one of the lowest degrees of participation, when compared with other European countries. Rarely are the HR mangers involved in developing the company strategies from the outset. More typically, they are involved most actively in the implementation stage.

Staffing practices

Many of the decisions on staffing practices in Bulgarian organisations in recent years are taken within the context of difficult external pressures. Managerial teams have limited options, and the space for seeking out effective solutions is small. Very often they are subordinated to political reasons, which have tended to take centre stage.

The dynamics of employment in the period 1994–96 show that in the bigger part of the surveyed organisations the number of employees has decreased in 40 per cent of the organisations surveyed. The factors at play here are undoubtedly the deep economic crisis and the unemployment that accompanies it. The data suggest that in a majority of the surveyed organisations the decrease of the workforce is a result of natural wastage, recruitment freeze, compulsory redundancies and early retirement.

In relation to selection mechanisms, the most common approaches are: application forms – in 49 per cent of the organisations, one-to-one interviews – 36 per cent, and references – 17 per cent of the companies surveyed. The aptitude tests, interview panels, psychometric and graphology tests are used significantly less. The Assessment Centres also have little popularity. They are used by only 1.4 per cent of the organisations surveyed.

As a whole, flexible staffing in all its forms is significantly less popular in Bulgaria than in the other European countries. According to the results from the survey, despite its high popularity elsewhere and the undoubted advantages that it offers, it is only used in a minority of cases in Bulgaria. Some of the flexible working practicies applied across European countries are not implemented within Bulgarian organisations mainly because of the lack of legal regulation. Some flexible forms are still the subject of informal arrangements. With regard to this there is the biggest gap to be closed between other Bulgaria and European organisations. Presently the most popular mechanisms are: the fixed-term contracts, shift work and temporary/casual work (see Appendix, Figures 13AI.1–13AI.5).

The difficult dynamics of the period of transition to a market economy, in Bulgaria require activation of the education, qualification and training activities of the personnel. The survival of the organisations to a large extent depends on the qualities and adaptiveness of the workforce, as well as on the ability of the managerial teams to develop and apply flexible strategies for the training and development of the employees. A majority of those surveyed state that the main and most hard to resolve problems they encounter daily are caused by the gap between the contemporary skill/knowledge requirements of the organisation and the real ability and performance of those employed.

Training and development

The survey highlights that a majority of the surveyed organisations ascribe a significance to training and development activities. More than half of the respondents have policies for training and development (58 per cent). The Bulgarian companies, despite their limited financial resources, are currently third biggest spenders after France and Sweden, in terms of the percentage of the annual wages and salaries bill spent on training and development activities.

The perceived priorities for the future differ from those in the other European counties. The respondents suggest that the following areas will prove important over the next 3 years: computers and new technologies (56 per cent); marketing and sales (52 per cent); quality management (52 per cent); management and supervision of the staff (49 per cent); customer service skills (47 per cent); strategy formulation (42 per cent); business administration (34 per cent) and health and safety of the work environment (30 per cent). The skills associated with strategy formulation are not highly valued, thus there is a lower than expected interest in this area. In comparison with other European countries, in Bulgaria the importance of management and supervision as a training area is undervalued as well.

Compared to all other European countries, the Bulgarian organisations are well behind in the assessment of employee training needs. They are systematically analysed in only 42 per cent of the surveyed orgnisations. Where it is done, the most commonly used methods are: management requests, training audits and employee requests to be trained. The analysis of projected business/service plans and performance appraisal are methods less frequently employed.

Half of the surveyed organisations suggest that they are monitoring the effectiveness of the actual training given. The preferred methods here are: informal feedback from line managers, formal evaluation immediately after training and informal feedback from trainees.

Generally therefore in the field of training, education and qualification, there is little by way of substantial evidence which suggests the use of a more systematic approach. Its potential is not perhaps as of yet fully understood and this is one of the directions where most effort must be put in order to reach a higher level of effectiveness in the training HRD area.

Payment

The trend towards the individualisation of payment as a tendency is observed in Bulgarian organisations also. Bulgaria is among that group of countries most often (in 65 per cent of the surveyed organisations) applying schemes of individual merit performance pay. Relative to other European countries, Bulgarian and Dutch organisations are the most likely to have increased variable pay. For all categories of staff, group bonuses are used most commonly as a means of differentiating pay. The data show that the strategies for linking the results with pay have most commonly been introduced in the period 1991–93 and revised more laterly in the period 1994–95.

The systems for performance assessment, nevertheless, are not yet widely applicable. Where they are used, they apply to all the different staff categories to some degree: manual staff, professional/technical staff, clerical staff and mangers. However, the low level of take-up would seem to suggest that they do not, as of yet, believe that it was any significant role to play in motivating employees. Many Bulgarian organisations do, however, use their customers as the means of assessment – in 28 per cent of the cases – which is the highest value for all surveyed countries.

Communications

The results of the survey show that in common with their European neighbours, many Bulgarian organisations are currently devising strategies and policies for development of communications (in 46 per cent of the organisations surveyed written communication policies exist. Conversely, in 24 per cent of cases they remain unwritten, while in 15 per cent of cases no such policies exist).

Practice shows, however, that qualitative and quantitative changes to business communications are not occurring. In the majority of the surveyed Bulgarian organisations, during the past 3 years the methods used for communicating with the employees on major issues have not changed. There is no evidence of the introduction of more democratic communication methods. The use of verbal methods has increased the most, followed by communication through written methods, team briefings and representative staff bodies. Less common are increases in the use of video (the increase is in only 2 per cent of the organisations), computer and electronic systems (increases have been reported by 10 per cent of the organisations). The use of joint management/employee consultative committees and work committees has increased at half the pace reported in Finland, France, Holland, Belgium and Denmark. The formal briefing of managerial and administrative teams on strategic and financial problems in the companies are one of the lowest in the surveyed European countries.

CONCLUSIONS

The results from the survey provide the possibility of highlighting a number of key areas in which effort will likely have to be made in order to speed up the process of transition to a more modern type of HRM.

On one hand, those surveyed highlight a number of key challenges in the HRM area that they will face over the next 3 years: personnel training and development, recruitment and selection and pay and benefits. On the other hand, the areas where Bulgarian managerial methods and practices fall behind those of the developed European countries show more precisely the necessary directions for future development. Most urgently efforts are needed for:

- the reconstitution of the subject of HRM and for gaining greater approval of its role and functioning in Bulgarian organisations;
- the active participation of the HR manager in the development of the organisational strategies;
- the widespread introduction of contemporary techniques and methods for recruitment and selection of the staff;
- the diffusion of flexible staffing practices in all its forms;
- the introduction of a more systematic approach to the education and qualification of the staff;

- the endorsement of the practice of performance appraisal and the introduction of modern methods for assessment;
- the modernisation of the methods and techniques for business communications.

The practical development of these areas will provide the possibility of building more effective systems of HRM and will likely assist in the future development of business in Bulgaria.

APPENDIX

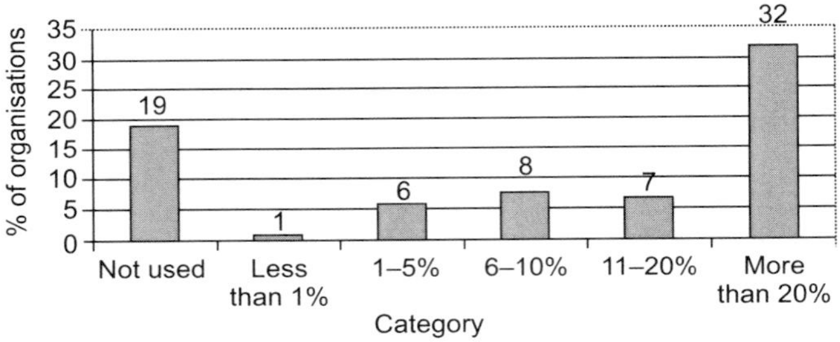

Figure 13AI.1 Percentage of organisations indicating the approximate proportion of the workforce on shift working contracts

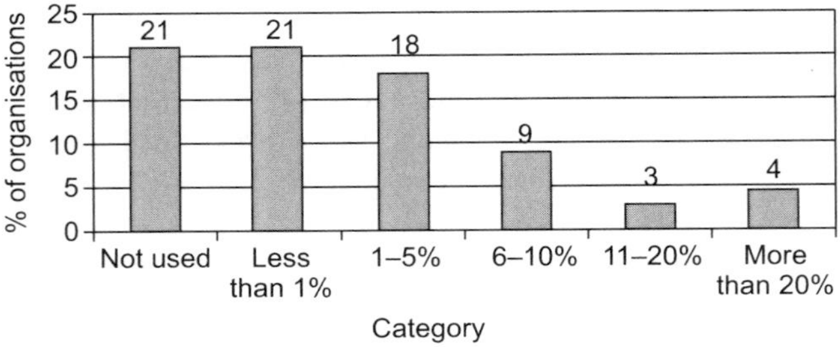

Figure 13AI.2 Percentage of organisations indicating the approximate proportion of the workforce on temporary/casual contracts

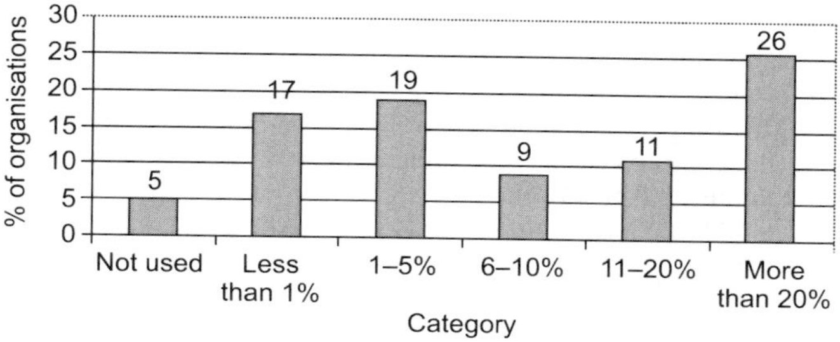

Figure 13AI.3 Percentage of organisations indicating the approximate proportion of the workforce on fixed-term contracts

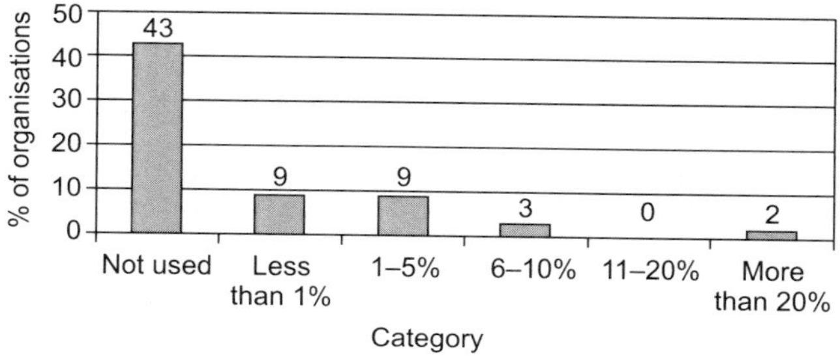

Figure 13AI.4 Percentage of organisations indicating the approximate proportion of the workforce on annual hours contracts

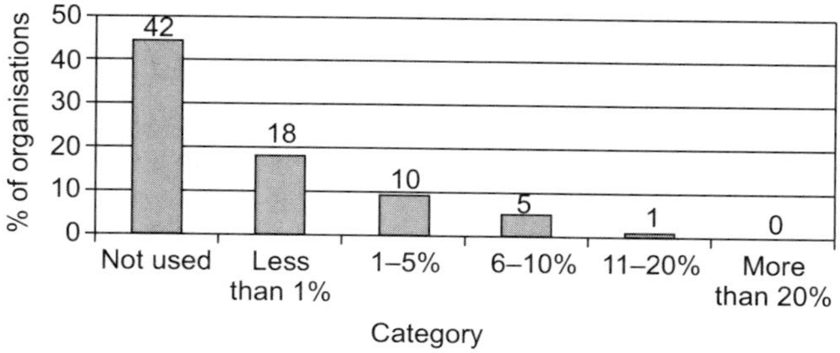

Figure 13AI.5 Percentage of organisations indicating the approximate proportion of the workforce on part-time contracts

References

Boeva, B. (1997) 'Corporate management – barrier or prerequisite during the transition of Bulgarian companies to market economy', UNSS-Multigroup, report at the National conference 'Bulgarian business during the transition to market economy,' April, Sofia.

'Bulgaria' 96 (1997) *Social and Economic Development*, Sofia, NSI.

Executive Report (1995) *The Cranfield Project on International Strategic Human Resource Management*, Cranfield, School of Management.

Further Reading

Andreeva, Z. (1997) 'State policy and strategy for regulation the unemployment in condition of transition to market economy', 'Business Week', International University, IBS 'Transbusiness-E', report at the National conference: Strategic human resource management in Bulgaria during the transitional period to market economy, June, Sofia.

Àtanassova, ì. (1997) *Selection and Training of the Personnel*, Sofia, Trakiya Ì.

Beleva, I., Dobrev, P., Zareva, I. and Tzanov, V. (1996) *The Labour Market in Bulgaria*, Sofia, Gorex Press.

Boyadjiev, D. (1994) *Human Resource Management*, Sofia.

Brewster, C. and Hegewisch, A. (1994) *Policy and Practice in European Human Resource Management*, London: Routledge.

Crowley, M. and Clifford, N. (1996) 'The contingent workforce: case evidence on part time work in Ireland', European conference on flexibility, Barcelona, 7–8 November 1996.

Hegewisch, A. (1996) 'Human resource management and contract flexibility in local government in the UK', European conference on flexibility, Barcelona, 7–8 November 1996.

Hristova, T. (1996) *Human resource management*, London, Princeps.

Lundblad, N., Lindstrom, K. and Waglund, M. (1996) 'Advantages and disadvantages of new strategies for flexibility in organizations', European conference on flexibility, Barcelona, 7–8 November 1996.

Mayrhofer, W. (1996) 'Warning: flexibility can damage your organizational health!', conference handout, November.

Paraplexandris, N. (1996) 'Flexible working patterns: towards a reconciliation of family and work', European conference on flexibility, Barcelona, 7–8 November 1996.

Ribarova, E. (1997) 'Strategies for behaviour at work and for survival of the personnel in the organizations during the process of adaptation to the market economy', *Business week*, International University, IBS 'Transbusiness-E', report at the National conference: Strategic human resource management in Bulgaria during the transitional period to market economy, June, Sofia.

Shopov, D., Stefanov, L. and Paunov, M. (1995) *Economics of labour*, Sofia, Jusautor.

Stoikov, L. (1995) *Corporate Culture and Communication*, Sofia.

The Price Waterhouse Cranfield Project on International Strategic Human Resource Management. Report 1990.

The Price Waterhouse Cranfield Project on International Strategic Human Resource Management. Report 1991.

Vatchkova, Å. (1997) 'Contemporary trends in human resource management in Europe and Bulgaria', 'Business week', International University, IBS 'Trans-business-E', report at the National conference: Strategic human resource management in Bulgaria during the transitional period to market economy, June, Sofia.

14 Human Resource Management in Australia: Towards a New Metaphor

Robin Kramar

INTRODUCTION

There are extensive reports of major changes in methods of management and employment policies throughout industrialised countries during the 1980s and the 1990s. Intense international competition and the internationalization of labour markets have reportedly encouraged innovations in the way work is organized and the way people are deployed and managed (Sisson, 1989; Blyton and Turnbull, 1992; Storey, 1992; Sparrow *et al.*, 1994; Kitay and Lansbury, 1995; Locke, *et al.*, 1995; Centre for European Human Resource Management, 1997). It has been argued these changes constitute a new approach to the management of labour. This approach has been labelled 'human resource management' and it is said to have replaced a 'personnel management' and /or an industrial relations approach to management (Mahoney and Deckop 1986; Dowling, 1990; Beaumont, 1991; Guest, 1991; Storey, 1992).

This chapter examines the extent to which the management of labour has changed in Australia during the 1980s and 1990s. It assesses whether these changes constitute a new approach to the management of labour and the degree to which the changes constitute an approach that is consistent with a HRM approach. The chapter also explores the factors which have encouraged these developments.

APPROACHES TO EMPLOYMENT MANAGEMENT

A number of models or typologies (Tichy *et al.*, 1982; Beer *et al.*, 1984; Beer and Spector, 1985; Walton, 1985; Hendry and Pettigrew, 1986; Kochan *et al.*, 1986; Purcell, 1987; Guest, 1991; Storey, 1992; Kochan and Osterman, 1994) have been developed to conceptualise, different approaches to labour management and to describe changes in labour management approaches during the 1980s and 1990s. Although these typologies differ in their specific characteristics, it is possible to classify older generic typologies and more recent generic typologies in terms of the root metaphor on which the models are based (Dunn, 1990). The root metaphor imputes 'meaning' to patterns of behaviour, which include 'philosophies', guiding principles (Legge, 1995, p. 32) and values.

The metaphors which describe the old generic typologies involve two components. The first component involves industrial relations issues and this has been conceived as warfare between trade unions and employers (Dunn, 1990). The second component involves a metaphor of the management of individuals in a day-to-day administrative way and in terms of legal compliance. The metaphor which describes the essence of new generic typologies is a process of partnership a new reality which involves processes of organisational and individual change. This metaphor of partnership places labour management as a central strategic management issue.

A common label for the old typologies is 'personnel management and industrial relations', while a common label for the new typologies is HRM. These typologies differ in their assumptions, timeframe, the roles of senior, line and specialist HR managers, the presence and role of trade unions and the nature of the policies used for managing labour. Table 14.1 details the characteristics of these two typologies. The characteristics in this Table have been organised into five groups: strategic approach to labour management; managerial responsibilities; bargaining, trade unions and communication; key levers for managing labour; and assumptions.

These typologies of personnel management and HRM are being used as stereotypes to describe bundles of employment policies and practices. It is unlikely an organisation will use all of the policies and practices in a particular typology, and there could be difficulties associated with locating an individual organisation within a typology. However, the construction of the typologies assumes a sufficient number of policies will exist to reflect a particular metaphor. Similarly, these typologies are built on the assumption that the 'rhetoric' of the formal, written policies are more often implemented than not and that they represent actual behaviour in the workplace. This assumption does not preclude the possibility of failure to implement some policies in some organisations. The typologies are used as a way of describing changes in employment policies in Australia.

Table 14.1 Typologies for approaches to labour management

Assumptions	*Personnel management and industrial relations management*	*HRM*
Role of conflict	conflict inherent in employment relationship	differences can be minimised and managed
Contract	clear delineation of employment contract	aim to go beyond contract, ie discretionary effort
Rationale for action	procedures are the rationale for action	'business need', the rationale for action
Main managerial task	monitoring	fostering partnership
Strategic approach		
Time frame	short-term	long term
Planning	reactive, *ad hoc*	proactive, strategic, integrated
Evaluation of labour management function	Cost minimalisation; avoidance of down time	maximum utilisation
Behaviour referent	norms, customs and practice	values, mission
Managerial Responsibilities		
Role: senior managers	concerned legal compliance; cost minimisation	consider labour management issues as part of the development of strategy
Role: line managers	advise HR managers about needs	undertake labour management activities as part of role
Role: Specialist HR managers	undertake employee management	provide advice to line managers and senior manager; manage culture and organisational change
Bargaining, trade unions and communication	trade unions are present and involved in negotiation of wages and conditions; involved in communication between employers and employees	limited presence and role; limited role in communications between employers and employees; role as worker advocates and service providers

Table 14.1 (Cont.)

Key levers for managing labour		
Pay	job value/evaluation/ grades; as per awards and collective agreements	performance based; based on individual/team performance
Labour-management	collective agreements and awards; national standards	individual contracts; certified agreements; 'brokered' agreements; enterprise focus
Job design	division of labour	teamwork
Conflict	temporary truces	manage culture
Communication	restrict flow	increased flow
Training and development	*ad hoc*	systematic; linked to business needs
Monitor performance	*ad hoc*, trait based	integrated with business needs
Job tenure	'life'	according to business needs
Career	vertical in one or small number of organisations	vertical, horizontal, a number of occupations within many organisations

Sources: Guest, 1987; Boxall and Dowling, 1990; Storey, 1992; Legge, 1995.

DEVELOPMENTS IN LABOUR MANAGEMENT IN AUSTRALIA

A number of studies (Callus *et al.*, 1991; CCH Australia Ltd, 1995; Department of Industrial Relations, 1995; Sheldrake and Saul, 1995; Kramar and Lake, 1997; Morehead *et al.*, 1997) that examine changes in labour management practices in Australia reveal that there have been significant changes in employment practices. These main features of these studies are described in Appendix I. They indicate there has been a change in the approach to labour management. They show the development of a long-term, strategic approach to labour management in many organisations, a change in the role of senior, line and HR managers in labour management, a change in the level of bargaining, a declining role for trade unions, more widespread use of direct communication with employees, the increasing use of performance based pay, teamwork, flexible employment practices, systematic linking of performance appraisals and training and development to business needs.

Strategic approach to labour management

A number of characteristics identified as part of the HRM approach indicate a strategic approach to labour management. These include the existence of mission statements, corporate and HR strategies, programmes to operationalise these strategies and evaluation of the HR department in terms of the utilisation of labour. A decade ago Stace stated (1986, pp. 1–2) that an 'increasing number of organisations in Australia are consciously linking HR strategies' and 'placing a great deal of importance on developing and maintaining the workforce behaviours and characteristics necessary to achieve organisational mission'. This strategic linking of employment policies to organisational needs has become more widespread (Deery and Nash, 1988; CCH Australia Ltd, 1995; Kramar and Lake, 1997). It is reflected in the widespread use of mission statements, corporate strategies and HR strategies. In 1996 more than 95 per cent of organisations employing more than 200 employees had a mission statement, 94 per cent had a corporate strategy and 84 per cent had a HR or personnel strategy. Of those organisations with either a written or unwritten strategy almost 84 per cent had translated these into HR programmes (Kramar and Lake, 1997). This suggests an approach in larger organisations that is consistent with the planning, timeframe and behaviour referent characteristics of an HRM approach rather than a personnel and industrial relations approach to labour management.

It is not possible to adequately assess the changes in the way the HR department is evaluated in terms of the criteria in Table 14.1. However, it appears, where departments are evaluated in Australia, there could be some concern with both cost and the maximum utilisation of labour. In the Cranet-E study of the 61 per cent of organisations that systematically evaluated the performance of the HR department, the most commonly used criteria for evaluation in 1996 were performance against objectives, feedback from line management and performance against budget (Kramar and Lake, 1997). The use of these criteria could suggest concern with cost minimisation, performance against budget, as well as a concern with the maximum utilisation of labour through feed back from line managers and performance against objective.

Managerial responsibilities

In many organisations the responsibilities for labour management are being redistributed between senior managers, line managers and HR managers. HR managers and line managers share responsibility for policy decisons in most labour management areas. HR managers are more likely to take responsibility in the areas of industrial relations, pay and benefits and, to a lesser extent, occupational health and safety (Kramar and Lake, 1997; Morehead *et al.*, 1997).

The responsibility of line managers increased in many areas in the first half of the 1990s. This was particularly the case in areas of occupational safety and health (53 per cent of organisations reported an increase in line managers' responsibility), training and development (50 per cent reported an increase) and recruitment and selection (44 per cent reported an increase). There has not been as great an increase in the responsibility of line managers for industrial relations and pay decisions (Kramar and Lake, 1997). There is some discrepancy between these results and the findings of Morehead *et al.* (1997, p. 86) who report that 'there were few notable changes in the ability of first line supervisors to make decisions on employee relations matters between 1990 and 1995, except for a small increase in decision-making with regards to levels of overtime and a decrease in regard to dismissals'. However, this discrepancy could be partially explained by the different time frames, samples and the issues examined as employee relations decisions/ responsibility.

As suggested by Table 14.1, a HRM approach would be indicated by senior management considering HR issues as part of strategy development and involving HR managers in this process. Senior HR executives are not well represented on the boards of companies. This occurs in only 40 per cent of organisations with more than 200 employees. However, in 47 per cent of organisations the Human Resource department is involved in the development of corporate strategy from the outset, while 31 per cent are consulted during the process of development.

Unfortunately it is not possible to determine from the surveys specifically the extent to which HR practitioners provide expert advice to line managers and senior managers. It can be inferred from the above discussion about their involvement with line managers and senior managers that HR managers are providing specialist advice. They also appear to have long-term experience in the labour management area, with 53 per cent of HR managers spending 10 or more years working in a specialist labour management area, and about 70 per cent being recruited from a specialist HR function. Most hold specialist qualifications. Almost two thirds of the HR managers in organisations with 200 or more employes hold a university degree and two-thirds of these are in disciplines such as business, economics, social sciences, the humanities and the law (Kramar and Lake, 1997).

Bargaining, trade unions and communication

The practice of enterprise bargaining which involves negotiating employment conditions and wages at the enterprise level is widespread. It has been used in an increasing number of workplaces during the first half of the 1990s (Department of Industrial Relations, 1995; Morehead *et al.*, 1997). In 1995 enterprise bargaining was widespread in all industry groups except in service industries including wholesale and retail trade, community, personal, accommodation, cafe, restaurant and property and business services (Department of Industrial Relations, 1995; Morehead *et al.*, 1997). Enterprise bargaining was more common in larger, unionised workplaces and those covered by federal awards. Particularly high levels occurred in the public sector, in utilities and communications services (Department of Industrial Relations, 1995; Morehead *et al.*, 1997).

Direct methods of communication between management and employees were increasingly used, while trade unions were less frequently used as a means of communicating with employees. In 1996 almost three-quarters of organisations had joint consultative committees and 4 out of 10 of these committees had been established in the period 1993 to 1996. During the same period more than 60 per cent of organisations had increased their use of team briefings, computer/electronic mail systems, direct written and direct verbal means of communication. At the same time almost 28 per cent of organisations reported a decrease in the influence of trade unions (Kramar and Lake, 1997). This finding is supported by Morehead *et al.* (1997, p. 335) who state that during the first half of the 1990s 'unions lost influence at the workplace level, both through a declining presence and where present, a declining level of overall activity'.

Key levers for managing labour

The surveys highlight that a number of policies have been used to improve productivity and facilitate change management. These include the increasing use of performance appraisals, greater flexibility in employment practices, job redesign, organisational development, culture change, employee consultation, the introduction of new technology and equipment, organisational restructuring and employee surveys (SCG, 1986–95; Callus *et al.*, 1991; CCH Australia Ltd, 1995; Kramar and Lake, 1997; Morehead *et al.*, 1997). 'Organisational change is now a common feature for a majority of workplaces' (Morehead *et al.*, 1997, p. 239).

The use of performance appraisals is a central part of a HR approach to management. In 1992, 40 per cent of organisations indicated that they used performance appraisals for some staff (CCH Australia Ltd, 1995, pp. 3–800). Cranet-E (1996) found a much greater use of performance appraisals, especially among management staff and professional/technical employees. About 90 per cent of organisations used appraisals for these staff, while more than three quarters of the organisations used them for clerical employees and almost half for manual workers (Kramar and Lake, 1997). Morehead *et al.* (1997) also found an increase in the use of performance appraisals, particularly in the electricity, gas and water supply, accommodation, cafes and restaurants, government administration, and health and community services. They found the use of formal performance appraisals was highest in the finance and insurance industries.

Unfortunately, it is not possible from these surveys determine the nature of the appraisal system used. However, the CCH survey found an increasing use of Management by Objectives (MBO) systems between 1985 and 1995. During this period, the percentage of organisations using this form of assessment increased from 52 per cent to 64 per cent (CCH Australia Ltd, 1995, pp. 12–700). It also found universal involvement of employees in the assessment process.

One of the most notable developments has been the increasing use of flexible employment practices. During the last decade the number of workers on either flexible employment contracts or flexible working hours, such as part-time or casual employment, has increased by almost 41 per cent. Casual employment covers employees who are excluded from non-wage benefits and are engaged as and when their labour is needed by the business. They are similar in many respects to the category of temporary worker in Europe. The incidence of part-time and/or casual work is increasing across all industries, occupations and for a variety of groups in the Australian labour market. However, younger and older workers, and women in sales and clerical occupations, are most likely to be engaged on the basis of flexible working arrangements (Burgess and Strachan, 1997).

The growing use of these flexible working practices is suppported by the Cranfield survey in Australia. In 1996, 59 per cent of organisations reported increasing their use of part-time employment during the previous 3 years. More than half the organisations increased their use of temporary/casual employment, fixed term contracts and subcontracting/ outsourcing arrangements. During the same period, 42 per cent of organisations increased their use of flexible working hours and 41 per cent increased their use of job sharing arrangements.

Another development has been the use of policies which facilitate working outside the employer's workplace. More than one in four organisations increased their use of home-based work and almost one in six increased their use of teleworking. The majority of organisations, however, still do not use these policies, and when they are used, they are available for only a small percentage of employees, usually less than 1 per cent (Kramar and Lake, 1997).

Labour market efficiency has also been sought through increased task flexibility. Between 1993 and 1996 many organisations redesigned jobs so they were wider and more open-ended. This was most evident for clerical and managerial staff. Of all organisations 56 per cent reported redesigning the work of managers and clerical staff so it was more open-ended and flexible. Almost as many organisations had redesigned the work of professional staff (49 per cent) and manual workers (42 per cent) so it was more flexible.

The research by Sheldrake and Saul (1995) found major changes in the work and job design of first line supervisors. They found that there had been a shift in their role from 'cop to coach'. This required a significant increase in leadership, communication, interpersonal and learning competencies. It also required them to be more proactive and resourceful problem solvers.

The increasing use of flexible working practices is similar to the trends in many European countries, particularly the United Kingdom. Although there are some differences in the actual extent of the increases in Australia and the United Kingdom, the greatest increases in both countries involved the increased use of part-time work, temporary/casual work, fixed-term contracts and subcontracting/outsourcing. Among OECD countries, Australia has recorded one of the highest growth rates in part-time and casual employment during the last 10 years (OECD, 1996).

In the first half of the 1990s methods of pay changed for many people in Australia. Increasing use was made of individual contracts, particularly in the property, business and mining industries. While awards were still common, there was a decrease in the award coverage of workplaces between 1990 and 1995 from 98 per cent to 96 per cent (Morehead *et al.*, 1997, pp. 205–30).

Pay for performance schemes became more common among organisations employing more than 200 employees between 1993 and 1996. About one-third of organisatons increased their use of variable pay and about one-quarter increased their use of non-monetary benefits. Managerial, professional and technical staff are most likely to receive merit-pay and other forms of pay for performance. Almost two-thirds of Australian organisations provide a merit-based scheme for their managers, while more than half provide this for professional/technical staff. Although clerical/administrative and manual staff are less likely to receive merit pay, almost 40 per cent of organisations provide merit pay for clerical/administrative staff and more than one in five organisations provide merit pay for manual staff (Kramar and Lake, 1997).

It is not possible from the surveys to assess the change in career paths, job tenure and the nature of training and development. However, Morehead *et al.* (1997) reveal that the extent of training received by all occupational groups increased between 1990 and 1995. In 1990 58 per cent of workplaces provided training and by 1995 this had increased to 68 per cent of workplaces. Professionals/paraprofessionals, technical staff and managers are more likely to receive training than clerical and manual employees (Kramar and Lake, 1997; Morehead *et al.*, 1997) with about 70 per cent of the first group of employees receiving more than three days training compared to about 50 per cent of manual and clerical employees (Kramar and Lake, 1997).

These developments reflect a change in the approach to employee management. Morehead *et al.* (1997, p. 331) report that 'there were often quite substantial changes in the way workplace relations were conducted' during the first half of the 1990s. Trade unions were less active in regulating employment and management were more likely to replace *ad hoc* and informal methods of employee management with methods which codify the relationship. These changes indicate a trend towards labour management practices which are consistent with a human resource management approach to labour management.

It is not possible to assess from the surveys the assumptions underlying the nature of labour management, nor is it possible to explicitly assess whether management is developing partnerships with labour rather than monitoring. However, an examination of the legislative, industrial and policy factors which have contributed to these changes provides an understanding of the factors which encouraged these developments and also an assessment of the assumptions underlying the employment relationship.

THE CONTEXT OF THE CHANGES

Australian governments, employers and many trade unions have supported a variety of reforms in the labour market as a way of making the market more efficient and internationally competitive. Since the early 1980s there has been a debate in Australia about the need for reform of industrial relations and employment practices and outcomes so that they promote productivity and efficiency (Dabscheck, 1995). One of the ways employers' groups and the federal government have sought to improve productivity is through the encouragement of the negotiation of employment conditions and wages at the enterprise level rather than the national level (Business Council of Australia, 1989; Department of Industrial Relations, 1995). These parties argued the centralised industrial relations system produced inefficiencies through the existence of multiple award coverage (Business Council of Australia, 1989; Hilmer, 1989), the proliferation of occupationally based unions, the 'flow on' of wage increases through an industry or occupation and the creation of narrow inflexible job structures (Drago *et al.*, 1992). Trade unions, particularly the peak body, the Australian Council of Trade Unions (ACTU) through its adoption of 'strategic unionism' and the various Prices and Incomes Accords (Accords) struck with the Australian Labour Party which became government policy also supported the concept of labour market reforms.

The Accords represented a new approach to wage determination and social policy. The approach sought to promote consensus, rather than conflict through industrial relations arrangements by developing an incomes policy which encompassed prices, wages, incomes, non-wage incomes, taxation, social policies and labour market principles such as industrial democracy and equity. The Accords indicated attempts to promote a new spirit of co-operation between trade unions and employers. They also represented a trade off of pay rises for non-income benefits, such as superannuation.

In 1987 the focus in federal industrial relations began to shift to enhance enterprise bargaining. At the same time there was an attempt to grant wage increases on the basis of productivity increases, rather than on the basis of cost of living increases and/or in response to increases in other industries and occupations. The introduction of the Structural Efficiency Principle (SEP) provided for wage increases on the basis of efficiency improvements resulting from changes in work and management practices, the reduction of demarcation barriers and improvements in training (Deery, 1995). Subsequent decisions of the Industrial Relations Commission (AIRC) further supported the achievement of enterprise improvements in productivity and efficiency through formal union–management agreements.

Federal and state governments have enacted legislation to encourage enterprise bargaining and the negotiation of employment conditions, such as flexible working arrangements which foster the efficient operation of the organisation. In 1993 the federal government enacted the Industrial Relations Reform Act. This Act was designed to facilitate the spread of enterprise agreements and to limit the role of the AIRC to one of assisting the parties to bargain in good faith using the process of conciliation, rather than the more interventionist role of arbitration. It sought to protect employees' interests by maintaining and strengthening the award safety net and introducing minimum entitlements (Department of Industrial Relations, 1995, p. 3). As a consequence of the Act, the AIRC reviewed its Wage Fixing Principles in 1994 and established a Statement of Principles which gave priority to enterprise bargaining.

The move to enterprise bargaining and enterprise agreements was further enhanced with the introduction of the Workplace Relations Act 1996. This Act provides for the simplification of awards by allowing them to contain only 20 'allowable matters'. It also allows for the negotiation of agreements between individuals or non-union collectivities and employers to have the same status as those negotiated with trade unions. In addition, it provides for a reduction in the arbitral role of the Industrial Relations Commission (IRC). These developments all encourage the view that the enterprise should be the focus for employment policies and that trade unions are not a necessary part of the process of negotiating these policies. Many anticipate that these developments will further encourage the implementation of flexible working practices because they are consistent with the business needs of the enterprise.

The major shifts associated with the devolution of employee management to the enterprise level in Australia and the introduction of other policies designed to foster organisational change were a consequence of the desire of managements to improve productivity and efficiency (Morehead *et al.*, 1997, p. 241). Australian workplaces were under pressure to become more competitive as a response to the internationalisation of the economy, the reduction in tariff protection, deregulation in the aviation and telecommunications sectors and privatisation in a number of sectors.

The adoption of flexible working practices was also promoted by individual firms seeking to manage their work and family responsibilities. In 1990 the federal government ratified an International Labour Organisation Convention (ILO Convention 156, Workers with Family Responsibilities). As a consequence the federal government established a Work and Family Unit in the Department of Industrial Relations to manage workplace issues highlighted by ILO Convention 156. Some large firms, particularly those in the service and finance sectors introduced career break schemes, working from home and part-time working schemes for employees with family responsibilities. However, often these schemes are introduced at management's discretion and are only available to the most valued employees (Kramar, 1997).

CONCLUSION

Labour management policies which seek to improve efficiency and productivity in Australia have been introduced in increasing numbers of workplaces. A greater number of organisations have attempted to link employment policies to corporate strategy. Line managers are responsible for a greater variety of employment policies and some HR managers are involved in strategic business decisons through membership of organisational Boards and involvement in strategy development. The role of trade unions has declined, bargaining about employment conditions and wages has shifted to the enterprise level and increasing numbers of organisations are introducing techniques to communicate directly with employees. Increasing numbers of organisations are also using individual contracts, pay for performance schemes, flexible employment practices, training, performance appraisals and broader job structures.

These surveys indicate that in many Australian organisations the bundles of employment policies are consistent with a HRM approach to labour management. They seek to promote a metaphor of organisational and individual change in an attempt to achieve economic efficiency and international competitiveness. However, they are unable to tell us if these policies are actually implemented in the workplace. They are also unable to inform us of the effectiveness of the policies in achieving organisational efficiency or in which circumstances particular policies are most effective in improving perfromance. The surveys are also unable to delineate the precise composition of the bundles of employment policies in particular workplaces.

Existing case studies that examine changes in labour management policies in Australia suggest that different types of labour management policies are effective in different economic environments (Dunphy and Stace, 1990; Stace and Dunphy, 1994). It has also been argued on the basis of other case studies (Kitay and Lansbury, 1995; Kitay and Lansbury, 1997) that the changes in labour management policies have not resulted in a qualitatively different social and economic order. These latter case studies demonstrate that organisations do not consistently introduce packages of new policies, but, instead retain some of the existing policies, as they introduce new ones.

In order to achieve an understanding of the above issues, further research needs to be done. Additional case studies that examine processes operating in the workplace, particularly the implementation of policies, would provide insights into the practices which are really occurring. Other case studies which explore the effectiveness of particular labour management policies in certain environments would extend the work of Dunphy and Stace. The surveys provide a rich source of data and these could be further analysed to show which policies are used in which sector of the economy and to reveal the subpatterns described in this chapter.

The surveys indicate that the metaphor underpinning labour management in Australia is changing to one of partnership, rather than administration and warfare. However, the impact of the policies on all the partners in the relationship requires further research. It is known there has been a favourable impact on shareholders and employers as labour productivity increases, and the number of awards in workplaces is decreasing (Morehead *et al.*, 1997). However, further research should explore the impact of these changes on employees quality of life and expectations concerning their working life.

APPENDIX I

Studies

Enterprise bargaining in Australia

A national survey of Australian workplaces with 10 or more employees conducted in October and November of 1994 examined the extent and type of changes introduced in Australian workplaces and the manner in which these changes had been introduced. The survey known as the Workplace Bargaining Survey collected detailed information about recently negotiated agreements and their effects. It also collected information from managers about the effects of the workplace changes and enterprise bargaining on employees. In total, 1060 managers were interviewed and 11 233 employee questionnaires were completed.

All the results of the survey have been weighted to provide estimates that are representative of Australian workplaces.

CCH surveys

National surveys of organisations across all industries were conducted by the Australian Graduate School of Management (AGSM) and CCH Australia Ltd (CCH) in 1989 and 1992. The 1992 survey that replicated the 1989 survey, was based on 796 respondents. The surveys sought information on the extent of strategic changes in Australian organisations, the links between these changes and human resources practices, and the implications of these practices.

Large organisations mainly from the manufacturing, finance, insurance and real estate industries, and conglomerates were the basis of the survey population.

A third survey conducted jointly by the AGSM and CCH is used in the chapter. This was a national survey of performance appraisal and management practices in 649 Australian private and public sector organisations. These organisations were drawn from a range of industries, with manufacturing, finance, insurance, real estate and public administration being well represented. They also varied in size, with 60 per cent having 100 to 999 employees.

Callus et al.*: The Australian Workplace Industrial Relations Survey (AWIRS)*

The survey was undertaken by the federal Department of Industrial Relations between November 1989 and May 1990. The results were published in 1991. The survey involved 2004 workplaces with 20 or more employees in all industries except Agriculture and Defence. Interviews with 4500 workplace managers and occasionally head office managers, and when present union delegates were undertaken. An additional survey of managers at 349 workplaces with between five and nineteen employees was also conducted. The surveys collected data on a wide range of matters including management and industrial relations practices, union structures, workplace relations, the management of change and industrial relations indicators such as voluntary labour turnover, labour stability, dismissals, absenteeism and industrial action.

Service industries dominated the survey population, both in terms of their share of workplaces and employees. Wholesale and retail trade represented 33 per cent of the workplaces, but only 19 per cent of employees, while manufacturing represented 17 per cent of the workplaces and 23 per cent of employees.

Morehead et al.*: AWIRS 95*

The survey was undertaken by the federal Department of Industrial Relations in 1995. The results were published in 1997. The survey involved 2001 workplaces with 20 or more employees in all industries with the exception of agriculture, forestry and fishing and defence. Interviews with the most senior manager at the workplace, the person responsible for day-to-day industrial relations and, where present, the union delegate were undertaken. A panel survey of 698 workplaces that had been interviewed in the 1990 was also undertaken. A small workplace survey of workplaces with 5–19 employees was conducted with the most senior manager in 1075 workplaces. The employee survey was distributed to a random sample of employees at the workplaces in the main survey. Topics in the main survey included union organisation, the role of union delegate,organisational change, communication, employment patterns, industrial agreements and industrial action.

Kramar and Lake (1997)

This survey is conducted as part of the Cranet-E research. The questionnaire includes questions on HR processes such as training, performance appraisal, compensation, employee relations, strategy, communication, selection and flexible employment. The survey included 331 organisations with 200 or more employees, of which 40 per cent were drawn from the public sector and 60 per cent from the private sector. All industries were represented, with organisations in the communication, finance and insurance, government and other (which includes statutory authorities) categories being well represented.

Employee surveys

Employee surveys are frequently used in Australia to benchmark attitudes, track the impact of change programmes and target change initiatives. Sometimes, the results are used as part of the assessment of management's performance. The results of surveys from one consultancy public domain are reported in this chapter.

Strategic Consulting Group (SCG)

SCG surveyed more than 30,000 employees in 20 organisations between 1986 and 1995. These organisations are drawn from the public and private sector and a variety of industries.

Industry Task Force on Leadership and Management Skills

In 1992 the Industry Task Force on Leadership and Management Skills was established to advise the federal government on measures to strengthen management development and leadership within Australian organisations. It was asked to identify effective management practices in a range of areas, to raise awareness of the need for improved leadership and management skills and to foster enterprise commitment to management development.

An extensive research programme involving 27 research projects was commissioned. Of particular interest to this paper was the research by Sheldrake and Saul (1995) that examined the impact of organisational change on the first line manager.

This research sought to explore the changing role of first line managers in organisations that had introduced substantial structural changes in workplace organisations through quality management processes, self-managing or semi-autonomous work groups and other changes in management practices. A total of 19 organisations participated in the study. Data was gathered from senior management in each organisation through in-depth interviews, from 10 line managers in each organisation through in-depth interviews and through questionnaires distributed to 298 first-line managers.

The majority of the organisations were drawn from the manufacturing sector and once again the organisations were large.

References

Beaumont, P. B. (1991) 'The US human resource management literature: a review', in Salaman, G. (ed.) *Human Resource Strategies*, Milton Keynes, Open University Press.

Beer, M., Spector, B., Lawrence, P. R., Mills, D. and Walton, R. E. (1984) *Managing Human Assets*, New York, Free Press.

Beer, M. and Spector, B. (1985) 'Corporate wide transformations in human resource management', in Walton, R. E. and Lawrence, P. R. (eds), *Human Resource Management: Trends and Challenge*, Boston, Harvard Business School Press, pp. 219–53.

Blyton, P. and Turnbull, P. (eds) (1992), *Reassessing Human Resource Management*, London, Sage Publications.

Boxall, P. and Dowling, P. (1990) 'Human resource management and industrial relations tradition', *Labour and Industry*, 3(2/3): 195–214.

Burgess, J. and Strachan, G. (1997) 'Growing workforce insecurity in Australia: trends, gender and policy issues', *12th Annual Employment Research Unit Conference*, Cardiff, Cardiff Business School.

Business Council of Australia – Industrial Relations Study Commission (1989), *Enterprise – Based Bargaining Units: A Better Way of Working*, Melbourne, Business Council of Australia.

Callus, R., Morehead, A., Cully, M. and Buchanan, J. (1991) *Industrial Relations at Work*, Canberra, AGPS.

CCH Australia Ltd. (1995) *Human Resources Management*, Sydney, CCH Australia Ltd.

Centre for European Human Resource Management (1997) *Cranet-G Results* (unpublished), Cranfield, European Centre for Human Resource Management.

Dabscheck, B. (1995) *The Struggle for Australian Industrial Relations*, Melbourne, Oxford University Press.

Deery, S. (1995) 'Industrial relations', in O'Neill, G. and Kramar, R. (eds), *Australian Human Resources Management*, Melbourne, Pitman.

Deery, S. and Nash, J. (1988) 'Organisational change and the role of personnel and industrial relations management', in Palmer, G. (ed.), *Australian Personnel Management: A Reader*, Melbourne, Macmillan Education Australia, pp. 164–78.

Department of Industrial Relations (1995) *Enterprise Bargaining Annual Report 1994*, Canberra, AGPS.

Drago, R., Wooden, M. and Sloan J. (1992) *Productive Relations*, Sydney, Allen and Unwin.

Dunn, S. (1990) 'Root metaphor in the old and new industrial relations', *British Journal of Industrial Relations*, 28(1): 1–31.

Dunphy, D. and Stace, D. (1990) *Under New Management: Australian Organizations in Transition*, Roseville, McGraw-Hill.

Guest, D. (1987) 'Human resource management and industrial relations', *Journal of Management Studies*, 24(2): 149–75.

Guest, D. (1991) 'Personnel management: the end of orthodoxy?', *British Journal of Industrial Relations*, 29(2): 149–76.

Hendry, C. and Pettigrew, A. (1986) 'The practice of strategic human resource management', *Personnel Review*, 15(5): 3–8.
Hilmer, F. (1989) *New Games, New Rules*, North Ride, Angus and Robertson.
Kramar, R. (1997) 'Developing and implementing work and family policies: the implications for human resource policies', *Asia Pacific Journal of Human Resources*, 35(3):1–18.
Kramar, R. and Lake, N. (1997) *Price Waterhouse Cranfield Project on International Strategic Human Resource Management*, Sydney, Macquarie University.
Kitay, J. and Lansbury, R. (1995) *Human Resource Management and Workplace Change*, Proceedings of an EPAC Roundtable, Canberra, AGPS.
Kitay, J. and Lansbury, R. (ed.) (1997) *Changing Employment Relations in Australia*, Melbourne, Oxford University Press.
Kochan, T. and Osterman, P. (1994) *The Mutual Gains Enterprise*, Boston, Harvard Business School Press.
Kochan, T., Katz, H. and McKersie, R. (1986) *The Transformation of American Industrial Relations*, New York, Basic Books.
Legge, K. (1995) *Human Resource Management: Rhetorics and Realities*, London, Macmillan Business.
Locke, R., Kochan, T. and Piore, M. (eds) (1995) *Employment Relations in a Changing World Economy*, Cambridge, Mass., MIT Press.
Mahoney, T. and Deckop, J. R. (1986) 'Evolution of concept and practice in personnel administration/human resource management', *Journal of Management* 12(2): 223–41.
Morehead, A., Steele, M., Alexander, M., Stephen, K. and Duffin, L. (1997) *Changes at Work*, Melbourne, Longman.
OECD (1996) *Employment Outlook*, Paris, OECD.
Purcell, J. (1987) 'Mapping management styles in employee relations', *Journal of Management Studies*, 24(5): 533–48.
Report on the Industry Task Force on Leadership and Management Skills (1995), Canberra, AGPS.
SCG (1986–95) *Summary of Attitude Surveys 1986–1995* (unpublished), Sydney.
Sheldrake, P. and Saul, P. (1995) 'First line managers: a study of the changing role and skills of first line managers', *The Report on the Industry Task Force on Leadership and Management Skills*, Canberra, AGPS.
Sisson, K. (ed.) (1989) *Personnel Management in Britain*, Oxford, Blackwell Business.
Sparrow, P., Schuler, R. and Jackson, S. (1994) 'Convergence or divergence: human resource practices and policies for competitive advantage worldwide', *International Journal of Human Resource Management*, 5(2): 267–99.
Stace, D. (1986) 'The value added organisation', *Report to the Government on Trends in Training and Development*, Stace Management Networks.
Stace, D. and Dunphy, D. (1994) *Beyond the Boundaries: Leading and Creating the Successful Enterprise*, Roseville, McGraw-Hill.
Storey, J. (1992) *Management of Human Resources*, Oxford, Blackwell Business.
Tichy, N., Frombrun, C. and Devanna, M. A. (1982) 'Strategic human resource management', *Sloan Management Review*, 23(2) Winter: 47–61.

Walton, R. E. (1985) 'Towards a strategy of eliciting employee commitment based on policies of mutuality', in Walton, R. E. and Lawrence, P. R. (eds), *Human Resource Management, Trends and Challenges*, Boston, Harvard Business School Press.

Part VI

Research in Comparative Human Resource Management

15 Coordination of Research Networks: Market, Bureaucracy and Clan in the Cranfield Network on European Human Resource Management (Cranet-E).

Wolfgang Mayrhofer

INTRODUCTION

The management of an international research network covers all areas that are well known in cross-border activities in the business field. Handling diversity, making use of economies of scale, dealing with cultural differences, working in multicultural teams, or balancing overall goals and local needs are some of the typical issues. However, international research networks cannot be equated with multinational companies. The networks differ in multiple ways: they have little or no formal and legal structure, less clear goals, and no profit orientation; their members have a greater degree of personal freedom due to a lesser degree of economic dependence (on the network) and the lack of position hierarchies, their members also work in small local units often consisting of only one or two persons and have to divide their attention between this and other activities such as teaching or additional research projects.

This chapter argues that despite these differences an international research network can use the same forms of coordination and control as a (multinational) company. It further claims that in order to contribute to the further existence of the network, to the efficient handling of the evolving tasks, and to a high quality output, managing the network requires the use of different forms of coordination and control at the same time. However, such a 'coordination mix' may lead to new problems like member ambiguity or conflict. These ideas are presented against the background of nine years of experience in Cranet-E, currently consisting of network members from 21 European and 5 non-European countries.

This chapter elaborates on these thoughts. It gives an overview of basic coordination and control mechanisms presently used in organisations and discusses their efficiency as well as the conditions for their use. It briefly presents the historical development and the main characteristics of Cranet-E and illustrates the use of specific modes of coordination and control in various areas of the network activities discussing the importance of their parallel and sequential use in terms of a flexible mix of modes. Finally, it develops some ideas that might likely influence the successful management of international research networks.

COORDINATION AND CONTROL IN ORGANISATIONS

Division of labour is one of the most prominent and seemingly inevitable characteristics of people working together. This is by no means a modern development, but has been reported throughout history. (Consider, by way of example, the rebuilding of the ancient temple walls in Jerusalem as reported in the biblical Book of Nehemiah, or the building of the pyramids.) Now, as soon as labour is divided, coordinating and controlling the divided efforts in order to secure (at least a minimum of) goal attainment becomes essential, the underlying assumption being that individual goals are, at the utmost, only partially overlapping and congruent with organisational goals (e.g. Barnard, 1968). Thus, coordination and control constitute a pervasive theme in the organisational theory and management literature (see, for example, Reeves and Woodward, 1970; Frese, 1974; Van de Veen *et al.*, 1976; Pfeffer and Salancik, 1978; Van Maanen and Barley, 1984; Schreyögg, 1996).

This chapter draws on a classic contribution by Ouchi (1980) describing three different basic mechanisms of mediation or control in organisations: markets, bureaucracies, and clans. Ouchi views organisations as 'any stable pattern of transactions between individuals or aggregations of individuals' (Ouchi, 1980, p. 140). Using this conceptualisation and a transaction cost and exchange theory framework (Gouldner, 1961; Williamson, 1975), he further specifies the characteristics and applicability of each coordination mechanism.

Market transactions involve contractual relationships which specify the terms of exchange. The three most typical forms of contracts are spot/sales contracts (all obligations are fulfilled at the spot), contingent claims contracts (specification of obligations, contingent upon all future states of nature), and sequential spot contracts (series of contracts for a short period of time). Due to bounded rationality and the opportunistic behaviour of the individual, the uncertainty and complexity of the environment, and the small numbers of market participants, sometimes no truly market relationship can evolve. 'In summary, the market failures framework argues that markets fail when the costs of completing transactions become unbearable. At that point, the inefficiencies of bureaucratic organisation will be preferred to the relatively greater costs of market organisation, and exchange relationships move from one domain into the other' (Ouchi, 1980, p. 134).

Bureaucracies substitute for the market through the imposition of bureaucratic mechanisms (hierarchical control, clear set of rules, etc.). They have two advantages over markets. First, they focus on the concept of the employment relationship which constitutes an incomplete contract. This means, the superiors can direct the actual work of the employees on a day-to-day basis thus reducing the problem of future uncertainty. Secondly, since the employees belong to a common organisation, there is the chance of an atmosphere of trust. In turn, this reduces the degree of opportunistic tendencies and the amount of control required. Nevertheless, the problem of control is crucial. 'When tasks become highly unique, completely integrated, or ambigous for other reasons, then even bureaucratic mechanisms fail. Under these conditions, it becomes impossible to evaluate externally the value added by any individual. Any standard which is applied will be by definition arbitrary and therefore inequitable' (Ouchi, 1980, pp. 134 f.).

Clans have their strengths in minimising goal incongruence, and at the same time tolerating high levels of ambiguity in performance evaluation. Clans reduce the differences between individual and organisational goals and create a strong feeling of community. Therefore, opportunistic behaviour is not very likely and not socially acceptable. Beyond that, clans do not require explicit performance evaluation. Since close personal and working relationships exist, there is a continuous exchange of feedback signals which can hardly be transformed to formal evaluation measures. 'This means that there is sufficient information in a clan to promote learning and effective production, but that information cannot withstand the scrutiny of contractual relations. Thus, any tendency toward opportunism will be destructive, because the close auditing and hard contracting necessary to combat it are not possible in a clan' (Ouchi, 1980, p. 137).

Based on these modes of coordination and control, Ouchi proposes an organsational failures framework that specifies the conditions under which each form will mediate transactions most efficiently (Table 15.1).

The normative requirements have to be shared by the members of the transactional network. The norm of reciprocity is a basic mechanism in social exchange and contains the conviction that an equal 'give and take' is the foundation of any social exchange. It seems to be one of the very few universal norms witnessed in all societies (Gouldner, 1961). Legitimate authority allows for a specific role for superiors. They can assign work to subordinates and audit their performance closely. Common values and beliefs lead to the existence of a certain level of harmony between the members of an organisation. Furthermore, they reduce the differences between individual and organisational goals and the probability of opportunistic behaviour (Ouchi, 1980: 137 f.).

Informational requirements are needed to guide the transaction processes. Prices are very sophisticated and precise forms of information for various 'goods' in an exchange process. Yet it is quite difficult to get 'correct' prices. Rules are more crude informational devices. They refer to specific problems. Therefore, it is hard to think of controlling an organisation solely by rules because of the great number of problems that could potentially arise. Traditions are more implicit than explicit rules. They are not very precise and heavily linked to the organisation's culture. New members are made familiar with traditions through various forms of socialisation (Ouchi, 1980: 138 f.).

Table 15.1 Organisational failures framework (Ouchi, 1980: 137)

Mode of control	*Normative requirements*	*Informational requirements*
Market	Reciprocity	Prices
Bureaucracy	Reciprocity Legitimate authority	Rules
Clan	Reciprocity Legitimate authority Common values and beliefs	Traditions

Source: Ouchi, 1980, p. 137.

CRANET-E

Cranet-E is a research network dedicated to analysing developments in the area of HRM in public and private organisations with more than 200 employees in a national, cross-national and quasi-longitudinal way (see Brewster and Hegewisch, 1994; Brewster *et al.* 1996). At the heart of the network is the Cranet-E survey. On a regular basis, a national sample of organisations with more than 200 employees is questioned on various aspects of HRM via questionnaires. The two most important objectives of this internationally, comparative survey were, at the outset: (1) to research whether a pattern of 'Europeanisation', i.e. convergence to a common pattern could be found over time, and (2) to identify whether changes in personnel policies towards a more strategic approach ('strategic HRM') have occurred. 'Thus, the general objective was to extend the range of internationally comparable evidence about particular policies and practices that have been seen as relevant to the concept of HRM' (Brewster *et al.*, 1996, p. 593).

History of foundation

In order to achieve these goals a research network of academics from France, Germany (West), Spain, Sweden and the UK was formed in 1989. Led by members of the Cranfield School of Management, UK, this team developed a first draft of the survey. Understandably, given the diverse conceptual and cultural background of the researchers involved, identifiying the most important issues of interest and prioritising them proved a very challenging task. Once a mutally acceptable draft had been established, this version was discussed with senior practitioners in each country, which led to further revisions to be discussed within the research group. After being tested with some sample organisations and further revision and discussion, the areas that were finally to be included in the questionnaire were identified.

Once consensus about the major issues to be included in the questionnaire was achieved the group had to create appropriate questions in a standardised format. The objective was to create a standardised questionnaire which could be used in the participating countries and at the same time, recognised the specific cultural, legal, economic, etc. context of each country. To ensure this, the translation-retranslation technique (e.g. Bauer, 1995) was used. Since one of the main objectives was to compare actual practice, the research team aimed at 'hard data' like numbers, percentages, ratio, etc. and not so much at estimations and attitudinal information. To reduce respondent and cross-country bias only two open-ended questions (on the three major challenges in the area of HRM and on the employee groups most difficult to recruit) were included.

The finalised questionnaire was mailed to public and private organisations by the research teams in each country. After collecting the answers locally the questionnaires were all sent back to the UK research team. Here, the data were checked, cleaned and encoded according to a joint coding frame, using a standard data processing package (SPSSX). Once this process had been completed, all members of the network got access to all data by receiving the data files of all countries.

In addition to the interpretation of the survey, panel meetings with senior practitioners, at which the preliminary results of the analysis were presented and discussed, took place in each country. This added some further insight into the national HRM situation through the 'qualitative' and 'soft' comments made and opinions voiced by the managers participating. In the first year, the results of the national panel discussions were fed into an international panel of experts. In subsequent years, due to the growing number of participating countries, no international panel meeting was held. However, the results of the national discussion with practitioners were fed back to the other partners in Cranet-E.

Development of Cranet-E

Since its commencement in 1989 with the five countries mentioned, the network has grown continually. At present, Cranet-E consists of research institutions in more than 20 European and 5 non-European countries, coordinated by the Cranfield School of Management, UK.

As the questionnaire used in the survey is rather extensive, the usual problem of response rate is aggravated. However, given the circumstances and with some country variation, Cranet-E overall achieves a quite satisfactory response rate. Table 15.2 shows more details on sample size and response rates

Current activities

The current activities of the network include four major areas. Each of these areas is, in its own way, a cornerstone of Cranet-E.

Table 15.2 Cranet-E – sample size and response rates in years of survey

Year	*Sample*	*Returns*	*Response rate (%)*	*Returns for organisations with more than 200 employees*
1989/90	25.200	5.628	22	5.098
1991	32.200	5.511	17	5.449
1992/93	37.360	6.426	17	5.316
1995	29.540	6.289	21	4.792

Source: Brewster *et al.*, 1996, p. 598.

Cranet-E survey

The survey is still the most important activity of the network. It is the core competence of Cranet-E, something which distinguishes this network from many other forms of research cooperation. In its ninth year of existence, Cranet-E has collected data on about 24,000 organisations. In the early phases of the collaboration, a survey was conducted on an annual or bi-annual basis. Today, it is the policy of the network to do a survey in all member countries every four to five years. There are two main reasons for this policy change. First, doing the survey with practically no time between two rounds puts the main focus on the collecting and processing of data, leaving little time for the analysis. Since both the specific data set in question and the cross-national nature of the research teams demand more time than the 'average, monocultural' project, Cranet-E, in its early history, demonstrated some weaknesses in terms of reporting and analysing the available data. This was taken care of by the change of periodicity. Secondly, the organisations contacted during the survey were reluctant to fill in such an extensive questionnaire every year arguing that, in most areas, no major changes will occur within so short a time span. For many countries and organisations this seems plausible, although there clearly are some exceptions (e.g. Germany–East).

The pattern followed for the surveys has hardly changed. Once the experiences of the previous round have been analysed and potential changes of the questionnaire have been discussed in the network, the research partners conduct the next round in their respective countries. The questionnaires are then sent to Cranfield, fed into data files and redistributed to the research partners who analyse the data further and hold panel meetings with personnel practitioners. One major problem is the synchronisation of the efforts in the various countries. Since available resources in terms of energy, money, and field entrance vary considerably from country to country, it is not easy to 'tune in' all countries to a common time perspective. In addition, new members very often do not fit into the networks cycle. Sometimes they may wait a considerable period for the next round to take place, while conversely sometimes the time left for organising the survey would be very short. Therefore, in some cases intermediate rounds of data collection are introduced.

Projects

Alongside the Cranet-E survey the research partners are involved with various joint research and teaching projects. Some of these research projects are directly linked with the Cranet-E survey, utilising the existing data in specific ways and generating new data. For example, the European Commission invited Cranet-E to generate a report on flexibility issues in the area of human resources. Other projects make only small use of existing data and have their origin in the personal contacts generated within the network. Similarly, there are joint efforts in the area of teaching. For example, a masters programme on European HRM has been established, integrating some of the business schools from within the network with other partners from outside.

Publications

From the Cranet-E survey as well as the other project activities, various forms of publications emerge. Naturally, the research partners publish on their own, especially in their home countries. Furthermore, cross-national teams of authors work together for various purposes, such as the 'official' publication of the results of the survey rounds and various books, special editions of journals, articles, or conference papers. It is one of the traditions within Cranet-E to encourage and stimulate cross-national collaboration wherever possible. Reflecting the different degree of centrality attributed to Cranet-E by the partners and the differing opportunities to participate in cross-border activities (e.g. some of the countries have very limited financial resources that do not allow for frequent travelling), not all partners take part in such joint activities to the same degree.

Meetings

The overview of the activities within the network given above indicates that the members of the network meet regularly at conferences, task force meetings, publication sessions, etc. depending on their degree of involvement with joint activities. In addition to these more or less individualised meetings, two traditional cornerstones allow for personal contacts and common working time: the annual spring and autumn gatherings. These meetings have a very typical pattern. They are hosted by the members in turn, usually last for one day and deal with various issues arising from the joint efforts. Very often, the local host organises a conference before or after the network meeting for the local practitioners and scientific community, using the expertise of the network members as well as other people for the event. Again, due to various restrictions and varying priorities, not all members attend all meetings. However, typically at least two-thirds, and often more, of the European countries are represented at these annual spring and autumn gatherings.

COORDINATION AND CONTROL MECHANISMS IN CRANET-E

Given the theoretical framework used in this chapter and the experiences drawn from working with Cranet-E as an international research network, this chapter will deal with the coordination and control mechanisms used. After discussing whether or not the requirements for the various modes of control are met with the three modes of control and their use within Cranet-E are explained. In a third step, the problems of a parallel and frequently changing use of coordination and control mechanisms in such a research network are discussed.

Requirements for different modes of control

The framework presented above indicates that the three modes of control are linked with different normative and informational requirements. Therefore, the extent to which these requirements are present in the Cranet-E will be briefly discussed.

Normative requirements

Reciprocity. Since the norm of reciprocity seems to be universally held in most societies one would expect to find it also within the network, as indeed one does. Most network members uphold a long term perspective, which leads them to develop frequent and regular exchange processes between themselves, on different levels. Consequently, the network members consciously apply the norm of reciprocity.

Legitimate authority. Compared to the norm of reciprocity, the question of legitimate authority within Cranet-E is a more subtle and critical one. Cranet-E is not a formal organisation with a clear set of positions and defined hierarchical relations. Similarly, there is no written statement dealing with the distribution of authority between network members. Since Cranet-E is not a commercial organisation, nobody formally 'owns' the network to a greater or lesser degree. In spite of this, there is such a thing as legitimate authority within the network. Existing authority draws its legitimacy from various sources (for a general view on power and authority sources see, e.g. French and Raven, 1959), the most important ones being:

- Seniority within the network: The longer a person and/or a country has been a member of the network, the more the partner is viewed as an experienced, proven, reliable member.
- Perceived centrality of Cranet-E for the member: Members of Cranet-E devote differing degrees of energy to the network. Due to personal preferences and outside restrictions they are not willing or able to put the same amount of work into network issues. The higher the centrality of Cranet-E for a member in the eyes of the other partners, the more authority is ascribed to that partner.
- Technical and social competence: The work of the network covers a great variety of aspects. Technical know-how, for example, specific methodological knowledge or international HRM know-how, as well as social skills, e.g. the ability to contribute positively to the emotional climate or to guide group discussions, are necessary to keep the network functioning. The more a member contributes in terms of technical and social competence, the more authority is lent to him or her.

Common values and beliefs. The existence of common values and beliefs in a group of persons from diverse cultural, national and professional backgrounds cannot be taken for granted. On the contrary, given this diversity one has to allow for a great variety of values and beliefs concerning most of the issues at stake. This definitely is the experience of Cranet-E. All the 'typical' phenomena in multicultural work groups also appear within Cranet-E, such as the difficulty in choosing an acceptable working language (English is being used generally, but sub-groups also use other languages among themselves), difficulties in interpreting the behaviour of others, or arguing on the basis of different national and professional traditions and taking these presuppositions for granted without conciously reflecting upon them. Beyond these differences, however, the members also have a shared set of values and beliefs. These centre around (a) the basic importance of HR issues in organisations, (b) the significance of international comparative research and (c) the non-hierarchical, peer-oriented way of cooperation within Cranet-E.

Informational requirements

Prices. Prices in the narrow sense of the word do not exist in Cranet-E. With very few exceptions, e.g. centrally produced reports or flyers that members can buy, no goods or services are bought or sold. Therefore, exact prices in the sense of a monetary equivalent for goods or services do not exist. However, in a wider sense, estimations about the 'worth' of contributions of individual network members in various areas of work do exist. Following this, the network or parts of it are willing to pay a 'price' for their efforts. This price is no monetary unit, but takes the form of other 'payments'. Take an example: A member of the network is willing to invest much of his or her time and energy into a task that is very important to the network and for which he or she is amply qualified. In order to 'pay' for this the network has to find ways of rewarding the member. This can be done in various ways, for example by tolerating frequent absences at important meetings, by inviting the person to contribute to joint articles and by accepting an uneven distribution of the work load for the said article, etc. As can be seen from this example, talking about prices in Cranet-E is not easy: It is not quite clear who or what determines the market prices. Opinions differ according to the worth attributed to a given contribution by different partners, one person can achieve different prices for one and the same contribution depending on which market segment he or she offers the 'goods' at. Nevertheless, there are at least some broad corridors of agreement about the pricing of member contributions.

Rules. In comparison to prices, rules are more crude informational devices. They attempt to cover issues that occur regularly and can also take the form of meta-rules that guide the formulation of rules and *ad hoc* decisions. On the basis of the work done to date, Cranet-E has developed a broad set of rules as well as meta-rules. The rules primarily cover the central aspects of the common work, especially the implementation of the survey and the analysis and interpretation of the results. At the meta-level, the main rule for the formulation of rules and *ad hoc* decisions is that, whenever possible, important steps and changes are to be decided upon through a process of joint discussion. As many network members as possible should have the opportunity to participate in the process. At the same time, the responsibility for feeding one's views into this process rests with the individual member, i.e. if members miss out joint meetings or do not respond to calls, there is no obligation to slow down the overall process. One quite specific characteristic of rules in Cranet-E is that they are not written down formally (although there are minutes from each gathering which contain the most important decisions made). With the exception of one area, the use and distribution of network data outside the network and the guidelines for publishing the results in countries other than your own, no formal 'rulebook' exists. This stands in marked contrast to some prescriptions in the literature that recommend a well defined set of written rules to define possible areas of misunderstanding and conflict in advance (Drenth and Wilpert, 1980, cited in Brewster *et al.*, 1996, p. 593).

Traditions. Traditions are located on a more implicit level than rules. They form part of the cultural pattern of a group or organisation. As in most other organisations in existence for nearly a decade, Cranet-E has developed a number of traditions that guide individual and collective behaviour. For example, joint dinners with a quite festive character during network gatherings represent the most enduring (and pleasant) traditions. At these dinners, the host's hospitality is praised and a lot of informal and personal information is shared among participants. At the symbolic level these dinners reinforce the bonds between members and convey the message that one feels at ease with the other members. Another tradition is that the respective host covers the expenses for board and lodging during the gathering. Again, this tradition is of high symbolic value – it signals to the other members that one's attendance is valued, that the host appreciates one's contribution, etc. Since the countries take turns hosting the gatherings, in the long run the expenses are more or less evened out, but the symbolic message is very strong.

Three modes of coordination and control

The last section highlighted that the normative and informational requirements for the three modes of coordination and control – market, bureaucracy, and clan – do exist within Cranet-E. This section goes one step further and describes one typical example for each mode.

Market. Some of the areas of cooperation within Cranet-E are co-ordinated and controlled by market mechanisms. In terms of the approach used, this requires the norm of reciprocity and a (more or less) clear understanding of the valuation of supply and demand, i.e. of pricing. A very typical example of this mode is the acquisition of partners for joint publications beyond the traditional overall report of Cranet-E and joint project results. In both cases, the search process for potential partners for a specific publication or a joint research or teaching project can be described as the search for the most attractive partner(s) in terms of 'goods' offered at a reasonable 'price'.

The 'goods' a Cranet-E partner can offer are manifold. Specific expertise in some area of national or international HRM, methodological know-how in terms of data sampling and analysis, conceptual and theoretical skills that help develop a framework of analysis, creative abilities (to avoid dead ends), resources at one's disposal in terms of money, time or secretarial manpower – these are the most important of the more obvious valuation categories. Further areas potentially constitute more intangible goods that can be exchanged. By way of example there is the reputation a members holds within a relevant target population such as, for example, the scientific community or research associations, the amount of experience with the hidden rules of a specific setting when formulating a research proposal or handing in a conference or journal paper, the degree to which a co-authorship would influence one's own reputation, the national affiliation of a member and the consequences of this for the joint undertaking, or the position in the internal transactional network of Cranet-E and therefore the link with a potentially 'powerful' person and a potential status profit.

It is clear that the worth of these goods is not objectively given per se. Rather than being an objective unit, the price is determined relative to the goals that one pursues by the joint undertaking and in the light of the contribution of other potential team members. One example: The individual chances of being invited to a joint publication *ceteris paribus* definitely decrease when a person's outstanding contribution is in the area of statistical analysis, but the publication is a conceptual–theoretical paper that does not demand any statistics. However, if one does not limit one's analysis to a *ceteris paribus* condition and takes into account the long-term nature of the network relationship and the great variety of projects, the picture might change. If most of the joint undertakings demand statistical knowledge and if there is a shortage of supply in this area because of a lack of specific manpower, then the situation is different. In the sense of pre-payment the person might be invited to the project to create a sense of obligation and debt to be repaid at a future occasion. Another example: Due to specific regulations some research grants are reserved for certain topics or regions, e.g. Eastern and Central European countries. In the recent past some of the network activities were focused on getting some of this money. Therefore, the mere fact of his or her working in a specific country made a person a potentially attractive partner for people applying for such grants.

Furthermore, there is another and probably even more tangible area that determines the choice of partners in mutual undertakings. Personal empathy, the attractiveness of a specific country or language proficiency, etc. constitute a further 'soft' and most often not directly technical relevant area that influences one's decisions. Depending on the importance of such considerations they can at times even override more 'rational' and directly goal-orientied considerations. However, even this area can be – with some difficulties – included into the supply–demand–price-thinking of the market view of coordination and control and thus into the argumentation above.

Bureaucracy. Bureaucracy is found in some areas, too. The term bureaucracy does not have any negative connotations in this context but is used within the theoretical framework of this chapter. Beyond reciprocity there is a need for legitimate authority as a normative requirement and rules as informational requirements. Probably the most typical example for the application of this mode is the practical handling of the Cranet-E survey.

In order to carry out the survey in the different member countries within a quite narrow time span, to secure a common structure of the survey, and to keep up high standards of data coding, a well-defined set of rules had to be developed. These rules cover the areas mentioned and express the common agreement on how to handle these issues. For instance, it is prescribed when organisations should be questioned and when the data has to be sent to Cranfield in order to get coded. There are two major sources for these rules. First, in the preparation phase of a new survey round, issues concerning the conduction of the survey are discussed during spring and autumn gatherings. Joint decisions are made that (should) guide the behaviour of individual country activities. In cases that are unclear or where conflict arises, these rules are used to solve problems. Secondly, sometimes it is hard to define these rules at the gatherings for various reasons like lack of information on the developments in some countries or very diverging points of view.

Furthermore, usually these rules do not cover all issues occurring during the process or have to be adapted and interpreted as the issues arise. Also, there are only bi-annual meetings, so in some cases you would have to wait for a comparatively long time span before a decision could be made. Therefore, the team at Cranfield holds a special position in the whole process. Since this team handles the data coding and input and has been involved since the beginning, it has acquired a special 'feel' for what is feasible and what is not. This gives them a special weight in the joint discussion process as well as factual power in actually adapting and interpreting rules during the handling of the survey.

In practice this means that for a certain area of work within the network the general formal equality of all network members is replaced by a hierarchical–bureaucratic model. The team at Cranfield is willing to take on this extra work, and the network members have enough confidence in the team to (a) acknowledge its increased weight in discussions about the practical aspects of conducting the survey and (b) to accept its modifications. In this way, the Cranfield team develops into gatekeepers and authorities in these areas. The resulting gain of this centralised approach is quite clear. Instead of getting lost in numerous discussions about the feasability of this or that (with the danger of an *ad hoc* adaptation without using long-term experience), a feasable and high standard of data coding and input is more likely to be achieved. At the same time, the dangers are obvious. Possible improvements as well as experimenting with new ideas might be slowed down or blocked if this would add to the work load of the central team without clear advantage. Thus, in the long run the evolution of the survey might be restricted.

Clan. Besides market and bureaucracy, the clan mode of coordination and control is used in Cranet-E, too. In terms of prerequisites it does not need only reciprocity and legitimate authority as normative requirements, but also common values and beliefs. Furthermore, traditions such as informational requirements are also needed. A very typical example of the clan mode at work is the control of behaviour of a Cranet-E member when representing the network to the public. Both market and bureaucratic mechanisms would fail and/or be too complicated to secure a behaviour that is compatible with the goals of the network. It is hard, for instance, to think of a set of explicit rules that prescribe the behaviour of a network member when writing an article or preparing a presentation about the control and coordinating mechanisms within Cranet-E that is precise enough to prohibit all deviations from the common understanding. Therefore, traditions based on common values and beliefs are used.

When presenting Cranet-E to an outside population, Cranet-E members face a number of choices: How much of the history should be told? What is the basic tenor of the presentation – critical, loyal, devoted, optimistic, scientific, etc.? How much of the implicit and often 'sensitive' issues can and should be revealed to the public? How concrete should the examples used be? What balance between realistic complexity and didactic simplification should be chosen?, etc. Since it is difficult to detect a functioning market with prices for these issues and there are no clear rules that guide the individual behaviour in a usable way, traditions and – from a more comprehensive point of view – culture is the adequate mode. With respect to the presentation of Cranet-E to the public there exists a rich tradition. For example, most conference presentations that use the Cranet-E data include a short section explaining the network. Especially through the presentations of key persons within the network considered to tell the 'authentic' story and through feedback from other network members concerning one's own section, a picture emerges over time. It becomes more and more clear what is a 'true', an i.e. accepted and balanced way of presenting the network to the public. *Mutatis mutandis* the same applies in the context of publishing articles and papers.

The more such traditions and a culture for presenting Cranet-E to the public emerge, the more they acquire normative force. That means, on the one hand they give comparatively clear guidelines about the corridors of meaning acceptable to (the majority of) other network members. At the same time, this guiding power makes it more difficult to deviate from certain core messages. At least such a deviation cannot be attributed to a lack of guidance. This again means that deviations are regarded as a very conscious decision *not* to follow a widespread tradition. In turn, this leads to questions about the reasons for such a decision which again has to be justified etc. It is clear even from this short sequence that the clan mode – as all culturally based coordination and control modes – represents a very strong and effective way of behavioural influence.

Betwixt and between: the mixture of modes

One of the most interesting things when re-constructing the use of control modes in Cranet-E is the existence of a mixture of control modes with no single mode clearly dominating. It is a frequently observed phenomenon that in 'normal' organisations not only one but a variety of typical coordination and control mechanisms are used. However, usually one of the mechnisms can be regarded as the primary mechanism. In Cranet-E we find two typical cases of mode mixture in this respect.

First, the mixture operates in a parallel way. This means, that in a specific situation it is not clear which mechanism is the primary one. The reasons for this can be manifold: Cranet-E has not developed any meta-rules guiding the decision-making in this area ('The decision which country is to host the next meeting is controlled through a combination of market and clan mechanisms!'), or such rules do exist, but there is disagreement about whether or not they apply, or there are different strands of argumentation coming to conflicting conclusions under different modes of coordination and control and therefore various modes are seen and promoted as the primary one. ('This questionnaire item is essential to secure the academic credibility!' – 'But it is too difficult to handle from a data entry point of view!')

Secondly, the mixture of coordination and control modes occurs in a sequential way. Often this means that there is a very clear and approved link between the area discussed and the mode of coordination and control that applies. However, the areas discussed either change very fast or it is not quite clear to which area a specific argument or conflict belongs. Both forms typically occur during network gatherings where broad issues are discussed and about 20 people take part in the discussion. It is very hard to create a solely goal-oriented discussion climate under these circumstances. Rather than strict goal orientation a collective trial and error style with many sidestreets, dead ends and a lot of 'theme-hopping' is typical for Cranet-E. As can easily be imagined, such a style of discussion touches upon many issues. Linked with those issues are differing modes of control. For an individual member it is often hard to decide where the discussion is at at a given moment and which arguments belong to which area. Therefore, one of the essential qualities in these discussions is the ability to flexibly switch between various areas and their attached coordination and control modes.

LESSONS TO LEARN AND OPEN QUESTIONS

Overall, the experience made by Cranet-E over the past years of active and functioning cooperation teaches us some things about the successful management of international research networks but it also leaves some questions open.

Use (and accept!) different modes of coordination and control?

The parallel and sequential use of different modes of coordination and control does create quite a bit of confusion and many difficulties. On the other hand, the different modes fit the areas were they are used best and lead to good results. Thus, there seems to be a positive net effect. The basic problem with accepting different modes of control is not necessarily the handling of the ensuing diversity, or complexity. Rather deeply rooted convictions seem to exist, in the sense of Schein's 'basic assumptions' as the most fundamental cultural level involved (Schein, 1985). These deeply rooted assumptions might favour one or the other mode as the 'one best way' of managing research networks. As soon as another mode of coordination and control is applied in one area in order to achieve results effectively and efficiently, these assumptions (for example, all network members have to have an equal vote at every decision; the academically best solution should under all circumstances be chosen) are violated. Since these assumptions are partly unconscious, they are not easily accessible. This in turn makes these conflicts difficult to discuss.

Develop meta-rules for the use of different modes?

Once a research network has decided, deliberately or through practical exercise to use different modes of coordination and control, the development of meta-rules seems to be crucial. Through a joint understanding of the difficulties of the modes applied and a common agreement on ways to handle these difficulties, a more efficient approach to task accomplishment is reached. Dealing with meta-rules at the same time heightens the awareness of the members of the dynamics in existence within the group. In this way, the importance of the individual contribution to the functioning of the group becomes clearer, thus valuing each individual. Such meta-rules need not be deliberately created in a conscious process. They can also gradually evolve over time, thus becoming a tradition or an emergent pattern without somebody centrally steering it (for the importance of emergent patterns in organisations see Mintzberg, 1978; Mintzberg and Waters, 1985). Indeed, sometimes it might be (at least in a first attempt) more sensible not to generate these meta-rules from the outset (a) without having had practical experience with situations with different modes and their handling and (b) relying on forces of self-organisation to do a lot of the work. Otherwise, the development of a 'comprehensive' and 'consistent' set of rules might take (too) much time, effort and conflict, at times in areas not seen as being particularely relevant.

Give new members of the network time to 'learn the ropes'?

Research networks often have to cope with a changing structure of their members. This is due to various factors, e.g. members leaving the academic sector or loosing interest in the research area, or the growth of the network. Regularly there is a very mixed population in the network. Experienced members and 'new recruits' are working side by side. In terms of the theme of this chapter this might pose some problems if (a) a clan mode of control is widely used and/or (b) meta-rules for application of modes to various issues are more implicit. In both cases, tradition, subtle reading of signs, 'understanding without words', etc. play an important role. For new members, this is even more difficult. Therefore, the new members need time to get accustomed to the 'way we do things around here' (which is, of course, just another way of expressing organisational culture). However, it is doubtful whether it would be a good idea to formally designate a mentor for new members. Although this might sound obvious to those familar with organisational socialisation and introductory programmes, the negative side effects might do more harm than good. The nomination of a formal mentor or clearly signals to the new member that he or she is a 'second class citizen'. Since research networks recruit new members usually on the basis of their expertise, this might send the wrong signal, possibly leading to irritation or more serious negative consequences. Maybe a more acceptable way of training new members would be to explicitly and actively encourage them to ask questions, seizing informal opportunities to make some background remarks ('socialise them'), etc.

Be aware that you have at least $n + 1$ accountants aboard?

Especially in areas in which a market mechanism guides the transactional processes over a considerable period of time, you can bet that there will be at least as many accountants and the corresponding number of profit and loss accounts as you have members in the network (and most likely that is an underestimate). Furthermore, it will become clear that the profit and loss accounting leads to divergent results because the standards for an 'even' account differ a lot. Due to factors like the number and amount of contributions over time, the different possible time frames, the different evaluation of one's own and others' contributions, or the great variety of contributors and the difficulties of attributing certain outcomes to certain persons, it definitely will be the exception rather than the rule to find a consensus about the overall picture of contributions. This inevitably leads to the fact that a research network has to develop a great capacity for 'forgiveness', i.e. for dealing with individual perceptions of an uneven distribution of 'workload and glory'. No instant recipes can be offered here, but attributional and cognitive dissonance theory on the individual level offers some mechanisms to cope with such phenomena.

Decide whether you want to be right or you want to get it right?

Especially when people from different cultures work together, there usually possess widely differing perceptions about a lot of issues. Directly linked to the phenomenon mentioned above, every individual has to choose whether he or she wants 'it' to be done in the 'right' way, which usually means his or her own way, or if one wants the network to achieve satisfactory results, even at the risk of one's own contribution not being valued the way it deserves. Probably one of the keys to success in this area is the choice of comparative measure. If one tries to be attributed for all the contribution one has chosen to give to the network in an absolutely accurate way (what again is the measure for this?), one might easily fail because of all the difficult measurement problems and attributional tendencies already mentioned above. If, however, one chooses, as a basis for measurement, the alternative of not being part of the network and, secondarily, is content with an adequate (not an optimal) level of satisfaction within the network, the situation is different. As long as the network is successful, chances are good that an individual calculation of costs and benefits will sum to a positive result. To put it more metaphorically: 'Does it matter that you yourself are a dwarf if you can have a lookout from the shoulders of a giant?'

References

Barnard, C. (1968) *The Functions of the Executive*, Cambridge, Mass., Harvard University Press.

Bauer, E. (1995) *Internationale Marketingforschung*. München.

Brewster, C. and Hegewisch, A. (1994) *Policy and Practice in European Human Resource Management*, London, Routledge.

Brewster, Ch., Tregaskis, O., Hegewisch, A. and Mayne, L. (1996) 'Comparative research in human resource management: a review and an example', *International Journal of Human Resource Management*, 7(3): 585–604.

Cartwright, D. (ed.) (1959) *Studies in Social Power*. Ann Arbor.

Drenth, P. D. and Wilpert, B. (1980) The role of 'social contracts' in cross cultural research *Internationel Review of Applied Psychology* 29: 293–306.

French, J. R. P. Jr and Raven, B. (1959) 'The bases of social power', in Cartwright, D. (ed.), pp. 150–67.

Frese, E. (1974) 'Koordination', in: Grochla, E. and Wittmann, W. (eds), col. 2263–73.

Gouldner, A. W. (1961) 'The norm of reciprocity: a preliminary statement', *American Sociological Review*, 25: 161–79.

Grochla, E. and Wittmann, W. (eds.) (1974) *Handwörterbuch der Betriebswirtschaft*, 4th edn, Stuttgart, Poeschel.

Macharzina, K. and Welge, M. K. (eds) (1989) *Handwörterbuch des Exports und der internationalen Unternehmung*, Stuttgart, Poeschel.

Mintzberg, H. (1978) 'Patterns in strategy formation', *Management Science*, 24: 934–48.

Mintzberg, H. and Waters, J. A. (1985) 'Of strategies, deliberate and emergent', *Strategic Management Journal*, 6: 257–72.

Ouchi, W. G. (1980) 'Markets, bureaucracies and clans', *Administrative Science Quarterly*, 25: 129–41.

Pfeffer, J. and Salancik, G. (1978) *The External Control of Organizations: A Resource Dependence perspective*, New York, Harper & Row.

Reeves, T. K. and Woodward, J. (1970) 'The study of managerial control', in Woodward, J. (ed.), 37–56.

Schein, E. H. (1985) *Organizational Culture and Leadership: A Dynamic View*, San Francisco, Jossey-Boss.

Schreyögg, G. (1996) *Organisation: Grundlagen moderner Organisationsgestaltung*, Wiesbaden, Gabler.

Van de Veen, A. H., Delbecq, A. L. and Koenig Jr, R. (1976) 'Determinants of coordination modes within organizations', *American Sociological Review* 41: 322–38.

Van Maanen, J. and Barley, S. R. (1984) 'Occupational communities: culture and control in organizations', *Research in Organizational Behavior*, 6: 287–365.

Williamson, O. E. (1975) *Markets and Hierarchies*, New York, Free Press.

Woodward, J. (ed.) (1970) *Industrial Organization: Behaviour and Control*, Oxford, Oxford University Press.

16 Comparative Research in Human Resource Management: A Review and an Example

Chris Brewster, Olga Tregaskis,
Ariane Hegewisch and Lesley Mayne

INTRODUCTION

In recent years it has become increasingly obvious that the study of HRM requires an international and a comparative dimension: 'the case for the comparative study of HRM takes little effort to establish' (Boxall, 1995: 5) and an 'international perspective is therefore needed' (Locke *et al.* 1995a: 139).

Research in this area is, however, rare. This is partly a result of the failure to recognise the need for such research and partly the result of the undoubted extra complexity created by international research. There is some welcome evidence that the number of soundly based comparative studies, while small, is growing. The aim of this chapter is to explore some of the complexities of conducting comparative international research and in particular internationally comparative surveys. The chapter begins by exploring some of the issues that shape international research design and then examines some of the practical problems inherent in such research. It ends with an examination of some of the problems faced in the creation and management of one major internationally comparative research project, the successive surveys carried out by Cranet-E and the steps that were taken to address these issues, providing the empirical background for the other chapters in this book.

ISSUES IN INTERNATIONAL RESEARCH

There are a number of fundamental issues to be considered in comparative research. These include conceptual issues (what is being researched and on what basis); and methodological concerns (how data is to be collected). In this chapter our intention is to focus on the comparative aspects of these issues and to emphasise the additional complications that international research involves.

Conceptual issues

International comparative research is fundamentally constrained by the perspective taken on the role of national context in management theory. Theories of management have tended to be constructed in one country (typically the United Sates of America: but theories from other countries show the same cultural specificity – the German Weber; the French Fayol, etc.). More recently, there has been a reaction to the dominant US model with attempts to construct other approaches, still claimed as universally applicable, in Germany (Kern and Schumann, 1984) and Sweden (Berggren, 1992). It has been suggested that other European researchers who argue for nationally distinct approaches to organisation (e.g. Child and Keiser, 1979, Maurice *et al.* 1979; 1980; Child, 1981; Lane, 1989; Sorge, 1991) show an implicit tendency to assume that one model, generally the German one here, is superior (Smith and Meiskins, 1995). This approach can also be seen now in US writers who have looked outside their own country and elevate the Italian (Sabel and Piore, 1984) or the Japanese approach (Vogel, 1979; Ouchi, 1981; Pascale and Athos, 1982; Womack *et al.*, 1990) as a model towards which organisations and nations should aspire.

Not surprisingly, there has been a related tendency for research to be designed in one country and transplanted, as if unproblematically, into another (Child, 1981). As a result the design and interpretation of results are taken from one national context, one national culture. This, still very frequent, error ignores the fact that knowledge of societies, of their language(s), their concepts, their values, their culture, is fundamental to understanding the behaviour of people within employing organisations (Hofstede, 1980; Laurent, 1983; Trompenaars 1985; Tayeb, 1994).

Partly as a result of these specific research trends, HRM theory has tended to remain highly ethnocentric in origin and has tended to focus on prescriptive as opposed to descriptive or analytical models. However, many specialist researchers (e.g. Adler, 1984; Smith, 1992;

Rosenzweig, 1994) warn of the problems in assuming the generalisability of theory: for this assumes the stability of factors across contexts – a demand which may not always be met in an international arena. Child (1981) noted that while there appears to be some degree of similarity in macro-level issues across countries there is still a high degree of variation at the micro-level.

There have been attempts to move beyond single variable models to theories which postulate complexes of influences. Thus there have been cross-national analyses that address both cultural and institutional diversity and technological and market contingencies (Child 1981; Negandhi, 1983; Poole, 1986, 1990; Lane, 1989; Sisson, 1989; Whitley, 1992a, 1992b; Jurgens, 1993; Jurgens *et al.*, Bean, 1994; Smith and Meiskins, 1995). Maurice, for example, has emphasised the social construction of categories and the importance of embedding research analyses in their appropriate societal context: he has called this the problem of comparing the incomparable (Maurice, 1989). In Europe alone such studies confirm the importance of small businesses in Spain, the plurality of regional channels in Italy, the role of Chambers of Commerce in Germany and so on. Research which is carried on (as many of the statistical surveys inevitably are) as if these differences did not exist will be correspondingly lacking in explanation. By contrast, of course, the societal studies are open to the critique of being excessively static and unable to explore variation within and between societies.

All these approaches, in so far as they allow a measure of freedom to the organisation to adopt various possible policies, have been termed 'strategic choice' approaches; a label applied by the researchers of the Industrial Relations Section at the Massachusetts Institute of Technology (Locke *et al.*, 1995a). These choices can clearly involve an international perspective for the firm, as is evidenced in the increasing research interest in the way that local subsidiaries cope with the pressures for local isomorphism against the imposition of practices from the parent MNE (Ghoshal and Nohria, 1989; Westney, 1993; Rosenzweig and Nohria, 1994; Zaheer, 1995).

A related conceptual research issue arises in relation to 'intellectual style' of the researchers. Each particular researcher will bring to the task of comparative study a particular set of assumptions about the focus of the research, i.e. should it be upon cultures and styles of management, or upon institutional arrangements, or upon national contingencies. Such assumptions will determine the kinds of results that are sought for and will tend to predominate over any attempts to identify areas of convergence towards some universalistic or organisational contingency theory or any attempt to identify divergent societal effects (Smith and Meiskins, 1995).

Each researcher also brings a particular degree of cultural knowledge and expertise to the task. This culturally rooted knowledge (or assumptions) will give the researcher easier access to understanding of his or her own society, or in some cases to two or even three societies, but it can make understanding of other societies more difficult. This can often result in researcher bias in the selection of variables for investigation and interpretation of data (Rosensweig, 1994).

This problem is most manifest when working in multi-cultural research teams; the issue of researcher bias can mean that the choice of subject matter and the type of research involved are contentious issues. At its simplest, some issues will be 'live' and controversial in some societies, unacknowledged or unremarkable in others. In the field of HRM, for example, studies of industrial relations might focus on strikes and disputes in a cross-Atlantic context; but on dispute resolution and conciliation in a Pacific Basin analysis (Brewster and Tyson, 1991). The area of equal opportunities policies is another where differing emphases can be identified: in Britain and the Netherlands, such discussions are generally concerned with addressing discrimination against women, ethnic minorities and people with disabilities; in France on the other hand, even though the proportion of black and ethnic minorities in the workforce is very similar, this is seen as a sensitive area in which questioning may infringe civil liberties (Brewster and Hegewisch, 1994). The MIT group of researchers found that changes in workplace practice tended to be explained by Americans in terms of 'strategic choice' at the enterprise level and by Europeans in terms of wider institutional structures (Locke *et al.*, 1995b); a point mirrored by Brewster (1995).

Methodological issues

Beyond that, different research traditions in different countries give rise to different expectations about the nature of *a priori* explanation expected in the construction of research projects. It has been argued, to take one significant case, that those trained in the United States tradition prefer to research against limited hypotheses, drawn from the literature and subject to unequivocal measurement; whereas other traditions, such as those in the UK, are typically less constrained, more pragmatic and more open to the development of theory rather than the testing of it (Brewster, 1995). Adding in the French tradition, for example, one could find other approaches, perhaps more concerned with the creation of overarching theory. None of these approaches is right or wrong (though they may initially seem so from the perspective of other approaches) and each has weaknesses, which have led to some 'uninformative' research, and strengths, which have enhanced our understanding of the topic.

The conceptual basis of the research will also influence the choice of countries in which to conduct the research. There are arguments for focusing on countries which are, in as many ways as possible, as similar as can be. If the distorting effects of very different population sizes, industrial segmentation, wealth, infrastructure and cultural values can be diminished, then remaining differences in the subject of investigation can be more clearly identified. The counter-argument suggests that it is precisely the differences between societies which illuminate and challenge the unacknowledged assumptions in the way issues are dealt with. A different form of analysis would lead researchers to focus on countries which have broader common boundaries (such as 'Europe') or which are major trading partners.

The issue of research approach also needs to be dealt with. The three dominant approaches to research are the case study, the eclectic summary and the survey: and these have been used extensively in cross-national research. The advantages and disadvantages of each approach is familiar territory (see recently McCarthy, 1994; Millward and Hawes, 1995).

The case study approach is better suited to the study of complex qualitative relationships (Morris and Wood, 1991): it is a more flexible and more informative way of exploring and defining and re-defining concepts than the survey (Yin, 1994). As the case study approach tends to be more exploratory in nature, it relies heavily on the interviewing and analytical skills of the individual researchers (Hyman, 1954; Kahn and Cannell, 1957). Case studies in international research which have included a substantial element of HRM include the work of Dore (1973); Ackroyd *et al.* (1988); Briggs (1988); Von Glinow and Teagarden (1988); Gleave and Oliver (1990); Beechler and Yang (1992); Saha (1993); Love *et al.* (1994); Easterby-Smith *et al.* (1995); and the team coordinated by Thirkell *et al.* (1995). The limitations of the case study technique in international research partly mirror those of the technique in a purely national setting. It is inappropriate for attempts to draw conclusions about the extent of difference between countries, for example; and in the attempt to use comparative case-studies to explore or explain different approaches to HRM the choice of cases and the problems of different national approaches will need to be carefully controlled.

There is also a strong tradition of national and sectoral comparisons using more eclectic methods, though these sometimes include case studies. Such industrial sector studies are based either on the notion that industrial sectors are internationally interwoven or that holding industrial sector constant will help to identify whether significant country influences operate and how they might impact on organisations. This line of research is exemplified by Gallie (1987, 1988), Smith (1990), Jurgens (1993), Jurgens *et al.* (1993), Oliver and Wilkinson (1992), Kenney and Florida (1994), Locke *et al.* (1995a), Zaheer (1995). In many of these studies there is a significant HRM component. Their explanatory power lies in their ability to go beyond the case study to provide more general evidence of differences and to utilise a much wider range of explanatory variables. The difficulties with such eclectic studies is made clear in a perceptive paper about the MIT project. This paper indicates that problems arise when different national teams take different approaches to the same broadly defined 'vantage points from which to view changes in employment relations in a given country' (Locke *et al.*, 1995, p. 142)

The survey is more appropriate for the quantitative measurement of differences (Babbie, 1990; Oppenheim, 1992). Hence, it is highly applicable for the collection of factual data or for gauging the strength of opinion or attitude on specific issues. Because the survey approach adopts the use of a standardised questionnaire format, the researchers' skills are utilised extensively in the questionnaire design phase, while the data collection phase (the administration or completion of the document) can utilise less skilled support or (Oppenheim, 1992), as is typically the case in mailed-out surveys, to be completed by the subject. When such an approach is being used in a cross-national context it brings into play the question of analyses and, related to this, the nature of the conclusions that can be drawn. A simple example would be the question of reward structures within two organisations in different countries. A comparison of pay rates is uninformative without detailed knowledge of purchasing power, lifestyles, cultural issues, state social security provisions, working hours and working lifetime details and so on, for each country. Such information cannot be collected through a survey. Use of a survey to establish comparisons of pay structures – to what extent are systems of remuneration linked to performance assessment or what is the differential from the top to bottom of the organisation – while still flawed, may be more valid.

Even with a carefully constructed survey approach, national differences have to be recognised – particularly in relation to different levels of regulation through employment legislation (see e.g. Whitfield *et al.*, 1994). 'Job sharing', for example, is more narrowly defined in several European countries than in the UK and under that more narrow definition is sometimes unlawful. Similarly, some countries prohibit private recruitment agencies, or provide an automatic right to trade union recognition, and therefore questions asking whether private recruitment agencies are utilised or whether trade unions are recognised would be of limited value there. Such differences may require careful adaptation of the survey questions. The central requirement is that the results mean the same thing.

Overall, interpretation of data is perhaps one of the most complex issues to address in cross-national methodologies. In some areas it is possible to place the results into the context of previous work in the field. This can be problematic in newer research areas where information may be limited, where the researcher risks misinterpretation and may be open to cultural bias. The most effective way to add depth to comparative cross-national survey research is through integrating the nomothetic and ideographic approach and obtaining qualitative data setting the results in context. Without some interpretative element the comparative data will be of limited value and lack explanatory potential.

If we are to address the explanatory obligation of cross-national research it is vital that research findings are placed in the national context. Research conducted jointly between researchers from different countries, working as multi-cultural teams (what Drenth and Wilpert, 1980 called Decentralised-Collective research), is one approach aimed at preventing a form of 'cultural domination' (or restricted viewing) by one country. It will also make the process of placing interpretation firmly in the national context more effective. Further, combining nomothetic and ideographic approaches provides depth to the thin broad framework of comparative studies. This process maintains standardisation in the measurement of variables whilst allowing a broader exploration of the 'why' factor.

PRACTICAL PROBLEMS IN INTERNATIONAL SURVEYS OF HRM

Two of the key practical problems in undertaking internationally comparative surveys of HRM are concerned with sampling frames and language translation issues.

Sample frames

A key issue in survey research is obtaining a representative sample. In single-country studies the difficulties of obtaining an appropriate sampling frame are numerous. The problems are compounded in cross-national research. The sample frame needs to contain a representative sample of the population being studied. Cross-national samples must be both consistent with the research aims and tap into similar samples across national boundaries.

Compared to surveys conducted within one country, international surveys require greater flexibility and more compromise in the establishment of appropriate databases. There are no internationally representative sources. At national level, where there is perhaps most comparability, this problem has been widely recognised (Hartmann, 1968; Visser, 1992; Wever, 1995). A primary source of empirical data used for the examination of trends across countries has been official statistical sources (Bean and Holden, 1992; Lane, 1994). This includes data produced by the International Labour Office (ILO), Eurostat, the official statistical office for Europe, and various national government sources. Not only are there considerable definitional problems with such data (Visser, 1992; Wever, 1995) but it tends to be either very general in terms of coverage of HRM issues or very detailed, and non-comparable, on highly specific issues such as working time or remuneration. There is a lack of empirical cross-national data on HRM.

The problem is even more marked at the organisational level. Analysis of any commercial mailing list, or international comparisons of professional bodies make this abundantly clear. Many listings which claim to be international in such publications as sector directories are partial and/or biased by a focus on or absence of representation from one or more countries. In addition listings from mailing list companies are not as comprehensive as they may first appear. Coverage varies greatly across countries and lists which are perfectly adequate in one country can prove patchy in other countries. For example, a study which drew a database from what is arguably one of the most readily identifiable sources (the *Fortune* 500) found that of 2045 parents and affiliates '423 of the addresses proved to be inaccurate or out of date' (Casson *et al.*, 1996). Less commonly used lists are unlikely to be more accurate. There is a similar, and in some countries even more problematic, difficulty with public sector coverage. In addition, there is a practical issue of cost; the costs of commercial or governmental lists can be very high in some countries.

The reality, therefore, is that, if we reject the proposition that research which is difficult or cannot be identical should not be attempted, all such surveys will require a degree of adaptability to what is possible.

The research sample (in a postal survey the mailing lists) thus have to take account of local conditions and use the best available list for each country involved in the research. This may involve, for example, co-operation from the national professional associations. Researchers have to address the possibility that this might constitute a source of bias; including only those organisations or individuals who are, by the nature of their membership of a professional association, likely to be more interested in the field. To some extent this is a general problem with postal surveys: since respondents cannot be forced to reply, those more interested or more positive about their practices may be more likely to respond. The important question concerns the nature and coverage of the lists.

Translation

The primary advantage of the use of questionnaires in cross national comparable research is the standardisation that can be attained. This is, however, not a straightforward issue. In such research it is important in standardising the questionnaire to ensure the 'correct' translation into each relevant language.

This may be achieved through literal translation (Elder, 1976). However in many instances literal translations are not sufficient as they fail to translate meaning and are consequently misleading. Therefore the translation process is as much a matter of meaning as it is linguistics. Take for example, the case of differentiating between the 'mission statement' and 'corporate strategy'. While most senior business leaders in most cultures would be familiar with the terms, an exact literal translation (where there is no direct correspondence to a commonly used national term) would often lead to terminology which would be unfamiliar to the majority of respondents in a particular country. In such cases it becomes important to achieve conceptual equivalence (Lincoln and Kalleberg, 1990).

This divergence in meaning attached to words highlights cultural differences. The problem is amplified when dealing with social as opposed to technical terminology (Rosenzweig, 1994: 30). The reason lies in the fact that social terminology linked to attitudinal or perceptual data is steeped in the history and traditions of the culture creating variation in meaning. For example Lincoln and Kalleberg (1990) reported difficulties in conceptual equivalence in the study of organisational commitment and job satisfaction.

One way to reduce conceptual and literal 'translation' problems is through the process of translation and retranslation (Brislin *et al.*, 1973; Brislin, 1976; cf. Hofstede, 1980).

CROSS-NATIONAL SURVEYS OF HRM

Clearly, our understanding of HRM issues in a comparative context is best approached using a number of methodologies. Although, comparative survey research remains rare there have been some notable examples. The European Foundation for the Improvement of Living and Working Conditions has conducted careful comparative studies of workforce involvement in the introduction of new technology and of flexible working practices (Bielinski *et al.* 1992). IBM and Towers Perrin conducted a global survey in 1991 which examined HRM issues, among other things. The survey covered 12 countries including 4 European countries, the UK, Germany, France and Italy; however the response rate was disproportionately biased toward the UK and included only very small numbers from some of the other countries. The aim in this instance was directed at understanding how organisations operate globally and therefore included MNC's only. In addition, the sample was restricted to those organisations identified by IBM and Towers Perrin as being the most effective in highly competitive environments (Towers, 1992). Given its focus, this survey relied heavily on attitudinal data, to ascertain the importance firms placed on HR concepts and practices as a means of attaining competitive advantage. It asked respondents to indicate how important they felt certain practices were in gaining competitive advantage. Sparrow *et al.* (1994), responsible for secondary analysis of the HRM aspects of this data, explore some of the issues surrounding the use of such data.

It has been pointed out that the collection of evidence of factual data rather than opinions not only reduces linguistic and cultural 'infection' of the data, but also lends itself more readily to the examination of trends (McCarthy 1994).

Another more recent research project which address HR issues is the International Organisation Observatory project. This is study of a wide range of organisational climate issues using a combination of 'factual' and attitudinal questions. This research was conducted in five countries although only part of the questionnaire dealt with human resource management issues specifically. Thus, there has traditionally been a lack of comparative data covering a comprehensive range of human resource issues.

The rest of this paper focuses on the approach used in what is known as the Cranfield Network on European Human Resource Management (Cranet – E) both as an example of some of the problems and opportunities involved in conducting international surveys of HRM policy and practice – and as an introduction to the data used in the other chapters in this book.

THE CRANET-E SURVEY

The Cranet-E project is based upon a survey of organisational policies and practices in HRM across Europe. Current publicly available European labour market data is far from comprehensive in the area of HRM practices. Available comparable labour market statistics, such as the EU labour force survey, are broad in their approach to employment, concentrating more on the type and size of employment than on aspects of HRM or personnel policy within organisations.

The Cranet-E survey was formulated from the outset as an internationally comparative survey. Its primary objective was to establish whether over time there was an increasing 'Europeanisation' (or convergence to a common pattern) of specific HRM practices in Europe. This potential Europeanisation is of course most plainly manifested in the (now) 15 countries of the European Union, though we did not restrict the survey to these countries. We were interested in whether increasing internationalisation would lead to a harmonisation of personnel policies.

A secondary objective was to establish how far there had been, in Europe, a shift in personnel policies towards 'strategic human resource management'. In other words, one aim of the survey was to gather data which might help to address questions of how far the range of personnel policies are planned, coherent and interactive with corporate strategies.

Thus, the general objective was to extend the range of internationally comparable evidence about particular policies and practices that have been seen as relevant to the concept of HRM.

Plainly, the Network takes a positivist approach to the research problem. The partners are not unaware of the essential difference between positivist and anti-positivist epistomologies (Blaikie, 1993) nor would we wish to deny that the mere systematic accumulation of facts as a research approach is less neutral than it seems. Our choice to study HRM and the debates, from different national cultures, that have led to the creation of the research instrument that we now use are sufficient to remind us of that. Nevertheless, we would argue that an outside world exists beyond individual cognition, even if it has to be interpreted through that mechanism, and we believe that at this stage of our knowledge there is much value in the accumulation of such facts as we can gather on an internationally comparative basis, however flawed that may be as a scientific process.

We are also attracted to the notion of pluralism (Reed, 1985) in the analysis of our data at least and would accept the interconnection in our research between the academic researchers and the practitioners: 'future generations of researchers and writers will have to get used to the unavoidable tension between the painstaking search for knowledge and the pressure for something that works' (Reed, 1985: 202)

The Network

To achieve these objectives an initial network of academics from five countries (the UK, France, West Germany, Spain and Sweden), was formed in 1989. This collaborative approach was chosen specifically to address a number of the design and interpretation difficulties discussed previously. As the programme of research has continued the network of academics has grown to include 18 countries in Europe and, in 1996, more beyond Europe.[1]

Suggestions from other researchers that such networks need to be buttressed by carefully written 'social contracts' that regulate all administrative, ownership and dissemination issues and any others that might cause disagreement or misunderstandings (Drenth and Wilpert, 1980) have proven to be unnecessary. Through continual contact, regular – twice-yearly – meetings, and a collegiate approach by all concerned the network has operated for over a decade now without such formalisation. However, as a precaution, a joint policy on dissemination has been agreed recently.

Inevitably, particularly given our objective of monitoring developments over time, the countries which joined the survey at a later date were more constrained and had less chance to influence the nature of the research, although extensive debates on the nature and the form of the instrument take place before each round of data collection.

A survey approach was adopted. Since the research was focused on comparisons of policy and practice, in size, sector and national terms, this was the appropriate methodology. However, the survey is supplemented with a more qualitative in-depth approach during the interpretation phase. All research involves 'trade-offs': as a survey based project the research gains significant advantages of comparability but intrinsically losses some explanatory value.

A key question concerned the level of the information needed. Given the limited resources available, an initial decision was taken to draw our evidence from specialist HR managers within employing organisations. Experts in the field have pointed out that, when attempting to gain a view of the structure and behaviour of social phenomena such as HR, it is important, though not unproblematic, to obtain a 'role-holder who can reasonably speak for the social unit concerned, reliably reporting its structure and behaviour' (Millward and Hawes, 1995: 72). The nature of the questions being asked demanded some degree of formalisation of process and someone who could provide us with an overview of HRM as it operated in the organisation. This pointed to organisations with a specialist HR or personnel department. Research in Germany for example (Semlinger and Mendius, 1989) suggests that the threshold for a specialist personnel function lies at a couple of hundred employees; thus only organisations employing at least 200 people were included. In some countries such as Denmark, the Netherlands or Spain, this definition excludes at least half of the working population, in others such as Sweden or the UK the small firms sector is less significant. However, the study of smaller employers would require a different questionnaire design which was not within the scope of this project. In the event, several of the countries chose to collect data from organisations of 100 employees upward although the comparative statistics that have been presented in articles to date are restricted to organisations of 200 and above to maintain comparability.

Mailing lists

Developing an appropriate mailing list is a key issue in all survey research. Some countries, such as Finland, have a comprehensive national company register, though these usually have limited coverage of the public sector. In general, however, such a luxury was not available and therefore other approaches had to be adopted. In some countries, including the UK, the primary mailing list was obtained from a private mailing list company specialising in the development of such data bases.

However, not only were such mailing lists found to be heavily country biased (even when they claimed to be 'European') but, again, they needed to be supplemented, particularly for the public sector. Professional associations, such as Personnel Management Associations, were very helpful, though mailing lists based on such bodies have to be treated with caution: membership lists, for instance, may be corporately or individually based depending on the country. In those countries with individual memberships care has to be taken to avoid duplication. In addition, such lists alone may not be comprehensive enough.

Public sector employment, in the sense of public administration covering central and local government, health and higher education, accounts for a substantial share of total employment in different European countries. Therefore it was important to ensure that public administration was properly represented in the survey. In countries such as Denmark, Ireland, Norway, Sweden and the United Kingdom public and private sector personnel management are reasonably well integrated; there is only one professional body for personnel management and there is an overlap in training courses and educational routes. Integration is also reflected in the composition of mailing lists and generally it was not necessary to supplement sector respondents. This was not the case in Finland, Germany, France, Italy, Portugal, Turkey or Spain. In Finland the national company register, which covered the private sector, was supplemented with a variety of independent listings; in Germany, individual local authorities will only participate in surveys if these have been approved by the relevant local authority federations. Therefore, a sample of organisations were selected from lists provided by the local authority federations. The federations did not support the annual repetition of the survey; without this official support the public sector response in the second year was negligible. In the third year a limited degree of support was secured from the federations and this was supplemented by national handbook listings for public sector education and health organisations. There was a similar, if not as formalised, experience in the Netherlands.

In summary, selecting an appropriate comparative sample is a complex task, inevitably involving compromise. For a survey such as ours, which is intended to show trends in HRM across Europe, the critical issue is to ensure that samples are as closely matched as possible to the reality of the countries being studied. Samples which are carefully matched between countries, but do not reflect the mix of organisations in each country are easier to manage, but make overall comparisons between countries problematic.

The questionnaire

The next phase was the design of the research instrument. This is where working as part of a collaborative cross-national research team can be most rewarding – while simultaneously being the most challenging in the issues it raises. The choice of major issues of interest and prioritising of them was established via bilateral and multilateral international discussions. This involved a great deal of negotiation and compromise among the collaborating research partners to arrive at a satisfactory research agenda that would ensure commitment from all concerned.

Once an initial draft of the areas of research had been agreed, the potential questionnaire was discussed with Panels of senior practitioners in each country; a questionnaire was formulated; tested with samples of organisations in each country and refined – following further discussion – to the final instrument.

As the number of countries has grown this process remains a lengthy one. Although, the development of close working relationships has generated a greater appreciation of different national practices and issues among the partners.

Once the issues to be researched had been agreed, the task of creating appropriate questions in a standardised format began. The aim was to produce a standardised questionnaire that could be used in all countries, while allowing for a recognition of national context in order to retain meaning. Thus, in recognition of the usual German practice the group 'manual workers' was split into two – skilled (Facharbeiter) and semi- and unskilled workers. Further difficulties arose in relation to German public sector terminology and special public sector translations had to be prepared to take this into account.

A process of translation and retranslation, followed by discussion of any differences that the process identified, was employed to ensure the transfer of appropriate meaning (Brislin *et al.*, 1973; Brislin, 1976; Hofstede, 1980). The dangers of this technique, and in particular the danger of assuming equivalence where none existed (Bulmer and Warwick, 1983) were recognised and addressed by two distinct means. First, differences between the first and second versions might arise from poor translation, from the fact that the concept was unfamiliar in the second language, or from structural or institutional differences. The two translations were, therefore the subject of detailed and sometimes lengthy discussion, aimed at ensuring that the same information was being collected. The translation was tested with the target population (i.e.

personnel/HR directors) to ensure that the terms and questions were comprehensible.

Secondly, as part of this process, but also as part of our objective of comparing actual practice, the questionnaire asked, wherever possible, for hard data (numbers, percentages or, where necessary, a 'yes/no') rather than attitudinal information. *Inter alia*, this reduces the chance of variation in responses arising from language or understanding rather than reality.

The number of open-ended questions was limited to two. These were coded in each country according to a framework developed mainly in the first year of the survey by analysing responses from the five countries included then (with 70 sub-categories for each variable). Survey research does, to some extent rely on 'self definition' and therefore reflects the evaluation of the respondent. Focusing on hard data and reducing the open-ended questions to a minimum does not eliminate this problem; but it does reduce it.

Data analysis

The co-ordination of the process of data analysis can create a number of logistical problems. It was decided that this process should be centralised, with the UK research team taking responsibility for processing the data for all countries. The primary reason for this was to ensure that at the end of the process we all had data that we could compare. Centralising the process ensured not only that one data processing package was used (SPSSX) and one coding frame but also that the checking, inputting and cleaning process was consistent for all data. All partners received data on disk, for analysis using their own statistical packages, also on hard copy and, where possible, they had access to the centralised database at Cranfield via a modem link.

In order to reduce the opportunity for misinterpretation and to add some depth in meaning to the data, each national centre meets with a panel of senior practitioners in each country to discuss their national results. It was felt that these national panels would add a further dimension to the research findings by providing qualitative comment and opinion setting the data into the national context. Each panel consisted of HR specialists from organisations within each of the major industrial sectors.

In the first year, the outcomes of these national discussions were used to feed into an international panel of experts. The expansion of the number of countries in subsequent years unfortunately made the gathering of similar panels too expensive. However, results from the national panel are fed back at a European level through the twice yearly meeting of the collaborating research partners.

This project has not overcome the problems of cross-national research identified above. There is no doubt in the minds of the collaborators on the project that opportunities have been missed and mistakes made. Nevertheless, the research has been successful in generating the most extensive body of comparable data on European HRM practice. The fact that the project has continued, and continues to be extended to new countries, provides some evidence that it has met a felt need for information and that comparative cross-national research of this kind, involving prestigious academic bodies and serious researchers is not impossible.

Key to the collection and, particularly, the interpretation of such data is the collaboration of experts from each country. Comparative research in which 'observers' or 'visitors' from abroad claim to be able to explain a range of issues in other countries has to be viewed with some caution. Our experience is that the excitement of working with colleagues from other countries far outweighs the difficulties that such co-operation involves.

1990–95 survey details

What was originally called the Price Waterhouse Cranfield Project began in 1989 with five countries. Since then data has been collect in 1991, 1992 and 1993 with the latest being completed in 1995/96 (see Table 16.1).

The number of countries participating has grown from 5 to 23 (for other research purposes separate surveys are still conducted in East and West Germany) and are represented in Table 16.1.

Data collection procedures and sample distributions for the years 1990 to 1992 are discussed in detail in Brewster and Hegewisch (1994). The remainder of this chapter will be restricted to a discussion of the 1995 data from which the articles in the book are drawn. In 1995 a total of 6289 questionnaires were returned from 15 countries. This gave a 21 per cent response rate (see Table 16.2). There was, as in past years, some variation in response rates across countries (see Figure 16.1). This may in part be due to differences in attitudes to surveys and

Table 16.1 Countries surveyed

1990	*1991*	*1992*	*1993*	*1995*	*1996*
Germany(W)	Germany(W)	Germany(W)		Germany(W)	
Spain	Spain	Spain		Spain	
France	France	France		France	
Sweden	Sweden	Sweden		Sweden	
UK	UK	UK		UK	
	Denmark	Denmark		Denmark	
	Netherlands	Netherlands		Netherlands	
	Norway	Norway		Norway	
	Switzerland			Switzerland	
	Italy			Italy	
		Finland		Finland	
		Ireland		Ireland	
		Portugal			
		Turkey		Turkey	
		Germany (E)	Germany (E)	Germany (E)	
			Greece	Greece	
			Austria		
			Czech Republic		
				Belgium	
					Poland
					Hungry
					Australia
					New Zealand

Table 16.2 European survey response rates

Year	*Sample*	*Returns*	*Response rate (%)*	*Returns for 200 plus employees*
1990	25.200	5.682	22	5.098
1991	32.200	5.511	17	5.449
1992*	37.360	6.426	17	5.316
1995	29.540	6.289	21	4.792

* 1993 data included in these calculations.

the disclosure of organisational details across countries. There were also variations in mail-out strategies; for example, in Greece companies were first approached by telephone before receiving a questionnaire.

The distribution of industry sectors is depicted in Figure 16.2. It is clear that the sample is dominated by manufacturing organisations which make up 48 per cent of the sample. Service and public sector organisations represent around one-third of the sample. This sector

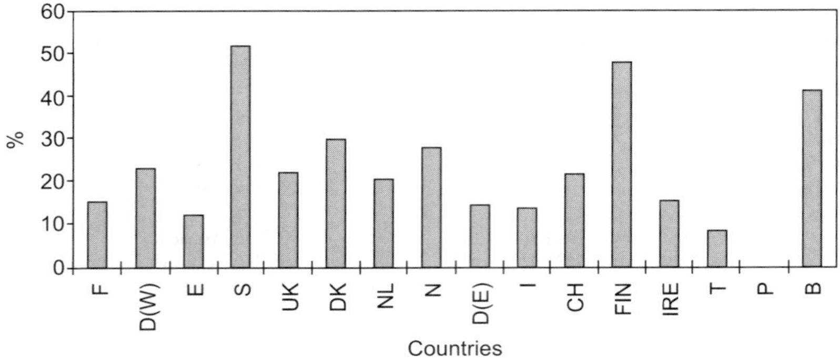

Figure 16.1 Response rates across countries for 1995

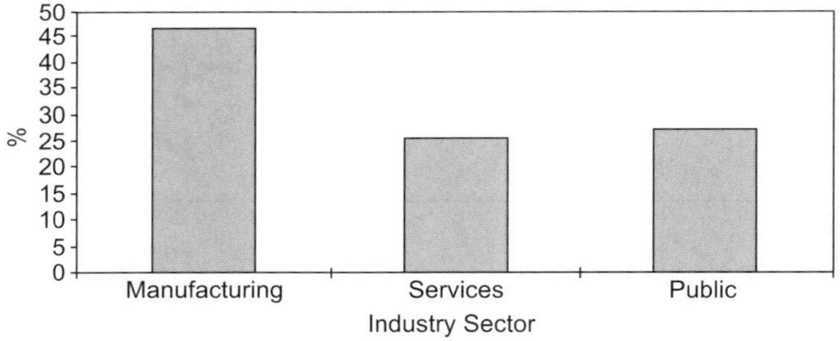

Figure 16.2 Survey industry distribution for 1995

distribution has remained relatively constant over the four years of the survey.

The size distribution breakdowns indicate that the sample is heavily represented by organisations employing more than 500 people (see Figure 16.3). Approximately one-third of the sample employs between 200 and 499 employees, one quarter employs 500 to 999 employees, with one in ten employing more than 1000. Again over the four year period the size distribution has remained relatively constant.

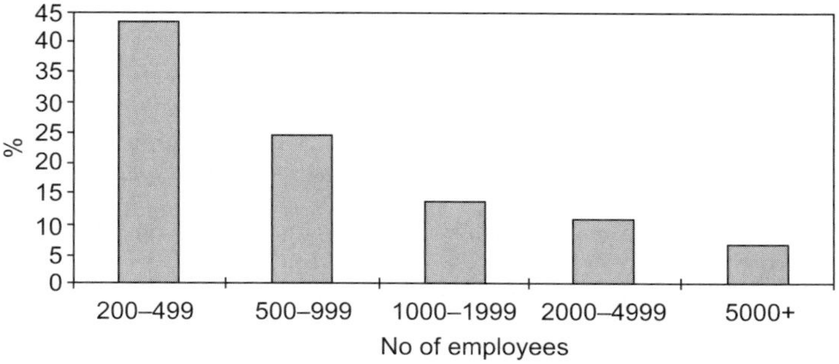

Figure 16.3 Survey size distribution for 1995

CONCLUSION

The significance of national differences has been demonstrated at both the conceptual and methodological level. If theories on HRM are to move forward we need to be wary of making assumptions about the universal applicability of practices across all national contexts, or the superiority of practices in one country over those in another. The same cautions need also be heralded with respect to comparative research design. For instance, lack of attention to language issues can result in inaccurate and misleading conclusions being drawn regarding organisational practice. One way of addressing such research bias is the formation of multi-cultural research teams or networks. In such cases it is important that all partners have an equal contribution leading to deeper discussion of the issues under investigation. Ethnocentric research networks will inevitably lead to the perpetuation of single country theories. However, it must also be acknowledged that comparative research demands compromise at all levels.

Note

1. The survey was conducted in Australia and New Zealand in 1996: and in Japan in 1999 and Canada in Autumn 1996.

References

Ackroyd, S., Burrell, G., Hughes, M. and Whitaker, A. (1988) 'The Japanisation of British Industry?', *Industrial Relations Journal*, 19(1): 11–23.

Adler, N. J. (1984) 'Understanding the ways of Understanding: cross-cultural management methodology Reviewed', *Advances in International Comparative Management*, 1: 31–67.

Babbie, E. R. (1990) *Survey Research Methods*, 2nd edn, Belmont, California, Wadsworth.

Bean, R. (1994) *Comparative Industrial Relations: An Introduction to Cross-national Perspectives*, 2nd edn, London, Routledge.

Bean, R. and Holden, K. (1992) 'Cross national differences in trade union membership in OECD countries', *Industrial Relations Journal*, 23: 52–59.

Beechler, S. and Yang, Z. J. (1992) 'The Transfer of Japanese–style management to American subsidiaries: contingencies, constraints, and competencies', *Journal of International Business Studies*, 3rd quarter: 467–85.

Berggren, C. (1992) *The Volvo Experience: Alternatives to Lean Production*, London, Macmillan.

Bielinski, H., Alaluf, M., Atkinson, J., Bellini, R., Castillo, J. J., Donati, P., Graverson, G., Huygen, F. and Wickham J. (1992) 'New forms of work and activity: a survey of experiences at establishment level in eight European countries', European Foundation for the Improvement of Living and Working Conditions, Working paper, Dublin.

Blaikie, N. (1993) *Approaches to Social Enquiry*, Cambridge, Polity Press.

Boxall, P. (1995) 'Building the theory of comparative HRM', *Human Resource Management Journal*, 5(5): 5–17.

Brewster, C. (1995) 'Toward a "European" Model of Human Resource Management', *Journal of International Business Studies*, 1: 1–21.

Brewster, C. and Tyson, S. (1991) *International Comparisons in Human Resource Management*, London, Pitman.

Brewster, C. and Hegewisch, A. (eds) (1994) *Policy and Practice in European Human Resource Management*, London, Routledge.

Briggs, P. (1988) 'The Japanese at Work: illusions of the ideal', *Industrial Relations Journal*, 19 (1): 24–30.

Brislin, R. W., Lonner, W. J. and Thorndike, R. M. (1973) *Cross-Cultural Research Methods*, London, Wiley-Interscience.

Brislin, R. W. (ed.) (1976) *Translation Applications and Research*, New York, Gouldner Press.

Bulmer, M. and Warwick, D. P. (1983) *Social Research in Developing Countries*, New York, John Wiley.

Casson, M., Loveridge, R. and Singh, F. (1996) The ethical significance of corporate culture in large multinational enterprises, in Brady, F. N. (ed.), *Ethical Universals in International Business*. Berlin, Springer.

Child, J. (1981) 'Culture, contingency and capitalism in the cross-national study of organisations', in Staw, B. M. and Cummings, L. L. (eds), pp. 303–56.

Child, J. and Keiser, A. (1979) 'Organisation and managerial roles in British and West German companies: an examination of the culture-free thesis', in Lammers, C. J. and Hickson, D. J. (eds), pp. 251–71.

Dore, R. (1973) *British Factory–Japanese Factory*, London, Allen and Unwin.
Drenth, P. J. D. and Wilpert, B. (1980) 'The role of "social contracts" in cross-cultural research', *International Review of Applied Psychology*, 29(3): 293–306.
Easterby-Smith, M., Malina, D. and Yuan, L. (1995) 'How cultural sensitive is HRM?: a comparative analysis of practices in Chinese and UK companies', *The International Journal of Human Resource Management*, 6(1): 31–59.
Elder, J. (1976) 'Comparative cross-national methodology', *Annual Review Sociology*, 2: 529–30.
Gallie, D. (1987) 'The social change and economic life initiative', ESRC Social Change and Economic Life Initiative, Working paper 1, Oxford, Nuffield College: 1–32.
Gallie, D. (ed.) (1988) *Employment in Britain*, Oxford, Basil Blackwell.
Ghoshal, S. and Nohria, N. (1989) 'Internal differentiation within multinational corporations', *Strategic Management Journal*, 10: 323–37.
Ghoshal, S. and Westrey, D. E. (eds) (1993) *Organisation Theory and the Multinational Corporation*, New York, St Martin's Press.
Gleave, S. and Oliver, N. (1990) 'Human resource management in Japanese manufacturing companies in the UK: 5 case studies', *Journal of General Management*, 16(1): 54–68.
Hartmann, H. (1968) *Der Deutsche Unternehmer: Autortät und Organisation*, Frankfurt, Europäischer Verlagsanstalt.
Hofstede, G. (1980) *Culture's Consequences*, California, Sage.
Hyman (1954) *Interviewing on Social Research*, Chicago, University of Chicago Press.
Hyman, R. and Ferner, A. (eds) *New Frontiers in European Industrial Relations*, Oxford, Blackwell.
Jurgens, U. (1993) 'National and company differences in organising production work in the car industry', in Kogut, B. (ed.).
Jurgens, U., Malsch, T. and Dohse, K. (1993) *Breaking from Taylorism*, Cambridge, Cambridge University Press.
Kahn, R. and Cannell, C. (1957) *The Dynamics of Interviewing*, New York, John Wiley.
Kenney, M. and Florida, R. (1993) 'Japanese Maquiladoras: production organisation and global commodity chains', *World Development*, 22(1): 27–44.
Kern, H. and Schuman, M. (1984) 'Rationalisation and work in German industry', in Kogut, B. (ed.).
Kogut, B. (ed.) (1993) *Country Competitiveness*, Oxford, Oxford University Press.
Lammers, C. J. and Hickson, D. J. (eds) (1979) *Organisations Alike and Unlike*, London, Routledge and Kegan Paul.
Lane, C. (1989) *Management and Labour in Europe*. Aldershot, Edward Elgar.
Lane, C. (1994). 'Industrial order and the transformation of industrial relations: Britain, Germany and France compared', in Hyman, R. and Ferner, A. (eds), pp. 167–95.

Laurent, A. (1983) 'The cultural diversity of Western management conceptions', *International Studies of Management and Organisations*, 8: 75–96.
Lincoln, J. R. and Kalleberg A. L. (1990) *Culture, Control, and Commitment: A Study of Work Organisation and Work Attitudes in the United States and Japan*, Cambridge, Cambridge University Press.
Locke, R., Kochan, T. A. and Piore, M. (1995a) 'Reconceptualising comparative industrial relations: lessons from international research', *International Labour Review*, 134(2): 139–61.
Locke, R., Kochan, T. A. and Piore, M. (1995b) *Employment Relations in a Changing World Economy*, Cambridge, Mass., MIT Press.
Love, K., Bishop, R., Heinisch, D. and Montei, M. (1994) 'Selection across two cultures: adapting the selection of American assemblers to meet Japanese job performance demands', *Personnel Psychology*, 47: 837–46.
Maurice M. (1989) 'Méthodes comparatives et analyse sociétale', *Sociologie du Travail*, 31: 175–91.
Maurice, M., Sellier, F. and Silvestre, J.-J. (1979) 'Societal analysis of industrial relations: a comparison between France and West Germany', *British Journal of Industrial Relations*, 17 (3): 322–36.
Maurice, M., Sorge, A. and Warner, M. (1980) 'Societal differences in organising manufacturing units', *Organisation Studies*, 1: 63–91.
McCarthy, W. (1994) 'Of hats and cattle: or the limits of macro-survey research in industrial relations', *Industrial Relations Journal*, 25(4): 315–22.
Millward, N. and Hawes, W. R. (1995) 'Hats, cattle and IR research: a comment on McCarthy', *Industrial Relations Journal*, 26(1): 69–73.
Morris, T. and Wood, S. (1991) 'Testing the survey method: continuity and changing British industrial relations', *Work, Employment and Society*, 5: 259–82.
Negandhi, A. (1983) 'Cross-cultural management research', *Journal of International Business Studies*, 14(2): 115–29.
Oppenheim, A. N. (1992) *Questionnaire Design and Attitude Measurement*, London, Pinter.
Oliver, N. and Wilkinson, B. (1992) *The Japanisation of British Industry*, Oxford, Blackwell.
Ouchi, W. G. (1981) *Theory Z: How American Business Can Meet the Japanese Challenge*, New York, Avon Books.
Pascale, R. T. and Athos, A. G. (1982) *The Art of Japanese Management*, London, Allen Lane.
Poole M. (1986) *Towards a New Industrial Democracy*, London, Routledge & Kegan Paul.
Poole M. (1990) 'Human resource management in an international perspective', *International Journal of Human Resource Management*, 1(1): 1–16.
Reed M. (1985) *Redirections in Organisational Analysis*, London, Tavistock.
Rosenzweig, P. M. (1994) 'When can management science research be generalised internationally?', *Management Science*, 40(1): 28–39.
Rosenzweig, P. and Nohria, N. (1994) 'Influences of human resource management practices in multinational firms', *Journal of International Business Studies*, 20(2): 229–52.
Sabel, C. F. and Piore, M. J. (1984) *The Second Industrial Divide*, New York, Basic Books.

Saha, S. K. (1993) 'Managing human resources: China verses the West', *Canadian Journal of Administration Science*, 10(2): 167–77.
Semlinger, K. and Mendius, H. G. (1989) *Personalplanung und Personalentwicklung in der gewerblichen Wirtschaft*, RKW, unpublished.
Sisson, K. (ed.) (1989) *Personnel Management in Britain*, Oxford, Blackwell.
Smith, C. (1990) 'How are engineers formed?', *Work, Employment and Society*, 4(3): 451–70.
Smith, C. and Meiskins, P. (1995) 'System, society and dominance effects in cross-national organisational analysis', *Work, Employment and Society*, 9(2): 241–67.
Smith, P. B. (1992) 'Organisational behaviour and national culture', *British Journal of Management*, 3(1): 39–50.
Sorge, A. (1991) 'Strategic fit and the societal effect: interpreting cross-national comparisons of technology, organisation and human resources', *Organisation Studies*, 12(2): 161–90.
Staw, B. M. and Cummings, L. L. (eds) (1981) *Research in Organisational Behaviour*, vol. 3.
Sparrow, P., Schuler, R. S. and Jackson, S. E. (1994) 'Convergence or divergence: human resource practices and policies for competitive advantage world-wide', *The International Journal of Human Resource Management*, 5(2): 267–99.
Tayeb, M. (1994) 'Organisations and national culture: methodology considered', *Organisation Studies*, 15(3): 429–46.
Thirkell J., Scase, R. and Vickerstaff, S. (1995) *Labour Relations and Political Change in Eastern Europe: A Comparative Perspective*, London, UCL Press.
Towers, P. (1992) *Priorities for Gaining Competitive Advantage: A World-wide Human Resource Study*, London, Towers Perrin.
Trompenaars, A. (1985) Organisation of Meaning and the Meaning of Organisation: A Comparative Study of the Conception of Organisational Structure in Different Cultures, unpublished PhD thesis, University of Pennsylvania (DA 8515460).
Visser, J. (1992) *Union Organisation: Why Countries Differ*, paper read to the Eleventh World Congress of the IIRA, Sydney.
Vogel, E. F. (1979) *Japan as Number One: Lessons for America*, Cambridge, Mass., Harvard University Press.
Von Glinow, M. A. and Teagarden, M. B. (1988) 'The transfer of human resource management technology in Sino-US co-operative ventures: problems and solutions', *Human Resource Management*, 27(2): 201–29.
Wever, K. S. (1995) *Negotiating Competitiveness: Employment Relations and Organisational Innovation in Germany and the Unites States*, Boston, Mass., Harvard Business School Press.
Westney, D. E. (1993) 'Institutional Theory and the multinational corporation', in Ghoshal, S. and Westney, D. E. (eds) pp. 53–76.
Whitfield, K., Marginson, P. and Brown, W. (1994) 'Workplace industrial relations under different regulatory systems: a survey-based comparison of Australia and Britain', *British Journal of Industrial Relations*, 32(3): 319–38.
Whitley, R. D. (1992a) *Business Systems in East Asia: Firms, Markets and Societies*, London, Sage.

Whitley, R. D. (1992b) *European Business Systems: Firms and Markets in Their National Contexts*, London, Sage.
Womack, J. D., Jones, P. T. and Roos, D. (1990) *The Machine that Changed the World*, New York, Rawson Associates.
Yin, R. K. (1994) *Case Study Research: Design and Methods*, 2nd edn, London, Sage.
Zaheer, P. (1995) 'Overcoming the liability of foreignness', *Academy of Management Journal*, 38(2): 341–63.

Index*

Note: page references to figures and tables are indicated by *f* and *t*.

*Index by Sue Lightfoot.

NATIONAL COLLEGE
OF IRELAND
LIBRARY